BUILDING
THE BONDS
OF ATTACHMENT

About the Author

Daniel A. Hughes, Ph.D., is a clinical psychologist in Waterville, Maine, where he specializes in child abuse and neglect, attachment, foster care, and adoption. He provides consultation to family services programs and also to therapists, case managers, and parents struggling with the treatment of attachment deficits in children. Dr. Hughes is the author of *Facilitating Developmental Attachment: The Road to Emotional Recovery and Behavioral Change in Foster and Adopted Children.*

BUILDING THE BONDS OF ATTACHMENT

AWAKENING LOVE IN DEEPLY TROUBLED CHILDREN

Daniel A. Hughes, Ph.D.

JASON ARONSON INC.
Northvale, New Jersey
London

This book was set in 11 point Veljovic by Alpha Graphics of Pittsfield, NH, and printed by Book-mart Press of North Bergen, NJ.

10   9   8   7   6

Library of Congress Cataloging-in-Publication Data

Hughes, Daniel A.
    Building the bonds of attachment : awakening love in deeply troubled children / by Daniel A. Hughes.
        p.   cm.
    Includes bibliographical references and index.
    ISBN 0-7657-0168-5
    1. Attachment behavior in children.   2. Adopted children – Family relationships.
3. Foster children – Family relationships.
    I. Title.
    RJ507.A77H837   1998
    155.44'5—DC21

    ISBN 0-7657-0237-1 (softcover)   98-13638

Printed in the United States of America on acid-free paper. For information and catalog write to Jason Aronson Inc., 230 Livingston Street, Northvale, NJ 07647-1726, or visit our website: www.aronson.com

Contents

Acknowledgments

I wish to begin by acknowledging my debt to many foster and adoptive parents, throughout the State of Maine and other states, who have challenged, taught, and supported me in my efforts to understand and assist them and their children. I have frequently learned from them and I have been constantly inspired by them.

I also wish to recognize the cooperative and creative contributions to this work made by many other therapists, case workers, and various other professionals who are themselves dedicated to finding ways to assist the unattached child become a full member of his or her family and community. There is not yet enough professional understanding as to the pervasive problems that these children manifest, nor with regard to the comprehensive interventions that are required to assist them. Professionals working with these children need to face their responsibility with humility, dedication, care, and creativity if they are to make a difference. I know many who are now doing that. We need to support each other in our work, recognizing that we are all searching for ways to be of help.

I wish to thank Jason Aronson Publishing Company for its willingness to present this work to the therapeutic community, and Ms. Cindy Hyden for her expert editorial criticism and guidance.

Finally, my wife, Barbara—who has been on her journey, which has been interwoven with mine for the past 27 years—has been a part of every insight that I have attained regarding facilitating attachment among unattached children. With Barbara, I have truly learned a great deal about attachment through our continuing bonds with our children, Megan, Kristin, and Madeline, who are at varying stages of their own unique and interesting journeys.

When Attachment Fails to Develop . . . Introducing Katie

In healthy families, a baby forms a secure attachment with her parents as naturally as she breathes, eats, and cries. This occurs easily because of her parents' bond with her. The bond guides her parents to notice her feelings and needs immediately and to respond sensitively and fully. Beyond simply meeting her unique needs, however, her parents "dance" with her. Hundreds of times, day after day, they dance with her.

There are other families where the baby neither dances nor even hears the sound of any music. In these families she does not form such attachments. Rather, her task, her continuous ordeal, is to learn to live with parents who are little more than strangers. Babies who live with strangers do not live well or grow well.

Katie, an abused, neglected, and poorly attached child, exists only in these pages. The same is true for Steven, her caseworker, Jackie, her primary foster parent, and Allison, her therapist, as well as the various secondary characters. But the great majority of events, experiences, relationships, thoughts, feelings, and behaviors described in this book have occurred, do occur, and will continue to occur in Maine, in the nation, and throughout the world. They will occur wherever there are children who do not know how to form a secure attachment with their parents. In my work as a psychologist, I have seen it occur countless times.

Through Katie, Jackie, and Allison, I present the general principles of intervention, both at home and in therapy, with poorly attached children. I hope that parents and therapists alike will readily recognize and identify with them. Their stories merit an appropriate and respectful response from social service agencies, therapists, courts, educators, legislators, and citizens. The unattached child needs our attention, our guidance, our love, and our help. She needs to become part of the human community.

I believe that the story format is best able to convey the affective tone and communications needed to make the interventions effective. I wish that I could say that Katie's story represents what really happens to most children with limited abilities to form attachments to their caregivers. Most have histories that prove to be far less successful than Katie's. Many disrupt from placements throughout their childhood and adolescence and enter adulthood without any relationships that provide them with a sense of being "at home." Many then enter into further unsatisfactory relationships that lead to deceptions, divorces, domestic violence, substance abuse, and ultimately to the abuse and neglect of their own children. The cycle of abuse is greatest among those adults and children who do not know how to form meaningful attachments.

The composite Katie Harrison is followed from birth until after her eighth birthday. During her first five years she is repeatedly abused—emotionally and physically. She also experiences profound emotional neglect from parents who ignore her, are indifferent to her, and who have no place for her in their hearts. Over the next 3 years Katie experiences a series of foster homes. The damage done to her by her parents remains alive within her affective core and greatly impedes her readiness and ability to form an attachment with her new caregivers.

Steven Fields is Katie's caseworker throughout her years in foster care. Steven is presented as a dedicated and knowledgeable professional who truly wants to be able to provide her with a chance to have a better life. However, her severe attachment problems are hard for him to understand, and he struggles with his questions as he tries to provide her with a placement and therapy that might offer her effective help. Steven's wife, Jenny, gives birth to a child, Rebecca, and it is through her early development that Steven is able to achieve new insight into Katie's deficits and needs.

Jackie Keller is Katie's fourth foster parent. Because of her care and commitment, as well as her training and experience with a former foster child with similar problems, she is able to provide Katie with a home environment that more closely approximates what she needs if she is to begin to form a secure attachment. Still, her life as Katie's foster parent is extremely hard. Jackie's commitment is tested by Katie's constant defiance, rage, and rejection of her.

Allison Kaplan is Katie's second therapist. Allison has specialized training and experience in working with children with serious attachment problems. She actively involves Jackie in the therapy sessions, and she consults with her about Katie's life at home and offers her support over the ordeals that she faces daily.

In my judgment, Katie, Jackie, and Allison can best be seen as transitional guides to providing these children with the type of life and experiences that they require. Further understanding, experiences, writings, and research will some day lead to comprehensive approaches that will provide greater hope for developmental progress. In my experience, it is the foster and adoptive parents who come to know and love these children who are leading the way. They are demanding that the professionals with whom they consult truly understand their kids. They also are expecting that their interventions make a difference. They have given their homes and hearts to these tragically isolated and unhappy children. The rest of us need to find ways to help them in their work.

1

The
Spiral
Begins:
The
Neglect
and
Abuse
of
Katie

On Tuesday, August 4, 1987, in Augusta, Maine, Katie Harrison was born and Steven Fields spent his first day working as a child protective worker with the Department of Human Services (DHS), State of Maine. While Steven was beginning to work with the abused and neglected children of Maine, Katie was becoming an abused and neglected child. Eventually she would be placed in the legal custody of the State of Maine. That day would not come for five years, one month, and nine days.

It's an unusual reality—a child in the custody of a State. Every adult citizen of Maine is responsible for Katie. If her parents will not raise her well, then all of the adults of Maine will do it. But in reality, Katie's reality, all of the adults of Maine are not what she needs to resolve her traumas and develop into a healthy child. Rather, she needs one family. She needs to have this family teach her to trust and to love, help her to heal and resolve her countless traumas, and develop an integrated self. Without such a family she will not begin to feel worthwhile, and she will not feel connected to others in the human community.

On November 10, 1987, Katie was in the crib where she had spent much of her first three months. It was getting colder in Maine and she was now almost constantly cold since her thin blanket was not sufficient for the weather. Being cold was unpleasant, as was the common soreness that she felt because her diaper was changed infrequently and she was bathed even less frequently. More acute and irregular discomfort came from her hunger. At times her cries brought food fairly quickly, while at other times she cried for long periods of time before being fed. Actually, sometimes she cried until she fell asleep, exhausted and still in pain. There were other times when she heard frightening noises that made her cry harder. On those occasions her mother Sally, or her father Mike, were not patient with her crying and they screamed at her as if that would calm her.

This day proved to be worse than average for Katie. She had not been fed and she probably was crying louder that usual. Mike screamed at her and then shook her by the shoulders and slapped her across the head. The pain was sudden, unexpected, and acute. Katie knew no other response but to cry louder. Mike slapped her again and put his face inches above her and screamed. Katie's world became total pain and chaos. Her arms and legs shook and flailed out, her back arched, and her cries made it difficult for her to breathe. Her eyes were wide and unfocused.

Sally came into the room and screamed at Mike to leave Katie alone and to never hit her again. She picked Katie up, spoke quietly, and rocked her. Sally continued to yell at Mike and her tension made it even harder for Katie to relax. Finally, Katie began to drink from her bottle, but she fell asleep before drinking what she needed. After two hours of restless sleep she awoke and cried for more milk. Sally was now sleeping and did not respond so eventually Katie fell asleep again, still hungry, troubled, and frightened.

Sally Thomas was 19 when Katie was born. She and Mike Harrison, who was four years older than she, had been together for eighteen months in spite of frequent conflicts and periodic separations. Sally wanted Mike to "settle down" and when she brought her wishes to him, he generally left in anger. Over time Sally kept to herself the resentment she felt about his lack of interest in working or getting married. He did get odd jobs but she generally found that he drank more and stayed out more with his friends when he was working. As a result, she had mixed feelings about him having a job. Usually it just caused more fights.

Sally was initially excited to have Katie. Her own mother, Helen, and her older sisters seemed to be pleased that she was a mother and she enjoyed her new status as an adult. She also had hoped that Mike would take an interest in Katie and want to help out with her and maybe even provide for her. When the opposite proved to be the case and Mike became more withdrawn and irritable than ever before, Sally began to resent Katie's constant demands. She found herself becoming increasingly impatient with her. She initially resisted this change in her attitude toward Katie because she had always told herself that she would do a better job raising her children than did her own mother in raising her. It seemed to Sally that during her own childhood her mother either yelled at her or ignored her. There seemed to have been little else. She had been sure that she and Katie would be different.

Sally knew that now she did not enjoy Katie very much. Katie might look at her and Sally would look away. She felt at times that Katie just wanted too much from her. Katie never seemed to be satisfied. Sally tried not to think about it. In some ways Katie seemed to be dissatisfied with her just like her mother always was. She couldn't even please her own kid! Sally was confused over Katie's reaction to her. At times she did not think that Katie liked her. She would play with her but Katie would not seem to be interested. She would feed and bathe her but Katie might cry thirty minutes later. She might cry when Sally held her or cry when she put her down. She did not feel that she knew Katie, and she did not feel much pleasure from caring for her. Being a mother wasn't what she had expected.

Sally thought about telling the nurse at the pediatrician's office that she really didn't think that she knew what to do when Katie cried. She wanted to tell her how hard it was and how tired she often felt. She wanted to tell her that being a mother wasn't what she had hoped it would be. But how could she say those things? How could she admit that she couldn't even raise a kid? Maybe she could ask for some help. Maybe someone could give her something to read. She had heard of a parenting class at Adult Ed at Cony High. Maybe she should take that. But who would watch Katie? Mike wouldn't. Instead, Mike would be annoyed with her for going off and doing something on her own. Sally ended up not thinking about her doubts. It seemed to be easier to just do what she had to do and then try to relax in front of the TV. She felt too tired to do anything else.

Katie, at 3 months of age, was actually not rejecting her mother. Her energies were going toward feeling safe and warm, being full, and making sense of her world. Inner feeling states led her toward food, sleep, or removing some discomfort. Sally was that part of her feeling states that best served to gratify her various needs. Sally did not exist to Katie apart from those needs. At times, Katie fussed and cried and Sally was there and Katie would feel better. But sometimes Sally was not there. Katie would fuss and cry over some discomfort and the Sally part of herself was not there to bring comfort. The discomfort continued and intensified and still Sally was absent. Katie could not bring comfort to herself because Sally was absent. She did not have confidence in herself because she did not trust a response from that part of herself, Sally, that should bring comfort. She did not have confidence in her "world" because for so long it provided her with nothing but varying forms of discomfort which were driven by hunger, sudden loud sounds, water that was too hot or too cold, or a continual soreness that was developing under her diaper.

On February 14, 1988 Sally may have made her last honest effort to raise Katie "right." Her father, Sam, who spent much of his life in the Portland bars and fishing boats, was coming to visit Sally with his new girlfriend, Tammy. If Sam held true to form he was likely to "settle down" for a few months until he lost interest in Tammy. His trip to Augusta to visit his daughter and granddaughter was for Tammy's benefit, but Sally didn't mind. She would show her father that she was a good mother who was making something of herself. He might even come again, to enjoy her family with the hope of being a part of her life.

When Sally began the day with Katie, she felt happy and capable. She fed Katie her bottle and then bathed her. Katie seemed glad to be with her. She smiled and splashed and seemed to respond when Sally played and laughed and acted silly with her. Katie did like her! She was doing a good job and her father would be proud of her. She put Katie down to sleep and got everything ready.

Katie was now 6 months old and on most days Sally wished that Katie could begin to take care of herself more. Mike never helped and he even resented Katie when she took Sally's attention away from him. Sally didn't often enjoy Katie anymore, but she did what she knew she was supposed to do, at least most of the time. She took some consolation in knowing that she was probably doing a better job with Katie than her mother ever did for her or her sisters.

Katie was increasingly confused because a subtle need that had been gradually increasing over the past three or four months was not being adequately met. Katie had one magical and pleasurable feeling state whenever Sally and Katie interacted in a playful and affectionate way. Katie would feel drawn toward Sally's eyes, her smile, and the musical sound of her voice. When Sally was dancing in front of Katie's eyes, Katie would feel arms around her and her body would rock and dance. At these times too, Katie would feel hands on her head and face and body. Those touches brought such pleasure when they accompanied Sally's face and voice! Katie was drawn more and more to those feeling states that were deeply connected to her experience of Sally. But they were not happening often. Katie would search for those eyes, and smiles, and hands, and arms, and very often not find them. At times they came along with the milk feeling state. But even then, more often then not, when Sally brought the milk she did not bring with it the playful and affectionate feeling state that would invite the reciprocal state in her that Katie wanted desperately to feel.

Katie awoke crying thirty minutes before Sally's father arrived. Sally carried her, sang to her, fed her, and changed her diaper. Sally was calm and hopeful initially, but when Katie did not stop fussing, she became tense. Mike could not stand her crying and she needed to have Mike stay calm. If her father were not coming, Katie would be back in the crib to cry herself to sleep and Mike would take off and she'd turn on the TV. That's the only way they could get through the crying. But her father arrived and she had to get Katie to stop.

As usual, Sam and Sally were awkward together after not having seen each other for a year or so. Initially Katie was a distraction as her father and Tammy laughed at how loud she screamed and they praised Sally for being able to raise her. Tammy, who wasn't much older than Sally, made it clear that she planned never to have a kid. Hearing Katie cry convinced her that she was right.

Eventually Sam gave Sally some suggestions about how to quiet Katie. She was not sure if he wanted to be helpful or if he had enough of the noise. Regardless, she didn't want his help. She knew Katie better than anyone and if she could not get her to stop crying than no one could. She took Katie into her bedroom and placed her in the crib.

Sam followed her and told Sally that she shouldn't leave Katie in bed when she was crying. Their interchange became increasingly heated and the focus moved from Sally raising Katie to how Sam had failed to raise Sally. Finally Sam exploded,

"Instead of talking to me that way you should be taking care of your kid!"

"I do take care of her. It's more than you ever did for me!"

"Why don't you go feed her then? That noise is driving me crazy."

"Then leave. That's what you've always done," said Sally.

Sam and Tammy left. Mike said that Sally had not handled that well. Sally didn't hear him. She could only hear Katie. She ran into her room.

"Shut up! Shut up!" she screamed as she pulled her from the crib and threw her toward the bed. Katie hit the side of the bed and bounced to the floor, with her leg awkwardly bent beneath her. Katie cried in acute pain. Sally screamed, shook, and covered her face. Mike swore and yelled and paced. Finally, Sally was able to call an ambulance. Mike told Sally to tell the people at the hospital that Katie rolled off the bed while Sally was getting her milk.

At the hospital Sally seemed to be in shock. She tried to care for her daughter appropriately, but she was emotionally withdrawn. She refused help when offered it by the hospital social worker. The hospital staff had reservations about the injury and the overall family situation, but decided that there were not enough questions to warrant an investigation by DHS. There were no previous accidents or signs of significant neglect.

When she brought Katie home, Sally seemed to be calmer with Katie than Mike had ever seen her be. But she could not forget how Katie had ruined her visit with her father. Katie would not hurt her again. What little pleasure Sally had felt when she was caring for Katie now became even less. At some level Sally knew that Katie wanted her to hold her, laugh with her, and play with her. She knew that her 6-month-old enjoyed nothing better than having her mother act silly with her, sing and dance, fuss over her, and run her fingers over her belly, arms, and neck, but Sally couldn't get herself to do those things very often. Katie was ruining her life; Sally wasn't going to go out of her way for her. Sally wasn't aware of making this decision. It was just the way it was. Actually, now it was the way it had been with her and her own mother. But Sally wasn't aware of that either.

Sally was right. Katie's entire being wanted to play and laugh and gaze at her mother. Katie's emotional life was developing rapidly at 6 months and it needed those experiences of reciprocal pleasure with her mother to fully emerge. If they were to develop, Katie's feelings of curiosity and joy and excitement were dependent on Sally having reciprocal experiences with her. Her emotional and neurological development were interwoven and needed to be activated by Sally's loving and sensitive frequent involvement with her. When Sally was absent, both physically and psychologically, Katie was lost and unable to proceed with her emotional and interpersonal development. Katie could not trigger these internal processes alone. She needed Sally to do it for her and with her. Increasingly, Sally did not.

Katie would often lie in her crib, fussing and crying. More often she would simply stare or engage in some repetitive hand and leg movements. She might fixate on some object in the crib or on the nearby wall, as if she were inviting it to interact with her. She wanted her world to respond to her feeling states and to share them. Getting little response, she began to overlook those states and to more often simply feel tense, isolated, and desperate.

When Sally was present, Katie had some awareness of wanting this special interaction with her. Anticipating that she would not get it, Katie would often look away from Sally or become more restless, as if she were trying to hide from herself what she was missing. Or she might become frantic, not being able to integrate the intense affect that Sally's presence was eliciting. At other times when Sally was particularly tense herself, such as after a fight with Mike, Katie would feel her mother's distress and she would fuss even more. At those times Katie would actually feel more calm and safe when Sally would leave. A profoundly sad reality for Katie was now developing. Unlike most infants who experience total delight in the presence of their mothers, Katie was very often anxious and ambivalent when Sally was present. She hoped for something from her mother, but she anticipated not getting it. Unlike most infants whose emotional and neurological development was driven by reciprocal enjoyment with their mothers, such developments within Katie were occurring slowly, with significant gaps, and lacking in adequate differentiation and integration.

On July 19, 1989 Katie was almost 2 years old. Months before, Sally noticed that Katie never cried. She and Mike had thought that it was strange, but they really didn't mind much. Katie whined a lot now and followed Sally around bugging her, but that was a lot better than her crying.

It had been almost eighteen months since Sally broke Katie's leg. For the most part, Sally was able to feed, wash, and clothe Katie on a fairly regular basis. When Katie began to crawl and then walk, Sally generally managed to keep an eye on her, prevent accidents, and keep her from bothering Mike. Sometimes she really did not care if Mike were bothered. Then Mike would scream at Katie and push her away with as much force as was necessary. Mostly though, Katie followed Sally wherever she went. She clung to her and whined when she learned some words. For a time Sally made a small effort to respond, even with a degree of enjoyment, but gradually she lost her sense of obligation to Katie and to motherhood. It was the seemingly constant barrage of demands that led to her almost complete withdrawal from her. Katie never seemed to be satisfied. She always wanted more from Sally. Sally had no more to give.

If there were any minimal benefit to this situation it was that Sally learned to deaden herself emotionally in a way that left her feeling little rage toward Katie. Mike could not do that. Katie could get him screaming at her in thirty seconds. Sally learned to ignore her whining and clinging and go on with her reading, eating, talking on the phone, or watching TV. Once in a while Sally might push her away when she clung to her leg and whined too loudly, but for the most part Sally went about her life without feeling much of anything toward Katie. She knew that she would not abuse her again. She also knew that she would do her job so that no one would criticize her mothering. Katie would be fed, clean, and well dressed. That would have to be enough.

That day in July started the way most days did. Sally got up with Katie, changed her, got her something to eat, and put her on the living room floor with a few toys while she got her coffee and toast and turned on the TV. Since Mike was sleeping and Sally did not want him yelling, she held Katie in her lap and made some effort to play with her puzzles and blocks while she watched her show. She explained to Katie how the puzzle went and she picked up the pieces that kept falling to the floor. Eventually she noticed that Katie was deliberately throwing the pieces on the floor. Sally became angry and she threw the remaining pieces and blocks across the room and spoke harshly to Katie as she roughly put her down.

Katie then asked for crackers and Sally gave her some and returned to her TV. When Katie asked for more, her mother continued to watch her show. After being ignored again, Katie threw a puzzle piece that hit Sally's arm. Sally yelled at Katie and threatened to hit her. Katie threw another piece and this one hit her mother's face. Sally leaped from the chair and slapped her daughter hard across the face. Katie then screamed and bit Sally's arm. Sally swore, and hit Katie again. Katie stared at her mother with hatred. She felt only rage toward this woman who hated her. Katie would no longer be afraid of her mother, nor sad at what was lacking between them.

Katie soon began to have frequent aggressive tantrums. Nothing that Sally or even Mike could do would stop them. She often got what she wanted when her anger was loud or destructive enough. She sensed that her rage would gain her some control over Sally. She liked seeing Sally get upset over her tantrums. Katie experienced a sense of power that felt good. Sally was mean and Katie was becoming good in finding ways to pay her back.

At the same time, Katie's wishes seemed to change. She no longer looked for enjoyment or nurturance from Sally. At some level she sensed that she was bad and could not expect such a relationship. She did not want attention or affection nearly as much as she wanted food or toys or other objects or wanted Sally to do something for her. When she got what she wanted she seemed to be content. If Sally did not give her what she wanted, Katie could get her upset, and that brought some contentment too. Having fun with Sally was no longer important to her.

On September 13, 1992, Katie entered protective custody in Augusta, Maine. She was now over 5 years of age. She had continued to change a great deal since she had begun her tantrums at 23 months. Before that, when Sally and Mike noticed that she didn't cry often, they didn't give it much thought. When they noticed that she didn't try to cling to them very much, they were pleased. Not that it was easier to raise her now. She always seemed to be angry and complaining and to throw herself or something else on the floor for what to them was little, if any, reason.

They really had to yell and punish Katie if they expected her to be quiet. But that strategy had its price. Often Katie got even with Sally for punishing her or for not giving her what she wanted. She was less likely to pay Mike back for his treatment of her. He slapped her hard when he was angry. Sally was safer and more fun to get upset. Once Sally refused to allow Katie to have any dessert. The next morning all of the chips and candy were gone. Another time Sally made her sit on the couch while Sally and Mike ate dinner. Later that evening Sally sat on the cushion to discover that Katie had urinated on it. Sally's hair brushes were missing, the toilet was stuffed up, the shampoo was spilled in the tub, and her favorite CDs were broken. Sally could not catch Katie being destructive or stealing something, but she knew that she was responsible and she would spank her often. What upset Sally the most was that Katie didn't seem to care. She would punish her more and more severely and Katie would look at her with resentment, indifference, or even pleasure. Somehow Katie seemed to be getting what she wanted no matter what Sally did.

Mike would get tired of Katie and Sally yelling and fighting. Sometimes he would grab Katie, push her into her room and slam the door. At times she would be in her room for hours or even the whole day. At other times he would blame Sally for Katie's behavior. Mike would find whatever Sally did to be lacking. Then they would scream and Katie would seem to be pleased. Often Mike would just leave. He might come back late at night drunk and have a hangover the next day. Katie would be quiet then. She knew Mike's unpredictable rage after drinking. Sally had trouble keeping quiet though. Often Mike would hit her and she might hit him back. But that made him worse, and Sally would get beaten. Katie would actually feel safer when her parents were fighting. If she stayed in her bedroom she'd be left alone. Also on the next day one of them might do something nice for her, if only to upset the other one.

Katie's mistake on September 13 was in allowing herself to get even with Mike rather than focusing her anger at Sally. That morning Katie spilled her cereal and Mike was in a particularly bad mood.

"You stupid ass." he said. "Can't you do anything right? Well, you're going to lick it up. Put your face on the table and start licking."

Katie yelled "No!" and tried to run from the kitchen. Mike grabbed her by her shirt, pulled her back to the table and pushed her face down onto the milk. "I said lick it up!"

He held her face in the milk and Katie screamed and fought. He held her more tightly, pushing her even harder against the table top. Then he began to wipe her face in the milk. "There, now you look like a pig, you little shit. Get out of here or I'll mop the floor with your hair."

Katie ran to her room where she screamed and threw her toys. When she heard Mike leave she was still enraged. She went back to the kitchen, took a carton of milk, brought it into his bedroom and dumped it over clothes in his bureau. She did show tears then, tears of anger and bitterness, not sadness or fear. Back in her room, however, she became frightened. She realized what she had done. Sally was not home. She knew of nothing that she could do if Mike returned.

Ten minutes later she heard Mike return home with a man, Kirk, who lived nearby. From her room she could hear them talking about his stereo system, which Kirk wanted to buy. Then she heard Mike walking into his bedroom.

She heard Mike scream, "That goddamn little bitch! That little fucking asshole! Where is she?"

He ran into her room and she hid on the floor behind her bed. He kicked her. He then dragged her by her hair into his bedroom and he threw his wet clothes on her. He kicked her again, spit on her, and began to urinate on her. She could not remember anything else happening, but could hear Kirk yelling at Mike and then Mike slamming the door.

Kirk left and told a neighbor who called the police. When they arrived, Katie was alone. Based on her appearance and Kirk's report, they took her to the hospital. They returned later and arrested Mike.

That night Margaret Davis, a child protective worker, brought Katie to her first foster home. Two months later, after a court hearing that was minimally contested by Sally, Katie entered permanent custody. The next day, November 9, 1992, she was assigned a Children's Services worker, Steven Fields, who had transferred from child protective services the week before.

COMMENTARY

Katie's first five years of life were characterized by specific incidents of physical abuse, verbal and emotional abuse, and long periods of emotional neglect. The endless acts of emotional violation to Katie's heart and soul through looks of disgust, screams of rejection, and the deadly silence of indifference were what led to her losing her desire to form an attachment with her parents. The trauma of sexual and physical violence is well documented. The "trauma of absence," which characterizes neglect, is less obvious to many. The cycle of abuse that leads inexorably from one generation to the next is powered most forcefully by the inability to enter and maintain meaningful attachments (see Egeland and Erickson 1987, Cicchetti 1989, Schore 1994). Regrettably, the absence of crucial affective interactions between parent and child is often not recognized by our society as being of sufficient importance to justify forcefully intervening in the life of a young child. As incredible as it may seem, there are reasons to be thankful that a child like Katie was abused by her parents, since that would justify initiating such intervention. Emotional abuse and neglect tend to be minimized by the legal system, although their long-term effects are profound.

Schore (1994), Greenspan and Lieberman (1988), Stern (1985), Mahler et al. (1975), and others describe the crucial role of attachment in the psychological development of the young child. (See Appendix 1 for a summary of the Developmental Attachment Patterns that are based on the work of these researchers.) Affective attunement, defined as the intersubjective sharing of affect, is central to the development of a secure attachment during the first year of life. Katie's attachment was severely damaged by the lack of sufficient attunement experiences with her parents. These experiences, the original dance of humanity, are the reciprocal interactions between the mother and infant that serve to regulate the infant's early affective life, especially those affects associated with joy and interest in her world. For attunement, Sally's affect would have to mirror Katie's, but they seldom did. These interactions are highly centered on eye contact, facial smiles and expressions, bodily movements, gestures, and touch. Through attunement the infant discovers her mother and in so doing, discovers herself. Katie discovered a mother who took little notice of her. Through her use of Sally as a mirror, Katie could only conclude that she, herself, was worthless and of no special interest or value. She would further conclude that Sally held little pleasure and joy for her. Sally would gradually become an object to manipulate in order to get things, or to attack when she became the source of discomfort. Any felt wish that Katie originally had to be a star in her mother's eyes or to snuggle closely to her magical warmth slowly faded during the thousands of times that Sally refused to dance.

Between the ages of 9 and 18 months, Katie would have been ready to enter into the world of social expectations. The toddler's behaviors are becoming increasingly organized as she integrates her own initiatives with her mother's socialization limits and directives. During socialization the toddler experiences shame, which is healthy and necessary for further stages of her development. The act of the mother saying "No" and limiting her toddler causes a healthy experience of shame during which the infant hangs her head, avoids eye contact, loses her smile, and is briefly motionless. During this experience, the toddler does not experience attunement with her mother and her expanding sense of self is felt as being diminished. In a healthy mother-toddler bond, the mother quickly reestablishes attunement with her child, and this enables her to integrate this socialization experience, to regulate her experience of shame and to remain in a secure, and even stronger, attachment with her mother. Early impulse control emerges and gradually the toddler is increasingly able to resolve the conflict between her wishes and the limits placed on her behaviors by her mother. From this integration emerges the next patterns, which involve increasingly complex cognitive developments. With language the young child is able gradually to identify and give expression to her inner life of affect and thought and she is beginning to reflect on herself. At the same time, she is internalizing her mother's wishes, affect, and behaviors. Sometime during the child's third year of life, she is able to enter into truly reciprocal, intentional interactions with her mother, and this skill continues to develop during the remaining years of her early childhood. This child has formed both a secure positive identity, as well as a secure, differentiated, attachment to her mother. Katie was not such a child.

In Katie's first 18 months, she experienced many fewer affective attunement experiences than are necessary for the development of her early sense of self, her affect and neurological development and regulation, and her emotional bonding with her mother. With an insufficiently developed sense of attunement with her mother, she was ill-prepared for routine shaming experiences and their effects on these early intrapersonal and interpersonal processes. However, her shaming experiences were far from routine. The extensive rejection, contempt, and disgust that she experienced when limited, greatly damaged her few early positive self-experiences. These pervasive shame experiences were made even more traumatic to her development because they were not followed by quick reattunement experiences that would bring her the reassurance needed to maintain any possibility that she could develop a stable and positive sense of self and a secure attachment. As a result, she denied her behaviors and experiences associated with shame and she increasingly reacted with rage in response to these hostile and self-negating realities. She stopped seeking or responding to any attunement experiences that might become available. Rather, her life became one of increasing emotional isolation from her parents, along with behavioral patterns meant to defensively control her environment, and early cognitive constructs that conveyed a sense that she was bad and that her parents did not value her and were not to be trusted. According to Schore (pp. 458–459), the severe pathological shame experienced by Katie greatly limited the capacity for internalization that enables a differentiated attachment, and greatly compromised her early schema of herself. Katie's shame was a cancer throughout her psychological self. It permeated every perception, experience, and behavior and left no air or light for her growth. For good reason, J. S. Grotstein refers to pervasive shame as the "black hole" of one's psychic life (quoted by Schore, p. 421). Kaufman's excellent work, *The Psychology of Shame* (1996), demonstrates the devastating effects of pervasive shame on first the development of one's affective life, and eventually one's very identity.

Katie's path was cut through a harsh and barren land. It began in terror—an infant lying among noise, cold, and pain. As she began to comprehend this land she moved into despair, a sadness that acknowledged what the core of her self screamed for and did not find. Terror and despair created her tears—tears that parched and cracked her heart, but which caused nothing to grow in her land. She was not soothed by any presence and affection from her parents, and she did not develop the ability to soothe herself. She did not seek to please her parents or become like them. She embarked on an isolated journey in which manipulation, anger, and control—

not love and autonomy—are crucial for survival. When this journey has become irreversible, it represents the death of the soul. At 2 years of age, Katie's path was following that direction.

Shame accompanied Katie along her path. Shame permeated her sense of self and it left its scent on every initiative and interaction that defined her young life. Shame is not a warm companion. It turns her away from moments of joy as well as feelings of worth and contentment, holding her head down and away from the disgusted gazes of her parents. Shame etches its message into her muscles, her heart, and her mind: You are flawed. You bring no joy to others. You are bad and without merit.

But Katie's shame, as is often the case, does not lie quietly, seeking not to disturb. Rather, it erupts in rage again and again. Not being given a place in the sun, it screams to blot it out for all. Near the sun, for those who have no place, there is pain. It screams: Yes, I have no worth. I am worthless. And so are you! I am hateful. And I hate you! I will not feel the pain that never leaves. I will give it to you!

Such was Katie, as she was brought to her first foster home. She could not, and would not, dance. She felt only the rage that she used to medicate her shame.

2

Enter the State: False Starts

FOSTER HOME #1—RUTH DALEY

When Katie entered foster care she was placed in the home of Ruth Daley. Ruth lived in Sydney with her husband, two children of their own, and another foster child, 3-year-old Dustin. Ruth had been a foster mother for a number of years, following a tradition started by her own mother a generation before her.

Katie's Children's Services caseworker was Steven Fields, who had recently transferred from the child protective services of the Department. Steven was excited about the transfer. He would no longer be investigating reports of abuse and determining the initial service plan. He had become very tired of trying to convince parents that abusing their child was wrong. He was weary of confronting their lies and absorbing their rage when he wanted to scream at them for violating their own children. He could not face more excuses, more blame flowing in every direction, and more indifference to the terrible physical, emotional, and mental scars that they left on their children. He had little empathy left for those parents, although intellectually he knew that they most likely had been abused themselves and had not received any help. Finally, he could no longer face the extreme doubt and fear that he felt whenever he decided to allow a child to remain in a home with the possibility of further abuse.

Now he would be working with the foster children who had been placed in protective custody. They would be in safe homes while he worked with their parents to see if they would be reunified with them. If the parents were unable or unwilling to work, Steven would be able to ensure that the child was provided with an alternative that could ultimately lead to his or her adoption into a stable and loving home.

The first case that Steven reviewed was Katie Harrison. He felt drawn to her when he saw her big brown eyes, short straight black hair, and her wide smile in the photo under her name. What a delightful looking 5-year-old girl. Steven quickly reviewed her file. She lived with Ruth Daley, who had been a foster parent for 10 years. Other workers found her to be competent and committed to the children in her care. Katie was now in a Head Start program. She had a therapist, Jan Temple, at the Mental Health Center.

He discovered that Katie's parents, Mike and Sally, were still together. He couldn't understand how Sally could stay with Mike after what he had done to Katie. Sally had weekly, one-hour visits with Katie that were supervised by a homemaker from Catholic Charities. She had completed a psychological evaluation that expressed some concerns about her functioning and general parenting. Sally agreed to begin individual counseling at the mental health center as well as to sign up for a parenting course. Mike had criminal charges pending and he had been advised by his attorney not to talk to a psychologist until after his case was heard.

Steven called the Mental Health Center and was fortunate to get through to Jan Temple. Jan indicated that she really didn't know Katie very well yet, having seen her only twice so far. She would be spending some time getting to know her and establishing a relationship. Right now she allowed Katie to choose whatever she wanted to do in her play therapy sessions. So far Jan found her to be a delight. Katie hadn't said much about her life with her parents.

Steven called Ruth Daly and arranged to go to her home and take Katie to McDonald's for lunch. It was about a twenty-minute drive from his office. Ruth and her family lived in an old farmhouse surrounded by large fields. Steven saw two dogs as he pulled into the driveway. He decided that Katie couldn't have asked for a better home.

Ruth was a friendly, down-to-earth woman who had lived in Sydney most of her life. She met Steven at his car and she showed him their small barn with a pony and two pigs.

"How are things going with Katie?" asked Steven.

"She's quite a handful so far. We're hoping that she'll settle in as she gets more used to living here. She's a strong-willed kid, probably had to be to survive. She does not like to be told what to do! She's also plenty rough on Dustin, my 3-year-old. I got to watch her a lot."

"How is she about the visits with her mother?"

"She goes OK but doesn't talk about them much. She never mentions her mother at other times either. She's likely to be a lot angrier and more easily upset for a day or so after the visits."

Just then Katie came running outside yelling "McDonald's!" Steven laughed and immediately liked this lively and direct child. Ruth introduced him to her and without pause Katie asked Steven if he would take her to McDonald's right then. He smiled and said that he could. He walked and she ran to his car. Steven saw this as an excellent beginning. No worries now that she might be afraid of him. He even figured that she liked him and was happy that he was her caseworker. He'd not let her down.

At McDonald's Steven discovered the amount of energy that was required to supervise this 5-year-old child. She did not hesitate to tell him what she wanted to eat, where she wanted to sit, when she wanted to play in the play area, and when she wanted her apple pie. He was only too eager to please her—she was so appreciative and enjoyable. She did fuss when it was time to leave, but what kid wouldn't? Steven tried to explain to her what his job was on their way back to Sydney. She wasn't interested. Nor was she interested in leaving on her seat belt. He had to tell her twice to put it back on. She paused and looked at him, but did what she was told. That wasn't too hard. She just needed some time to listen to what she was told to do. One shouldn't push her too hard; she'd eventually do it. He thought of making this suggestion to Ruth, but forgot about it when he was meeting Dustin and her own older kids. When he left he heard her hollering to Katie to put down Dustin's truck. She kept yelling, a little louder each time, as Steven walked to his car. He would have to talk with her about other ways to approach Katie.

Over the next few months Steven had gotten to know his first five children and he had been given fifteen more. His supervision indicated that he could expect five more in a few weeks so that he would have a full case load of twenty-five. The paperwork! The visitations between parents and children that he had to arrange and often supervise if there was no homemaker or aid available. The preparation for court! So many written documents to review, organize, and prepare for the Assistant Attorney General who would be representing DHS in court. The requests from foster parents also took much time and energy. Then there were the frantic phone calls from a foster parent indicating that a child's behavior was intolerable and that he or she would have to move within a few weeks. Steven would try to resolve the problem, but his efforts were too often unsuccessful and he spent hours finding another home.

It was after his second failure to maintain a child's placement that he got a call from Ruth Daly saying that Katie's behavior was getting worse.

"It seems like every day she does something that I have to get on her about," said Ruth. "Yesterday she threw Dustin's little bike into the pig pen and we didn't find it until this morning. What a sorry mess it was! The day before she stuffed up the toilet with some wash cloths, and a few days before that she stole the bracelet that Bill had given me for Christmas. We still haven't found it. And those are only the *big* things that she's done."

"How do you know that she took your bracelet?" asked Steven.

"She's the only one who was upstairs alone that morning when I missed it. Plus she had shown a lot of interest in it."

"Is anything bothering her now?" wondered Steven.

"Nothing I can think of. The visits are hard, but they've always been."

"Have you talked with her therapist?"

"Not about these most recent things. I usually fill her in on things before the therapy session. We'll be seeing her tomorrow."

"If it's OK with you I'd like to sit in on the meeting," said Steven.

"That's fine," said Ruth. "I'll see you there."

The next day, January 15, 1993 was busy, but Steven arranged his schedule to be at Jan Temple's office by 10 A.M. He did not want to lose this placement.

Ruth told Jan about the bike, toilet, and bracelet and added a few more that involved Katie swearing at Ruth, breaking her 15-year-old son's tape recorder, and putting a nail in the pig feed.

"I've tried everything," Ruth said. "I tell her not to do something and she listens fine and then does it anyway. When I catch her she lies about it even if I'm right there when she does it. If I tell her to stop doing something she wants to do, that's when she'll swear and try to hit me. And when she gets mad at someone, that's when she'll find a way to pay him back. She was mad at my son for telling me about her hitting Dustin, and two hours later his tape recorder was broken. Nothing seems to work. Time out, losing privileges, talking to her. We don't know what to try next."

Jan was an experienced therapist who had treated a number of foster children over the past ten years. She liked Ruth and had agreed with Steven that this was a good placement and needed to be saved.

"Katie has only lived with you now for about four months," Jan said. "She's still showing the signs of abuse that she probably received for four years. She's still a very mad little girl and she doesn't trust anyone much. I know that she's really hard to raise now, Ruth, but I'm hoping that if we can keep working with her, she eventually will begin to trust more and not be so hard. It will take a lot of patience, but I think that she can make it."

"Have you seen progress in therapy yet?" asked Steven.

"Nothing significant. She's an easy kid to work with. In therapy she doesn't present any of the problems that she's showing at home. She is showing some of her anger in her dollhouse play. She can be quite aggressive in her play with the parent dolls often hurting the children. I'm hoping that she can work through some of her fear and rage for how she was treated."

Turning to Ruth, Jan added, "Catch her being good and let her know how pleased you are. Pick your battles, overlooking some of her less extreme behaviors. Use time-outs, but only one minute for each year of her life. Use a timer and only start it when she is sitting in time-out without screaming at you."

"What should I do when she breaks or steals something?" asked Ruth.

"If you're sure she did it, give her a time-out and make her say she's sorry. Try to get your kids to not leave important things around where she can get them. Make their rooms off-limits to her."

"I'm afraid she'll find a way to break something," Ruth replied. "We can only watch her so much. She can be out of my sight for one minute and be into something."

"Maybe you'll have to put locks on the bedroom doors up high so that she can't reach them," Jan suggested.

Steven took notes of Jan's recommendations. Her early suggestion that Katie needed patience seemed important and he emphasized that to Ruth. He added that Ruth was important to Katie.

Ruth thought for a moment and then said, "So far I'm not so sure what I mean to her. If she left tomorrow I don't think that she'd give any of the family another thought."

Steven was not sure what to say. Jan broke the silence by suggesting that they meet again in a month and review Katie's progress. Steven and Ruth left for the waiting room and Jan went to get Katie for her session.

"Do you really think that Katie wouldn't care if I moved her tomorrow?" asked Steven.

"I'm afraid I do," replied Ruth quietly.

On January 27, 1993, Steven's wife Jenny gave birth to Rebecca at home on their king size bed. "She's so beautiful, so precious. She's ours." Jenny, lost in wonder, looked over Rebecca's body from her tiny toe nails to her dark brown hair. She touched her and pulled her closer and slowly rocked her and spoke to her, welcoming her into the family. Steven could not make out what Jenny was saying to Rebecca, but whatever it was, it was right.

For the next week Rebecca could not say or do anything that did not get a response from Jenny or Steven. Jenny's mom had come and Steven was happy to have her. Alice did most of the cooking and laundering and she managed to keep the house fairly neat. She also brought an air of confidence. Her approval of how Jenny and Steven were caring for the baby was important to them. She knew kids in ways that they didn't. She and Jenny talked more than Steven could ever recall. So far she was becoming a great grandmother.

Since Alice would be staying with them for one more week, Steven was able to go back to work without anxiety. He was greeted by a message from Jan Temple.

"Hi, Jan, I just got back. What's up?"

"The last three weeks with Katie in her foster home have been as difficult as ever. Ruth seems to be wearing out. I've begun to talk with Katie about her behaviors at home, but she wants none of it."

"Has Katie done anything serious?" he asked.

"No, unless you would call her constant defiance, anger, and destructiveness serious. We have a behavioral specialist here who could consult with us about developing a behavioral management plan for Ruth. That might give her some tools that would be more effective than what she's doing now. Do you want me to set up a meeting with him?"

Steven replied that it probably would be a good idea to develop a more effective way to get through to Katie. "Get it set up and let me know. I'll make sure I can attend. I'll give Ruth a call and offer her my support."

When Ruth answered the phone she spoke with Steven for ten minutes about Rebecca before he was able to ask about Katie.

"I just don't know how to get through to her," said Ruth. "She's a great kid but she does not want to be told what to do. If things are going her way she does fine. But my goodness, that's not the way life is all the time. She will not tolerate not getting her way."

"Why don't I talk with her," said Steven.

"That would be great," Ruth replied, "When I talk to her I get nowhere. In fact, she seems to be thinking that she's somehow winning."

Steven told Ruth about the meeting with the behavioral specialist and he arranged to see Katie the next day.

On February 6, 1993 Steven picked up Katie for another trip to McDonald's. He would let her buy what she wanted, then they would go into the play area for awhile. After having fun she would be more likely to cooperate when he talked with her about her problems. As they headed back home Steven told Katie about Ruth's concerns. He asked her why she thought she was getting into trouble so much. Katie's manner changed immediately. She seemed to be sullen and tense. He repeated his question and she replied: "Ruth isn't fair to me. She's always yelling at me but she never yells at Dustin. She likes him!"

Steven suggested to her that Ruth did like her. He suggested further that Ruth might get angry at her behaviors, but not at her.

"Yes she does!" said Katie. "She never lets me do anything. She's mean to me!"

Steven did not know what to say. He did not think that arguing with her would change her mind. Maybe if he told Ruth about Katie's feelings Ruth could reassure her and try not to get angry with her so much.

"You're in a good home, Katie," said Steven. "I'll try to help you and Ruth get along better. I want you to be happier with your mom."

"She's not my mom! I don't like her anyway," said Katie.

When Steven got back to Ruth's home she asked how it went.

"She thinks that you like Dustin more than her," said Steven. "She seems to need reassurance that you do care about her."

"I don't know what else I could do to show her I care about her and want to help her," said Ruth.

"When she does something wrong could you tell her you do care about her and only are correcting her to teach her what is right?" suggested Steven.

"I'll try to be more careful when I scold her," replied Ruth. She did not seem too optimistic that Steven's suggestion would help.

Back at the office Steven asked Barbara, a colleague, for ideas. "She's in a good home but I don't think that she believes it. How can we get through to her?"

"She probably doesn't know how to be 'good,'" replied Barbara. "It can take a long time before it gets better. Some kids just never do."

"Why not?" asked Steven.

"I wish we knew," said Barbara. "If Ruth can hang in there maybe Katie will begin to trust her. But if Ruth gives up on her, she may never trust anyone."

Steven was troubled. What could he do? "It seems to me that Rebecca trusts me and Jenny more in 1 week than Katie trusts Ruth after 5 months. Why can't Katie get it?"

"Rebecca was never abused and neglected. Katie has a lot of reasons not to trust. She needs more time. Your job is to help Ruth to give Katie more time so that she won't have another reason not to trust."

"Ruth isn't sure that Katie really cares about staying with her," said Steven.

"She must care. She probably doesn't know how to show it."

"Well," said Steven, "she had better learn how soon or we may have a big problem."

On February 11, Steven and Ruth met Bill Jenkins, the behavioral specialist, at Jan's office. Steven liked Bill. He seemed to be a reasonable man who wanted to help Ruth and Katie. They all presented him with Katie's behaviors over the past five months.

"I think we have to begin finding ways for Katie to experience some success," said Bill. "She's in trouble so often that she probably has given up all expectations that she can do better. We should start with a reward system that is easy for her to succeed in and gradually build up the demands. Why don't we start by developing a list of behaviors that we want her to increase, behaviors we want her to decrease, as well as things that she likes that we can use as rewards."

For the next forty-five minutes Bill helped Ruth to identify very specific behaviors that needed to change in one direction or the other. He also determined from her what Katie really liked to do so that he could make these privileges contingent upon appropriate behaviors. He identified three behaviors—no aggression, following directions, and asking for permission—that they would focus on first. He broke each day into blocks of time and suggested that Katie receive one play coin for each of the three behavioral goals that she attained in every block of time. She could trade in her coins for rewards each day, or she could save her coins for larger rewards available each week. Bill suggested that Ruth start by making it fairly easy to get the rewards so that Katie would "buy into the program" through having early successes. They would review the success of the program in two weeks. Ruth seemed to be very motivated to try the plan. She would explain it to Katie that evening and start the next day. Steven felt some cautious optimism that this plan would help.

Three days later Steven called Ruth to find out how the plan was working.

"So far so good," said Ruth. "Katie seems to be interested in getting the coins. In fact she is quick to remind me if I owe her some. She's not aggressive so often and she is more willing to do what I tell her. She's not spending them so far. She's saving them to buy a doll next week."

When they met with Bill, Ruth was not as pleased as she was initially. She said that Katie got her doll, but after two days she broke it. "Now she's working to go to McDonald's. She's not getting the coins as fast as she did earlier, but she's still doing better."

Bill made some modifications in the program. Katie would have to spend some of her coins each day, rather than be able to save them all.

They met again in two more weeks and Ruth was becoming somewhat discouraged. She indicated that Katie would still get coins, but again, not as frequently as she once did. She seemed to take some pleasure in the fact that she had discovered how to earn rewards, while at the same time maintain many of her previous problem behaviors.

"Yesterday she hit Dustin and knocked him down. Ten minutes later she gave me five coins to watch a video. She had a smile that seemed to be saying 'ha, ha, you have to let me watch it even if I did hit Dustin'. I wanted to take her coins and throw them away, but I didn't. She got her movie."

Bill suggested that Ruth modify the program again, but not make it harder to earn rewards. He was reluctant to have Katie lose coins for certain behaviors out of fear that a negative cycle would emerge again. Katie also would get a special reward at the end of each day if she was not aggressive the entire day.

In March they met again with Bill. Ruth was now even more frustrated.

"If she wants something a lot, she will follow the program perfectly. As soon as she gets it, she'll be as aggressive and oppositional as ever. Or if for some reason she doesn't particularly want any reward, she'll do whatever she wants that day and not try to follow the plan at all. Then if she changes her mind and wants the reward, she's as mad as ever at me for not giving it to her."

Bill suggested that Katie was learning that she had to follow the plan if she wanted rewards. She was testing it now and once she realized that Ruth would follow through with the plan and not reward her, she would be more likely to comply. He then suggested changing the value of the coins in order to increase the reinforcement for Katie's behavior, which was of greatest concern to Ruth.

By the end of March, Bill acknowledged that Katie's behavior was not significantly different than how it was when the program began seven weeks earlier. When she wanted something she easily did what it took to get it. Nothing carried over afterward. Bill still feared that if Ruth made it harder to get the coins, or if Katie lost coins that she earned already, her motivation would be even less.

In April and May, 1993, Steven and Ruth spoke three times each week about Katie. Their conversation consisted mostly of Ruth reporting something new that Katie had done. Steven initially would ask various questions, trying to understand her motives so that they would know how to prevent it from recurring. But why would she scratch the paint on the minister's car when he came one afternoon for a visit? Why would she destroy her own mattress with a fork? He could begin to understand why she took crackers and cookies. But why would she take dirt and put it in the toaster? Why did she scream and swear and kick at Ruth for telling her to put her clothes in the drawer? Why did she hide behind the door and jump out at Ruth or Dustin as they walked past? Once Ruth was so frightened that she jumped, lost her balance, and twisted her ankle. Katie seemed to like the video *Aladdin*. So why did she put it in five inches of water in the sink? Steven met with colleagues to discuss what he could do to improve the situation.

"Why not try to be sure that Ruth gets respite from Katie one weekend a month?" one suggested.

"She'll be 6 in August," said another. "She might be able to attend a summer recreation program that would help."

"There's a parenting program at the Mental Health Center that might be helpful to Ruth," said Steven's supervisor, Kathy. "You might offer it to her. She'd probably appreciate the offer even if she doesn't want to enroll."

"Also, you mentioned that Katie's behavior is somewhat worse after visits with her mother. Ask Jan if she'd be willing to write a letter recommending that the visits be discontinued until Katie has begun to stabilize in her functioning."

"But how do we get Katie to stop acting like she's the worst kid in the world, or like she's in the worst home in the world?" asked Steven.

"Steven, if there was something that you haven't tried that might help, Jan, Bill, or Ruth, or one of us would have suggested it by now," said Kathy. "I know how hard you want this to work. You're doing the best you can. So is Ruth. She needs your support now. Just listen and reassure her that this is not her fault."

Steven replied, after a long pause, "You're right. But Katie's just a little 5-year-old. She can be so cute and friendly and helpful. Why won't she stop the rest? I know she was abused, but it's been eight months. Ruth has been so good to her. Jan's a good therapist. When will it end?"

On June 17, 1993, Katie's placement with Ruth ended. Katie and Dustin were outside playing at the swing set with Ruth watching them closely from the open kitchen window while she relaxed after lunch. They were chasing each other around the slide, laughing together more than Ruth could recall them ever doing. Katie could have caught Dustin but she was careful not to and he laughed harder. Katie looked at Ruth, seemingly for approval that she was playing so nicely with Dustin. Ruth smiled and yelled that she'd get them each a popsicle since they were playing so well together.

As Ruth opened the freezer she heard a scream. She hurried to the window to see Dustin on the ground with Katie standing over him. In horror, Ruth watched Katie pull back her foot and kick Dustin in the head. Ruth yelled, "Katie, no!" and ran outside. As she approached, she saw Katie kick him again and then run behind the swing. Ruth went to Dustin, who was screaming and crying on the ground. She held him and tried to calm him. She looked toward Katie and caught her breath. Katie was watching her and Dustin with a smile that Ruth had never seen before. Katie seemed excited and pleased, not frightened or angry. Katie was happy!

Ruth took Dustin inside to tend to his bruises. She checked him over and held him until he stopped crying. Katie then came in and demanded her popsicle!

"You hurt Dustin, Katie," said Ruth. "You're not getting a popsicle. Tell him that you're sorry."

"You said I could have a popsicle!" screamed Katie.

"No Katie!" said Ruth. "Not after what you did to Dustin. Say you're sorry."

"I hate you!" said Katie. "I'm not sorry! I hate you!"

Katie ran outside again, while Ruth continued to try to comfort Dustin. Finally she went looking for Katie. She found that Katie had begun to throw rocks at the pony in the pasture. As Ruth approached Katie ran toward the road. Ruth hesitated, not knowing if it would make matters worse if she ran after her. She decided to return to the house and watch her from the windows. Her decision worked and Katie slowly returned to home in about thirty minutes. She walked past the kitchen where Ruth and Dustin were and looked angrily at them both. She was mad at them! Didn't she have any awareness of what she had just done?

That evening Ruth and her husband decided that Katie would have to be placed elsewhere. The next day Ruth called Steven and, with both sorrow and guilt, informed him that Katie would have to leave soon. Steven could say nothing. He knew that Ruth was right. He would have to find a home for Katie that had no small children. He finally reassured Ruth that he knew that she had done the best that she could.

COMMENTARY

What motivates the poorly attached child often does not resemble the more normal motivations of childhood. For this reason, the usual reinforcers are not likely to be effective for any period of time. Concrete reinforcements and activities may work briefly, but such external objects have little inherent motivation. Generalization from such objects to relationships are unlikely to ever occur since relationships themselves have little reinforcing value. The typical reinforcers of the poorly attached child are not common to most kids. They include being in control of the feelings and behaviors of others and winning every power struggle. These children also love saying "No!" and maintaining their negative view of themselves and others. They also find it reinforcing to be able to need no one, and to avoid both experiences of reciprocal fun and love, and also having to ask for favors and being praised.

Most often the stickers and "m&ms" selected to direct children into more socially appropriate behaviors are no match for the very powerful reinforcers that developed within them during the first two years of life. When parents present such children with clear and specific behavioral plans, they are making a mistake. They are telling the child what is important to them, now making him more able to know how to gain control and cause them distress. It is similar to having the coaches of a football team presenting the opposing team with their game plan prior to the contest.

Traditional play therapy is often not effective in facilitating the development of attachment between a child and his parents. Play therapists tend to leave the parent out of the therapeutic process with the exception of providing parent counseling in separate sessions. When we want the child to begin to form an attachment with her new parent, we should seriously consider bringing that parent into the treatment sessions. And while play therapists stress that the therapeutic relationship is the vehicle for therapeutic progress, children who have not successfully formed an attachment with a parent are not likely to be able to form a relationship in an hour or two a week that will have an impact on their profound attachment deficiencies. Also, much play therapy tends to be fairly nondirective. Since poorly attached children compulsively need to maintain control, they are often unlikely to relinquish that control when they have a choice. They will then be able to avoid indefinitely experiences of both attunement and shame.

Many foster parents are similar to Ruth. They are very committed to providing the foster children in their care with a family experience similar to what they provide their birth children. They often work for weeks and months with a foster child who is presenting severe problems that disrupt their family life, only to discover that if they raise the poorly attached child in a manner similar to how they raised their birth children, the results will not be the same. But the principles and strategies needed for raising these children are often difficult to incorporate into a parent's routine child rearing initiatives and responses. For the foster care system to be adequate in providing stable and therapeutic homes for children with significant attachment problems, it must develop and maintain special foster homes provided with highly specific recommendations that have some probability of success in assisting the child to learn to form a secure attachment.

For the foster care system to be more responsive to the needs of our children, it must be able to respond quickly and appropriately to these children's placement needs for security and continuity. Each child should have only one temporary placement prior to moving to a permanent home, either back with the birth parents or into an adoptive home. One of the preconditions for the development of severe attachment problems is multiple placements. Yet many children experience multiple placements in our foster care system. Although developed to safeguard, protect, and nourish these vulnerable children, our system often can fail as profoundly to meet their psychological and developmental needs as did the original family's abuse and neglect.

Foster parents critically need sufficient training to be able to begin to understand the effects of abuse and neglect on the daily functioning of their child. They need to know how to most effectively raise this child, who may well have significant deficits in his affective, cognitive, and behavioral development. Ruth, a competent and committed foster parent, did not have the knowledge and intervention strategies that she needed if she was going to effectively engage a child as damaged as Katie, and lead her into the realities of attachment and healthy family relationships. When Katie's first placment ended in failure it certainly confirmed in her mind that she was a bad girl and that no one would ever really love her. Ruth might have been nicer than Sally to her, but Katie would have to conclude that Ruth ultimately saw her as Sally did. Namely, she was a child who was not worth the effort.

Steven quickly found that he had monumental responsibilities in trying to provide his foster children the comprehensive services that they needed. These children often require various psychological, medical, educational, and social services, all of which need to be coordinated if their various needs are to be adequately met. At the same time, he needs to be working on the reunification plans with Katie's parents. He has to monitor the services that they are receiving and insure that the visitation arrangements are in place. He has to communicate constantly with lawyers and prepare reports for the court. If he fails to maintain adequate paperwork, he could hurt Katie in court much more than he might help her by spending time with her.

To provide truly effective services for children in foster care requires a great amount of time, money, training, and commitment from significant members of our society. If Katie could have been maintained in her home with Sally and Mike, through teaching her parents how to notice and respond to her developmental needs, and providing them with other psychological and social services, she would have had an easier time. Preventive services, services initiated at birth, early childhood education, and family support services all should be in place in order to prevent the need for children like Katie to enter the foster care system. Given that, however, when parents like Sally and Mike either refuse to or are unable to benefit from such services, we must have a strong and effective foster care system that is able to meet children like Katie's developmental needs. We cannot endlessly attempt "family preservation" programs while the children in such programs continue to experience emotional abuse and neglect and remain at risk for physical and sexual abuse. Living in circumstances of emotional abuse and neglect for months is causing signficant psychological damage to the minds and hearts of these children. When mental health and social services providers refuse to recognize that reality, we all have little reason to hope that our society will ever take the developmental needs of these children seriously.

FOSTER HOME #2—KAREN MILLER

On June 25, 1993, Steven went to Ruth's home to bring Katie to her new home. The most suitable home that he had been able to find was with Karen and Ken Miller, a fairly young couple who had become foster parents nine months earlier. They had a few short placements that seemed to go well. There were no children in the home. Karen would be home most of the time. She had a part-time job with a local business and she had daycare arrangements when necessary. They were excited about taking Katie because of her age and the likelihood that she would be able to stay with them for awhile. When Steven spoke with Karen she even suggested that she and her husband might be interested in adopting Katie if that became possible. Steven informed her that the plan was for Katie to eventually be able to return to live with her parents, if they were able to meet the terms of the service agreement.

When Steven had told Katie that she would be moving to Karen and Ken's house, she only asked if she could bring the toys and clothes that Ruth had given her. When, in the most supportive way possible, Ruth explained to Katie the reasons for the move, Katie seemed indifferent to her support. She showed no emotion until later, when she became excited about moving and spoke about it as if it were an adventure.

During the drive to Karen and Ken's house Katie spoke constantly about nothing relevant. When she paused for breath, Steven said, "I'm sure you're sad about having to move."

"No, I'm not," she replied. "This is a better home because you said there are no other kids."

"But you'll miss Ruth. You've lived with the Daleys a long time. Maybe you can visit them after awhile."

"I won't miss them. Ruth was mean to me. This is going to be more fun."

When they arrived, Karen and Ken were waiting on the porch. Steven introduced them and Katie gave them each a hug and called them 'mom' and 'dad'. She began asking questions about their home and she was pleased during the tour, followed by a snack of cookies and milk. She immediately ignored Steven and spoke to her new parents. When Steven went to leave, she took no notice of him. Neither did Karen or Ken who were enthralled by this charming child.

Later that week Steven called Karen to check on Katie.

"She's such a good kid. We really enjoy having her," said Karen. "Once in awhile she gets angry when we tell her to come for dinner or to get ready for bed, but it's nothing major. I think that she likes being here."

"I'm glad that it's working out so well," said Steven. "Any trouble with taking food or destroying things?"

"None at all," said Karen. "You know, I think that maybe Ruth was a little too hard on her about eating. We give her plenty of food at meals and snacks too and she doesn't take anything to her room at night."

"Well, again, I'm glad that she's off to such a good start."

"Maybe I shouldn't say this, but I really think that Ruth just wasn't the right mother for her. Katie tells me how much she was yelled at and how often she got punished. She needed more understanding and patience than Ruth was able to give."

Steven defended Ruth and indicated that Katie's behaviors had been very difficult. Later he shared Karen's comments with Barbara. They both agreed that Karen was minimizing Katie's responsibility for her difficulties. Barbara expressed the fear that Karen might have to learn the hard way how serious Katie's problems seemed to be.

Over the next few weeks Karen continued to tell Steven how well things were going. He called Jan who indicated that in therapy Katie was somewhat more resistant. In fact, she seemed to be complaining about therapy and Karen had asked Jan if therapy might no longer be necessary. Jan suggested that they continue for another few months and then reevaluate it.

On August 4, Steven stopped by the Miller home to give Katie a birthday present. A big family party was underway and Katie had no interest in Steven or his present. Karen was busily enjoying the activity and Steven decided that things could not be going much better. He met Karen's mother, Anne, who spoke with pleasure about Katie. As he talked with Anne he discovered that Katie apparently was demonstrating some behavioral problems that Karen had not told him about. The next day Steven called Karen to ask about the problems hinted at by her mother.

"Oh, Mom worries too much," said Karen. "Sure Katie is not perfect but we're managing well. She peed on the couch once and she was really sorry about it. She has had a few other problems like that but nothing major."

Steven began to wonder about Katie's placement but could not be sure if there were more problems than Karen was willing to acknowledge. With other kids in his caseload demanding his attention, he had little choice but to assume that Karen would tell him if she really had some problems with Katie.

On September 16, 1993, Jan called and said, "We have a problem, Steven. Katie is mad at Karen for not buying her some candy when they stopped at K-Mart before today's appointment. She seems to have decided to get Karen in trouble for not buying it."

"Is she making up lies because she didn't get what she wanted?" asked Steven.

"I don't think they're lies," said Jan. "She said that Karen had tied her to a chair because she would not sit for a time-out. There are marks on her wrists that look like rope marks. She also said that Karen slapped her and scratched her face. There is a scratch mark. She gave other examples that have a ring of truth to them. Then she asked me if I would yell at Karen and tell her to get Katie some candy."

"What other examples?" asked Steven.

"She said that Karen has called her a little bitch. She said that she was locked in a closet and also that Karen forced food into her mouth. But the scary thing for me is that Katie was really upset that I was going to call you. She does not want to move. She said that Karen is a great mother because she always buys her things and lets her do what she wants. She just wants that candy bar."

Steven indicated that he would be right over. Jan said that she would wait with Karen and Katie until he arrived.

At Jan's office, while Katie stayed in the waiting room, Steven asked her to tell Karen what Katie had said. As Jan talked Karen became upset and tense. She quickly said that the rope marks were caused accidentally when Katie was playing with some rope. Karen had never tied her up. As Jan continued, giving one example after the next, Karen began to cry.

"Why isn't she ever satisfied?" Karen finally asked. "We have given her so much. Nothing is too good for her. But she still wants more. And when I finally say 'no' she screams at me and says that I'm mean to her. She's never satisfied with me!"

"Did you slap and scratch her?" asked Steven.

"Yes, yes, and I've spanked her too." Karen replied. "It's just that sometimes I can't take it. She's always mad at me. She'll only do what I ask if I'll give her something. Sometimes I get so mad I just want to hurt her like she's hurting me. I couldn't stand it."

"You could have asked us for help," Steven said quietly.

"You would have thought it was my fault. I thought it would get better. I thought that someday she'd realize how much I love her. I just wanted her to be happy with us. I hated it when she told me that she didn't want to live with me."

"I'm sorry that this has been so difficult, Karen. I wish that you had told us. Maybe we could have helped before it got to this point. I'm afraid with all that has happened that we'll have to move Katie."

"No!" wailed Karen. "I do love her and won't do any of those things again. Please give me another chance."

"Even if you were able to control your anger at Katie, and ask us for help, I'm afraid that so much has happened that Katie would not be able to change while living in your home. I don't think that it would be fair to you or Katie to keep her with you, Karen. I'm sorry."

Jan agreed with what Steven said and supported Karen. She then called in Katie and they told her that she would be moving.

"No!" screamed Katie. "I want to stay with Karen. I lied. She hasn't done anything wrong."

"Yes I have," said Karen. "You don't have to lie for me. You weren't wrong, Katie, I was."

"I want to stay with Karen. She buys me things and lets me watch TV. She lets me play more than Ruth did," said Katie.

As Karen cried, Katie stared at her but showed no emotion herself. She eventually went with Steven with no difficulty and when she got into his car she immediately told him that she wanted to go to another home "like Karen's."

At the office Steven found some crayons and paper for Katie while he went to tell his supervisor, Kathy, about the crisis. She supported his decision to move Katie and they began searching for a home. Kathy recalled a recent foster child who was returned to his parents' custody.

"Susan Cummings is a good foster parent, Steven. From what you've said about Katie, I think that she could manage her. Why don't I give her a call?" She was back in ten minutes to say that Susan agreed to take Katie immediately and would consider keeping her indefinitely but wanted to learn more about her first.

Steven breathed easier as he drove Katie to Karen's to get her things and say goodbye. Katie would be going to her third home.

COMMENTARY

Katie's response to the move from Ruth's to Karen's home is not unusual for children who have difficulty forming attachments. Such children show no grief when they leave a home that they may have lived in for months, if not years. Their lack of emotion seems to reflect how their relationships with their foster or adoptive parents contain no depth. Their parents are there to be used. They are objects whose function is to meet their immediate concrete needs. Such objects are interchangeable. Their parental value is determined solely by the percentage of times that they gratify their wishes. Since these children are never satisfied for long, they inevitably became dissatisfied with their current foster parents. They are usually quite willing to move to another home.

One might speculate that Katie was hiding her feelings of grief from others. She might be pretending that her feelings were shallow in order to minimize the rejection that she felt. However, Katie truly had not begun the internalization process with either Ruth or Karen that would have elicited the feelings of loss and abandonment. Katie was a very "selfish" individual who had very little empathy for others and did not experience her parent as a separate person with whom she cared to bond. She needed to be "selfish" because her sense of self was fragmented, filled with gaps, and covered with shame. All of her psychic energy was spent trying to find band-aids that would hold her self together, repair her wounds, and cover over her emptiness. Band-aids could not hold such a child together; she needed a mother. A mother who could so hold her that she would learn to develop her "self" in a differentiated and integrated manner. Katie's attachment with such a mother would be the mold from which to fashion her self. The joy and interests that would emerge from such an attachment were needed if she were to be likely to give up her "selfish" preoccupations.

Katie's immediate desire to call Karen and Ken "Mom" and "Dad" is not unusual. Such comments do not reflect a favorable emotional response to her new parents. Rather, they are simply her efforts to establish control over these new parental objects. She is saying, "I really like you a lot. Now you have to be nice to me and give me what I want." Regrettably, she does not know how to "like" someone. But she does know that parents want to think that they are special to their child so she tells them that they are.

Katie, and the actual children whom she represents, are excellent at manipulating adults in new relationships. They are able to be charming, polite, friendly, and helpful when they think that they will get something from such behaviors. Most adults assume that such behaviors, while being superficial now, will lead to something with deeper reciprocal affect. They are then likely to be extra nice to Katie, not wanting to jeopardize the "good" start. They want to "reinforce" their new child's appropriate behaviors. Karen waited quite a while for some reciprocity to Katie's interactions. When it failed to come, in spite of her "doing everything for her," she became enraged at Katie's rejection of her as a mother. What she did not know was that Katie never thought of her as a mother. To Katie, Karen was a servant, not a mother.

Although most foster parents are more like Ruth, some are similar to Karen. They may or may not have the right motives in taking children into their homes. Poorly attached children are likely to elicit strong emotional responses from the adults who care for them. Foster children will often compulsively try to recreate the abusive situations that they experienced in their original home. They also often manifest extreme emotional and behavioral outbursts because of their poor affect regulation, self-control, and self-reflection. They often trigger emotional responses that reflect their foster parents' own unresolved issues from their own childhood. When foster parents have such unresolved significant problems they eventually abuse the children in their care, either emotionally, physically, or sexually. When that occurs, the severe problems that the child had when entering their home are made worse by the maltreatment that they subsequently received by the adults chosen to keep them safe.

Caring for poorly attached children is an extremely difficult 24-hour-per-day task. It requires a high degree of personal maturity, self-control, empathy for their child's inner life, and ability to tolerate long periods of stress. In order for foster parenting to be done well, there needs to be a high level of screening, training, and support. Even then, there remains the risk that a given child will prove to be too difficult for the foster parents. When that occurs, our solution to the tragedy of the abuse and neglect of children, only makes the problem worse. We need to be committed to reducing these system failures as much as possible. Our commitment must begin with the individual foster parent. If that parent is not emotionally mature and skilled as a parent, nothing that we do in the overall system will suffice.

FOSTER HOME #3—SUSAN CUMMINGS

Susan Cummings reminded Steven of Ruth Daley. She had a relaxed air of warmth and confidence. She clearly enjoyed her work and seemed pleased to meet Katie. Her husband, Richard, ran a local oil dealership and left her to run their home. She had two "grown" children—Beth, who was away at college, and Dick, who was living on his own and working for his dad. She had two other foster children, 9-year-old Jessica and Dan, who was 12. She was about to leave to pick up Dan at soccer practice and she invited Katie and Steven along for the ride.

Katie did not waste a minute getting Susan's attention. She jumped into the front seat of the car. Susan suggested that she get in the back with Jessica. She looked hurt, almost rejected. Steven intervened and said that he would get in the back so that Katie could get to know Susan. His offer seemed to work as Katie immediately became cheerful and talked with Susan all the way to the school soccer field. She was calling Susan "Mom" as if she had known her for months. Susan enjoyed answering her questions about school, her room, and whether or not she liked McDonald's. Katie also wasted no time telling Susan how Karen, her last mother, had abused her in various ways. Susan reassured her that she would not do those things to her. Steven was glad that Katie had addressed that issue so directly with Susan. He was puzzled though, at how quickly she had begun to speak of Karen in such a negative manner. Steven interrupted their discussion to say that Karen had really tried, but simply did not have enough practice taking care of kids to know what to do in hard situations. Katie turned to Steven and with a tone meant to end all debate, said "She was mean to me and I don't like her."

Back home Dan and Jessica offered to show Katie her room while Susan talked to Steven. Katie immediately replied, "I want Mommy to!"

"Why don't you go with Jessica, Katie. She'd love to show you around," Susan suggested.

"I want you to do it." Katie was almost tearful.

"OK, honey. You'll have to wait a few minutes while I talk to Steven."

Katie sat down to wait. Jessica and Dan left the room. Steven decided that he would call the next day to tell Susan more about Katie. When he left, Susan showed Katie her room.

Katie seemed to settle into Susan's home fairly well over the first few months. She wanted to be with Susan a great deal, talking to her about anything and wanting to know everything. Only when Richard came home from work would she give Susan a rest. Richard immediately liked her. She was so friendly and affectionate. She tried to be helpful and was disappointed when he was busy and could not do something with her.

Jessica and Dan were much less favorably impressed with Katie. She did not want their help. She seldom played with them unless she needed them to do something for her. Whenever they went to Susan to talk or relax she would try to get between them and Susan. If they hugged Susan, she would stop whatever she was doing and hug Susan twice. She would interrupt their conversations and find things that she needed Susan for whenever they asked for help.

Susan initially asked Jessica and Dan to be patient. Katie simply needed extra attention until she felt comfortable with the family. Later she would ask Katie to wait her turn, "I need to be with my other kids too." She thought that Katie was beginning to accept her need to 'share' Susan with the other two. Then she noticed that when she spent some close time with Jessica or Dan, Katie would take or break something of theirs. They would become enraged at Katie. Susan would calm them down and correct Katie. She thought that Katie would stop but the pattern seemed to become stronger. Jessica and Dan did not like their "new little sister."

On November 13, 1993, Dan was outside helping Richard finish raking up the leaves, which they would later be spreading in the gardens. Dan hurried to keep up with his "dad," always looking for Richard to nod and say "good job." Never before had Dan had a father who wanted to be with him and appreciated his efforts and abilities. When Richard had managed to attend his last soccer game, Dan felt a degree of pride and joy that he could barely contain.

Richard enjoyed Dan. He was a good worker. He was quick to learn. In some ways Richard was closer to Dan than he had been with his own son Dick, when Dick was Dan's age. Funny how that happened. Dick seemed to grow up so fast. They never seemed to have time to do much together. Richard was planning to go hunting with Dick for two days next week. That would be good. Dan wanted to go. In a year or two, Richard thought, the three of them might go together.

Katie and Jessica were playing at the swing set behind the house. That was unusual. They were together without fighting. Dan saw them too. He also saw Katie, now sitting at the top of the slide, playing with his Gameboy.

"Katie, I told you not to play with that," Dan yelled. "Put it back in the house."

Katie ignored Dan. He yelled again. Katie looked up, stared at him, and then went back to the game.

"Katie!" Dan screamed as he threw down the rake and ran toward her. She still ignored him. "Give me that!" he yelled as he reached the swings.

"No!" she screamed back and then she suddenly threw it into the driveway.

"Katie I hate you!" yelled Dan as he ran to his game. He picked it up and there was nothing on the screen. He tried to get it to operate but it wouldn't.

Dan turned and ran at Katie, still sitting on the top of the slide. Richard yelled to Dan to let him handle it, but Dan did not hear him. Katie tried to escape by sliding down but Dan arrived at the same time and pushed her as she was halfway down. Katie fell over the side, landing on her back and letting out a piercing cry.

Richard watched Katie fall and he ran to her, pushing Dan aside.

"Get in the house!" he yelled at Dan.

"But she broke my Gameboy!"

"Shut up and get out of here. I don't want to see you!" Richard replied. He bent down and attended to Katie. She reached for him and he held her as she cried. Susan came out, they fussed over her to see that she was all right, and Richard went looking for Dan.

He went into Dan's room and shouted, "Don't you ever touch her again!"

"She's always breaking my stuff!" Dan shouted back through his tears.

"I don't care what she breaks of yours, she's just a little girl and you will not hit her again if you want to live here!"

Dan became motionless as if he were hit. He stared at Richard. Finally, in a slow and calm voice, he said, "Maybe I don't."

"Well it's your choice. Let me know what you want." Richard left him alone.

Susan later went to Dan to quietly explain that he was much bigger than Katie and could hurt her. She knew that Katie sometimes did not treat him well, but he had to control himself around her. If he were patient with her maybe she'd start to treat him better.

"Mom, I can't stand her. Ever since she came here nothing is the same. Dad always takes her side and yells at me. Why does she have to live with us?"

"Dan, when you came here two years ago you had hard times too. Remember Johnny who lived with us then? You were so jealous of him. He couldn't stand you either."

"But that was different, Mom. I was never mean to him the way Katie is. And she just wants to get me and Jessica in trouble all the time. She doesn't try to get along at all, Mom."

"You just have to keep trying like we all do, Dan. Katie has had a hard life and she's still a little girl. She needs our patience," said Susan.

Dan stared long at Susan. "I had a hard life too, Mom."

On December 18, 1993 the Cummings family were beginning their Christmas preparations. This was the most enjoyable season for Susan. Decorating the house, baking special breads and pies, and selecting just the right gifts were activities that she truly treasured.

Richard and Dan had just brought in the tree and they were standing it in the traditional spot in the dining room. The table was set in the corner so that there would be plenty of room for presents to be placed between now and Christmas with most of them mysteriously appearing on Christmas eve.

Susan had become concerned that Katie really was not "settling in" as she had expected. It was now three months. She was still very mean to Jessica and Dan. She would pout and complain whenever she did not get something that she wanted. She had begun to take things from Susan. Just last week her wedding band was missing from the sill above the kitchen sink. She found it in Katie's backpack. Katie's teacher had called to say that Katie was showing off her "new ring" at school. When she confronted Katie she got no response. Katie seemed to "shut down" when confronted with something that she had done. Susan would say what needed to be said and Katie would wait till she was done and then walk off. Susan suspected that Katie was neither sorry nor committed to change her behaviors.

Susan hoped that the Christmas season would help Katie to begin to relax and begin to be a regular, happy kid. Jan Temple had said that it wasn't likely to happen that quickly. Jan thought that Katie wasn't likely to begin to trust for another year or two. Susan prayed that Jan was wrong.

Susan, Jessica, and Katie were unwrapping the ornaments and other tree decorations and placing them on the table, waiting until the tree was ready. Each year Susan would give each child a new ornament for themselves. This tradition was an important part of Susan's own childhood. Last year Jessica had been given a lovely white ornament in the shape of a swan. Jessica loved it and had pleaded to keep it in her room when they were wrapping up the ornaments at the end of the season. Susan explained that not only would her special ornament be safer if kept in the box with the others, but it also would retain its magical Christmas quality if she could see it only during this season.

Jessica was thrilled to see it again. She carefully unwrapped it and placed in the center of the table. She stared at it and gently touched it.

Eventually the tree was ready and they began the process of turning it into "The Tree." Susan gave each child the ornaments, one at a time, and they found the place on the tree that was "just right" for each one. Jessica and Katie each went to put an ornament on the same spot. Jessica got there first and Katie yelled. Susan told Katie to find another spot and she did, though only after her usual pout.

A few minutes later Susan looked up to see Katie look toward Jessica, smile, and then drop a book on Jessica's white swan. Susan and Jessica both screamed and Dan and Richard looked up. Jessica ran to the table and lifted the book off her shattered ornament.

"Why did you do it?" Susan grabbed Katie's arms and yelled at her.

"It was an accident," Katie replied.

"I saw you do it. You did it on purpose. That was a very bad thing to do!" Susan continued to hold Katie by the arms and stare into her face.

"You're hurting me! Leave me alone!" Katie screamed at Susan.

"No I'm not! I'm not going to let you go until you tell me why you did such a mean thing!" Susan's anger continued.

"You better let her go, Susan," said Richard. "Maybe it was an accident."

"It was not! I saw her do it!" Susan turned to Richard. "She's going to tell me why!"

"You're hurting me!" Katie continued to scream.

"You better let her go," Richard said again. "You might be hurting her!"

"I am not!" Susan yelled at Richard. "Let me handle this."

"Now you go to your room, Katie. What you did to Jessica was very mean and you're not going to have a Christmas until we deal with this," Susan yelled. Katie screamed and ran to her room.

"Don't you think you're overreacting?" Richard asked. "Maybe she did do it on purpose but she didn't realize how important it was to Jessica."

"She did realize it. She knew what she was doing and she enjoyed hurting Jessica. I saw it and you didn't." Susan was becoming annoyed with her husband.

"Let's just drop it, Susan," said Richard.

"You can drop it but I'm not. She's going to face what she did."

Richard dropped the streamer that he had been attaching to the window and left the room. They heard him slam the door. Susan by now was holding a crying and shaking Jessica in her lap.

"I'll get you another ornament, Jessica," said Susan.

"I want my swan!" cried Jessica.

"I'll find another swan just like that one," promised Susan.

Dan stood for a time by the tree. "She always ruins everything!" He ran from the room and went outside, looking for Richard.

During the next two weeks the Cummings family celebrated the Christmas season with the same activities and traditions that they had always done. Susan was not able to get Katie to "face" what she had done. Susan stopped trying and instead worked harder to have a good Christmas for the family. She and Richard did not feel as close as they usually did at this time of year. Susan felt sad often during that time. She had lost something special to her. Katie got her presents and she seemed content. In fact she almost seemed to be peaceful. This may have been the best Christmas that she had ever had. If she noticed the mood of the rest of the family, it did not interfere with her own. Actually, it may have helped her own.

On the morning of January 27, 1994, Steven sat at his desk planning his lunch break. Jenny had given him a list of things to bring home for Rebecca's first birthday party later that day. Steven also wanted to bring something home that he had picked out. Something that would delight his daughter. He would find something later.

Steven received a call from Susan. His anxiety rose just as it had done at every phone call over the past four weeks. Katie was not doing well at Susan's despite everything they tried. Steven and Jan had met with Susan. Jan had seen Katie for extra sessions. But so far there were no signs of progress. During the last meeting when Jan had told Susan that Katie had only been at her house for four months and that it took time for a child to begin to trust her new parents, Steven felt dread. He had heard and said this before. Katie had been in foster care for sixteen months and receiving therapy for fourteen months. Ruth and Susan were excellent, experienced foster parents and Karen had really tried to give Katie a good home. What could he do next? What was going to happen next?

"Steven, I'm losing it with Katie," said Susan. "Lately she is getting up at 4 A.M. The alarm on her bedroom door has stopped her from roaming the house, but she has discovered it to be a great way to get us. She deliberately sets it off when she awakens and wakes the whole house too. She always has an excuse. She either has to use the bathroom, or she fell out of bed, or she had a scary dream. I tell her those reasons are not acceptable but she does it anyway. It's hard for us all to get back to sleep. Even Richard is losing patience with her."

"She really is giving you guys a rough time lately. Any ideas yet why she might be doing so poorly?" asked Steven.

"I really don't. It seems like every day I'm trying to come up with a new explanation for her behaviors. I try everything. Maybe I'm too strict so I give her more attention and go easier on the consequences. Then I think that maybe I'm too easy and I tighten things up. Then I think I'm too inconsistent and I set up rules and routines to try to cover everything that happens. Whatever I do seems to have no impact on her."

"Has there been any effect from the antidepressant medication that Dr. Veilleux decided to try?"

"Not yet. He did say it would take a few weeks and she's only been on it for ten days. It just gives her something else to complain about. 'Why do I have to take medicine when Jessica and Dan don't,'" Susan replied.

"Do you explain that it's not a punishment but simply a way to help her to be happier?" Steven asked.

"I do, but she doesn't listen. I think that she would take medicine cheerfully if it were her idea. She always wants to be in charge! She would argue if I gave her ice cream and the other kids celery. She'd want both the ice cream and the celery and she'd want to decide what to give them. There's nothing that happens that she doesn't want to control," Susan said wearily.

"I guess the honeymoon is over, Susan," Steven said, for nothing better to add.

"I'm beginning to think there never was a honeymoon, Steven. Her 'good' behavior over the first few months seems to have been an effort to charm me and Richard. I think that she even thought that we might get rid of Jessica and Dan. All of her negativity seemed to be directed at them. Now she is sending it toward us all, even Richard. Yesterday Richard asked her to get his gloves for him when he was leaving for work. She refused to do it for him. He didn't say anything but he stared at me when he left. He seems to want me to fix her. Or he might be blaming me for her problems, I don't know. We don't seem to be able to talk about Katie without one of us getting upset."

"How are the other kids managing things?" Steven asked.

"They avoid her. If anything, they might be doing better since she's been getting into trouble more with me and Richard. I think they might be relieved that we now see her for who she is. She's not the sad and troubled angel that she first seemed to be. I probably give them more understanding than I did before over their anger at her. I still worry about Richard and Dan though. They're not as close as they were before Katie came," Susan said.

"I'll try to stop by later in the week. I hope you can hang in there. She's bound to get better eventually," Steven suggested.

"I hope so. But it sure would be nice to know when," Susan replied.

As he had done many times, Steven updated his colleagues on Katie's current functioning. They knew how important Katie was to him. She represented his hope to really be able to make a difference with children who had been abused and neglected. He had met her shortly after her fifth birthday. Certainly he could ensure that she was provided with a good life.

On the way home that evening he stopped in a local hardware store and glanced at their small toy section. There on the top shelf sat the largest, happiest, stuffed lady bug that he had ever seen. When Rebecca ripped off the paper covering his present later that evening she squealed with delight. Steven felt proud of his contribution to Rebecca's first party. She insisted that the lady bug share her crib and Jenny somehow found the space.

The first year for Jenny and Steven as parents had been busy, tiring, fulfilling, and challenging. They had never worried so much before about anyone or anything. At the same time they both felt no regrets. Rebecca brought so much to their lives. She needed so much and they had to work out schedules so that they shared the responsibilities. But Rebecca had a way of making time vanish. Steven might play with her for an hour, making strange sounds and faces, crawling after her, showing delight and surprise at her countless gestures and movements. They would crawl around the dining room table, first one chasing and the other screeching and then they would change directions and it was the other's turn to howl. Their fun and excitement were mutual. Steven gradually sensed when Rebecca was tiring and he intuitively slowed his pace and gestures and vocalizations. Soon Rebecca would fall into his lap, put her thumb in her mouth, and become quiet. He would wait for her cue that she rested enough. She would then get up and generally wander to some other activity.

Steven had initially sat in awe at Jenny's relationship with Rebecca. When they were together nothing else seemed to exist. Jenny always seemed to sense Rebecca's moods and intentions as they were being expressed and she would respond in a way that meshed just right with her daughter's emerging inner state. They would stare at each other for endless minutes, with Rebecca on her back on Jenny's legs. They would smile and move their heads and scrunch their eyes and nose in time with some unheard music. Those first twelve months seemed to have been designed for Rebecca and her mother. Their union at birth still seemed to exist. Rebecca was becoming herself while dancing with Jenny.

On March 8, 1994 Susan was called by the principal at Katie's school. Katie refused to return another child's snack that she had taken. When her teacher went to take it from her she kicked the teacher and ran from the room. The teacher and her aid eventually were able to carry Katie to the office of the principal, who promptly called Susan to come and take Katie home. She was being suspended for the next day as well. This was the principal's first experience with suspending a first grader.

When Susan brought Katie home she noted that Katie acted as if nothing had happened. She ignored Susan's talk in the car about trying to hurt her teacher. When they entered the house Katie ran to the TV and turned it on. Susan turned off the TV and informed Katie that she needed to spend some time in her room before doing some school work that the teacher had given her. She told Katie that since the other children were in school she would have her school work at home.

"No I won't. You can't make me!" Susan was not surprised at Katie's response. Katie's defiant attitude had become the norm.

"Katie, I want you to go to your room now," Susan said and prepared herself to take Katie to her bedroom.

Katie screamed at Susan, "I'll kick you too!" Given warning, Susan tried to protect herself, but as she reached for her arm, Katie still managed to kick her leg hard. She spun Katie around and pushed her toward her room. Katie reached up and grabbed onto Susan's hair. Susan's glasses fell and both she and Katie landed next to them on the carpet. Katie screamed that she hurt her leg. As Susan released her Katie leaped up and ran toward the kitchen. Susan followed, yelling for Katie to stop. Katie grabbed the portable phone and threw it through the bay window. Katie darted outside. Susan followed but Katie ignored her yells to return. She leaped in the car and locked the doors. She refused to let Susan in. Susan went for her keys and returned to see Katie's look of hatred from the front seat. Susan turned the key and the door release popped up. Before she could open the door Katie had pushed the release down again. This must have happened twenty times before Susan retreated to the kitchen. It was cold outside and Katie did not have her coat on. After an hour of waiting she tried to open the car door again. Katie again managed to keep the door closed. Finally Susan became concerned about Katie's health in the cold so she called Richard from his office to come home. When he arrived, Katie was still locked in the car and refused to let them in. Richard and Susan had to open both front doors at the same time in order to get to

Katie. Richard had to carry her to her room. She screamed and swore at him and managed to scratch his face. She then destroyed her bedroom.

Steven felt intense discouragement when he met with Susan at Jan's office before Katie's therapy on March 11. Katie had been with Susan for about six months and her problems were worse than ever. She had been in foster care for eighteen months and what had been accomplished? He turned to Jan and asked what they might try next.

"I wish I knew," Jan replied. "We might consult with Bill again about another behavior plan. We need to try to get a positive attitude back toward Katie or I'm afraid we'll have a vicious circle that won't do her or anyone else any good."

"I haven't given up yet," Susan said. "What's a bay window as long as Steven will pay for a new one. But we have to find some way to get through to her. She's not like Jessica and Dan who seem to want to do better. When they mess up they seem a little sorry anyway and are almost grateful to get some consequence so that it's over with. But Katie, she doesn't care. It's the rest of the family's fault. Give her a consequence and we'll pay for it, as if we have no right to be so cruel to her."

"Did you ever see any effect from the medication?" Steven asked.

"No, Steven," Susan responded. "And Dr. Veilleux has tried another that he thought might reduce her rage outbursts. That hasn't helped either."

"Let's meet next week with Bill. A new behavior plan might give us all a fresh start," suggested Jan. Steven and Susan agreed and Jan suggested that she meet with Katie and try to understand what's going through her mind now.

In therapy Katie would have nothing to do with discussing her recent behaviors at school and at home. Jan knew that if she pressed too hard Katie would insist on ending therapy early that day and they would be locked in a power struggle over her need to stay until the session finally ended. Jan accepted her refusal and became hopeful that Katie might nonverbally express her recent experiences when she chose to play with the doll house. Katie's play had its usual intense, driven quality. The child figure was quite aggressive. On this occasion the child went further. She took the furniture from the entire house and placed the pieces in a pile in the living room. She left the baby upstairs. She then pretended to set the furniture on fire and the entire house burned down. The baby, of course, died. Jan wondered if the baby represented Susan and her family or Katie herself. Probably both, she thought. When she suggested that to Katie she received a "Shut up!" with more force than usual. Maybe she got through to Katie. If so, would it do any good?

During the next few weeks Bill helped them to develop a behavioral program that focused heavily on the positive. Katie had various rewards available to her for maintaining fairly appropriate social behaviors. Misbehavior was overlooked, or she was simply told that the rewards would be available to her as soon as her behavior was on target again. Katie learned the system very rapidly. For a few days she seemed to be responding favorably. Then Susan began to note that as soon as she got a reward her behavior would get worse. Susan was cautioned not to expect this to happen or Katie might act to meet the expectation. Susan tried to avoid anticipating anything after the reward, but Katie's behavior still became more aggressive and defiant. Maybe she was communicating something negative to Katie without being aware of it. She tried harder, but nothing changed. She soon began to feel somewhat disappointed when Katie earned a reward. Somehow that wasn't what was supposed to be happening.

Early in April, 1994, Susan again met with Steven, Jan, and Bill. Katie's behavior might be somewhat better, but for some reason she didn't feel better. She tried to explain it.

"I think that Katie might be doing a little better because she's able to get what she wants more now than before. She knows that when she does something wrong she really won't lose out on anything that she most wants to do. It's not hard for her to hold it together enough to get what she wants and then she doesn't care for awhile and she does whatever she wants to annoy the rest of us. Then when she wants something again, she turns it on, and gets another reward."

"That's a start," suggested Bill. "She is aware of the connection between good behaviors and rewards. This is something to build on. If she does it enough, eventually she should start to take pleasure in doing good for its own sake. Be sure to verbally reinforce her good behaviors."

"I'm careful to do that, Bill," said Susan. "But so far I haven't seen any sign that she cares about anything I say. She does it to get the reward. But only when she wants the reward. When she doesn't care about it, she does what she feels like and its often something that the rest of us don't like."

"But again, it's a start," said Jan. "Since things are better at home now maybe eventually she will begin to want to get along better with the family so that she is liked and praised for what she does."

"She never had these positive reinforcements when she was young, Susan," said Bill. "It will take some time before she begins to associate the concrete reinforcers and then the social reinforcers with her good behaviors. Once that happens, you'll begin to see that she is trying harder to please you and do what you're reinforcing."

On May 1, Susan was making preparations for the annual early-spring family cookout that had been a tradition in her home for a number of years. Dick and Beth would be home and Susan and Richard's parents would be there as well. Susan's brother Mike and his family were also planning to come.

Susan hoped that Katie would be OK for the family gathering. While she really had not seen any improvements over the past few months, there were no outrageous behaviors either. She again thought that Katie was doing better because she was getting what she wanted more. She was still hurtful, oppositional, and selfish. Susan did not feel that Katie was any closer to her. Katie still lied almost constantly and tried to get away with whatever she could. Susan and Richard were pretty good at biting their tongues and not reacting to these behaviors. When Katie did what she was supposed to do, they were able to praise her and she got her reward.

Katie was in a good mood that morning and even offered to help prepare for the cookout. Susan thought that she might be competing with Jessica to see who could be the most helpful. If that was her motive, it was all right with Susan! She'd have enough jobs for them both. She'd simply make sure that they worked separately.

"Jessica, why don't you vacuum the living room and TV room. After that you can make the lemonade. Katie, I'd like you to stay here and help me get the food ready."

Both girls readily agreed and Susan began preparing the food. She had Katie wash the vegetables for the salad while she prepared the ground beef for hamburgers that her husband would cook on the outdoor grill. Katie was quickly bored with washing the lettuce and Susan could see that she'd have to do it over herself. She suggested that they trade tasks and Katie again agreed. They worked for only a few minutes when Richard called her outside to inspect their garden.

Fifteen minutes later, Susan's parents, Harold and Margaret Woods, arrived and joined them in the garden.

"It's going to be a great summer. We figure we'll have enough food to feed half the town," Susan said to her parents. "Glad you're both feeling well today." Susan worried about her parents' recent health problems. "Would you help me finish up in the kitchen, Mom? Your salads are the reason we have this cookout every year."

"Sure. And if I believe that I'd believe that Harold and I just won the lottery," Margaret replied as they walked toward the house. "How are all the kids doing?"

"So so," Susan said. "I still don't think we're doing much for Katie. You just can't get through to her."

"Well, you can only do your best. And your best is good enough for most kids," said Margaret.

When they entered the kitchen, Jessica was making the lemonade and Katie was not there. "Where's Katie?" asked Susan.

"She went to her room," replied Jessica.

Susan went to check the hamburgers. She figured that she'd have to squeeze them harder than Katie could do. They looked like they'd fall apart before they got on the grill. Susan took one in her hand and began to form it into a ball. Something was wrong. It didn't feel right. It didn't look right. She inspected it more closely. It smelled awful. Something was wrong with the meat. But she had just bought it fresh yesterday. She turned to Margaret. "Smell this, Mom."

"Yuck!" Margaret replied. "That's not hamburger."

Susan had a bad feeling when she thought of Katie in her room. She took one of the hamburgers and walked through the house to her bedroom. She knocked on the door, entered, and immediately knew that she was right. Katie had that look about her that meant that she had done something wrong.

"What did you do to the hamburger, Katie?"

"I didn't do anything!" Katie yelled.

"Katie, this smells awful, what did you put in here?"

Susan then became aware that the smell was much worse in Katie's room. Also, it was now more familiar. She walked in, and looked behind the bed. On the floor were Katie's soiled underpants and a towel that was smeared with feces.

"Katie did you put your poop in the hamburger meat?" Susan screamed.

Katie's look removed all doubt. Katie was pleased! She had done something that would really upset Susan. She was enjoying Susan's look of horror.

"Katie, you did!" Susan continued to yell. "Why did you do that? What a mean and disgusting thing to do! Why did you do it?"

Katie did not answer. She only stared at Susan. She didn't appear to be frightened. If anything, she seemed to want Susan to yell at her and maybe even hit her. She wanted to get Susan to hate her!

Susan didn't know what to do or say. Tears came to her eyes. She felt like rubbing the meat in Katie's face. She wanted to drag her into the kitchen by her hair and make her clean it all up and tell everyone what she had done. Susan could not accept such feelings. She could not feel anything toward Katie. She was beaten. She had done what she could for this child for eight months. Now she could only cry. She left Katie's room, saying nothing more to the child. Susan needed to be with her mother. She needed to grieve with her mother. Katie did not grieve. She was as content as she was capable of being.

When Susan called Steven to tell him that he would need to find another home for Katie, she did not feel anger or guilt. If she felt anything, it was sadness. She had failed. It didn't hurt as much as it first did. Her mother had helped her to come to terms with it. But she was still sad for Katie. She was not yet 7 years old.

Steven took the news with resignation. He was as upset over the meat incident as Susan was initially. What was Katie thinking? Who could raise this child? What could he do with her?

He consulted with Kathy, his supervisor, who arranged to consult with Dawn at the Central Office regarding placement options for Katie. Susan had said that she would be willing to keep her to the end of the school year, which gave them four or five weeks.

The next day Steven summarized the past twenty-one months in Katie's life for the other workers and for Dawn. He had pulled together the various symptoms that she had manifested in all of her placements. The more he listed her problems, the worse they seemed. He questioned his own experiences with Katie, which, for the most part, went fairly well. He was impressed with her energy, initiative, and general expressiveness. While she did seem self-centered and pushy at times, her behavior showed little of the oppositional and aggressive behaviors shown in her homes. For whatever reason, she wasn't making it in the homes that were provided for her.

Dawn asked if they considered one of the therapeutic foster home programs in the area. Kathy indicated that she was thinking the same thing.

"What's different about these homes than our regular homes?" asked Steven.

"In general the parents receive more training and support than the regular homes. They receive a higher board rate and are expected to be more actively involved in the child's treatment. While many of our regular foster parents are as skilled and committed as are these parents, they are a resource that you might consider if you cannot find the right home among the regular DHS homes," Dawn suggested.

"I'd support that, Steven," Kathy said. "We have to do everything we can to get the right placement for her. She can't afford any more moves after this one."

"I just don't know what any home can give Katie that Susan and Ruth didn't give," Steven said. "Somehow we're missing something."

"Would you say that Katie has difficulty forming attachments with her foster parents?" asked Dawn.

"She sure has difficulty getting along with them if that's what you mean," Steven replied.

"Does it seem to matter to her when she is moved or does it seem that one home is as good as the next to her?" Dawn asked.

"I don't think it matters. Ruth and Susan don't think so either. Her other parent, Karen, thought that she meant something to Katie, but the moment she left she seemed to forget her."

"Also would you consider her to be manipulative and controlling? Will she always have an excuse, lie, and blame others?"

"That's Katie," Steven replied.

"Why don't you have her evaluated by Allison Kaplan in Farmingdale. She's done a lot of work with children who have difficulty forming an attachment to their foster or adoptive parents," Dawn suggested.

"Some of our kids have seen Allison in the past," Kathy said. "She did a good job. Her therapy isn't like what most therapists offer."

"What's the difference?" Steven asked.

"Well, she's kinda pushy with them. She really challenges their behaviors. But she also gets the foster mom involved and actually works on teaching the child how to be nurtured by the mom. Why not ask her to evaluate Katie; she's a psychologist."

"You should know that there are some questions around Allison's work. I know that she often holds the child in therapy, whether or not the child wants to be held. Some folks think that might be too intrusive," Dawn said.

"Well, why don't I call her and talk with her about Katie. At least maybe she can see her and give us some ideas about the most appropriate placement for her."

"Sounds good. Let me know what you find out," Kathy said.

The next day Steven was able to reach Allison Kaplan. She sounded interested in Katie and indicated that she would be willing to evaluate her. She asked for a summary of her history prior to and after she entered foster care. She also wanted to speak with her foster mother. Steven felt hopeful that she might help him to understand Katie. He was most encouraged when Dr. Kaplan said that she knew of a foster family that might be suitable for Katie. She had just finished working with Jackie Keller, a foster mother, and her foster son, Gabe, who was recently placed in an adoptive home. Jackie was taking some time off now, but had expressed interest in taking in another child soon.

COMMENTARY

Children who manifest significant difficulty forming a specific attachment with their foster and adoptive parents tend to have a variety of symptoms that create moderate or extreme difficulties in the major areas of their life. These symptoms affect their abilities for basic biological regulation, affect modulation and integration, behavioral organization, and the development of language and cognition. (See Appendix 2 for a list of the most common symptom patterns of unattached children.) Katie definitely manifested such pervasive problems during her three foster placements. Her various symptoms reflected a significant inability to form a selective attachment with her caregiver. The same symptoms also reflected a lack of continuity of the self from one experience and affective or ego state to the next. Such continuity of self depends a great deal on a continuous and secure attachment figure during the first two years of life.

Katie's behavior toward Jessica and Dan did not represent the normal jealousy among siblings or even the jealousy of a child who doubted that she were as special to her parents as were her siblings. Rather, Katie wanted affection from Susan only when she saw her siblings seeking affection. She had no interest in affection itself. She wanted to keep Susan as her servant and hers alone. If Susan were attending to the other children she would not be available for Katie.

The same dynamic entered Katie's perception of Susan and Richard's marriage. She wanted each parent to serve her and relate to her, not to each other. Nothing would make her happier than to be able to create a conflict between Susan and Richard. Since Susan was the primary caregiver, most often she perceived her as being the "bad" parent and Richard as the "good" parent. When she had a conflict with Susan, she would immediately seek out Richard for sympathy. When she was able to cause them to argue over her, she would become as happy as she were capable of being.

In general, poorly attached children have many conflicts with their new mother and then turn on their charm the moment the father comes home. Many are quite accomplished at manipulating the father into thinking that the mother might be too harsh and then encouraging her to "lighten up" a bit. Nothing will discourage and infuriate a mother of a poorly attached child as much as seeing her husband be so manipulated and then turn to see her child smile at her behind her husband's back. She then finds herself competing with her child for her husband's heart and mind.

Katie was successful in causing splitting among the members of her foster family. Many foster children are equally successful creating splitting among all of the professionals with whom she relates. Her cries for sympathy at school creates disagreement between her teacher and parent. Her carefully placed comments make her therapist question the decisions and comments made by her case worker. The case worker, in turn, begins to second guess the medication prescribed by the psychiatrist or the decisions made by the previous case worker. When the child is really successful, most of the professionals eventually agree that the parent is probably the reason that the child has not made progress. Such splitting increases the difficulty in being able to successfully assist a child like Katie. The adults involved need to be aware of the risk that such splitting may occur. They need to have developed open communication with and confidence in each other's abilities, knowledge, and commitment to a particular child. If the adults differ, they need to openly work to resolve their differences, with respect for each other's views. Since the parent is the most important person in the child's treatment, the professionals should share their recommendations and concerns and then accept the decision of the parent. If parents are treated with respect, most often they will be very receptive to assistance and ideas when their own efforts are not effective. It is hard to fail when we want so desperately to make a difference in the life of such troubled children. If we begin to blame and not support each other, we will have become like the children we are treating and will be of no help.

Generally, Katie's first motive in interacting with others was to be able to manipulate them to give her what she wanted. If she got her parent to do what she wanted, she would be satisfied temporarily. However, the objects or activities that she wanted never brought her any inner satisfaction or enjoyment. She would then make her next demand and her satisfaction with her parents depended primarily on whether they again did what she wanted. Sooner or later each parent realized that granting her request did not make her feel safer or more trusting. When they began to refuse her requests, Katie would begin to respond with anger at how unfair and harsh they had become. In her mind they caused her to be angry, and it was their fault that she was destructive, aggressive, sneaky, and defiant.

Katie and those like her do not experience remorse for hurting others. They have little empathy for others and little guilt for their behaviors. Empathy and guilt presuppose a basic attachment with a parent, during which the parent's values and beliefs were internalized. Her parent is a person, not an object, and the attached child experiences empathy for her distress and guilt when she is responsible for it. Katie did not reach that developmental level. She remained lost in shame, an emotion that focuses on the self, not the other, and which, in healthy families leads to socialization and internalization. With Katie, shame led back to her own worthlessness and to her hatred toward others who did not serve her and so were equally worthless. Feces in the hamburger was to her an amusing representation of her contempt for the efforts of others to enjoy themselves. Mutual enjoyment necessarily excluded her and she would not tolerate it.

As is often the case among those who try to raise poorly attached children, Steven, Jan, and Susan would look at recent events in Katie's life to try to understand what might have precipitated her symptoms. Frequently parents and professionals spend a lot of time trying to identify the "triggers" as if that would enable them to help the child to better manage those stressors. What is not given enough attention is understanding the roots of the symptoms, which, when we are talking about unattached children, lie among the thousands of experiences that occurred during their first two years of life. We can work diligently on identifying and trying to limit every "trigger," only to eventually become discouraged and begin to blame the child or each other. More valuable professional and parental energy needs to go toward providing the child with the therapeutic experiences—at home and in the office—that will address the developmental and attachment deficiencies that originated years before.

3

A New Approach: Understanding and Treating Children Who Refuse to Form Attachments

ALLISON KAPLAN, Ph.D.

On May 12, 1994, Katie met Allison when Susan and Steven brought her to Allison's office. She had not yet been told that she would be leaving Susan's home sometime after the school year ended. Allison met them in the waiting room and directed Katie to remain there while she talked with Susan and Steven. There were various toys in the room and Katie didn't mind staying.

Steven immediately noticed Allison's capable, relaxed manner. She appeared to be a calm and comfortable person and he sensed that she enjoyed her work. She was in her early forties and had an air of confidence about her with her graying, light brown hair, a few freckles, and lovely smile. Her office reminded him of someone's living room more than a professional space. There was a large couch that held a variety of pillows, some of which seemed to have fallen to the floor. There was a rocking chair near the center of the room and a large stuffed chair near the window. The drapes over the windows also made him feel that he had entered the warm home of one of his foster parents.

Allison questioned Susan in detail about the past eight months. Steven noted that she was clearly not blaming Susan for the disrupted placement. If anything, she was expressing admiration for how hard Susan had worked to help Katie.

"If only Katie had worked half as hard as you, Susan, we wouldn't be talking about her having to move," Allison suggested.

"Let me summarize what you've told me about her. She's an angry and controlling child who always insists on getting her way. She often does mean and hurtful things, especially if someone 'crosses' her or if she has just had a lot of fun and excitement. She is affectionate when she wants something from you or if she has done something wrong. She's frequently lying and stealing and generally she seems like a 'dark cloud' in your house. Originally she was able to split you from the other kids somewhat and then split you from your husband, who thought that you were too hard on her. You tried a behavioral plan that she

71

seemed to play with—using it or not depending on whether she wanted something at the time. You don't think that you or anyone else really mean anything to her. You have to watch her around animals or younger kids. When you set a limit and consequence, you know that you'll either have a fight on your hands then or you'll pay later in some way. Does that about cover most things?"

"That's Katie, Dr. Kaplan. I don't mean to seem too negative about her but that's the way she really is," Susan said.

"My impression, Steven," Dr. Kaplan said, " is that her first foster mother had basically the same experience when Katie lived in her home."

"That's right," Steven replied, "And it's my impression that Ruth was as competent and committed to Katie as Susan has been."

"Why don't I bring her in now. I'd like you both to stay," Allison said.

They agreed and Allison went to the waiting room. Steven heard some commotion from Katie but they both entered Allison's office in a few minutes. Katie went directly to Susan and sat close to her.

"Katie didn't want to stop playing with the toys," Allison said. "So I told her that she needed to come in here with us and she had a choice. She could walk in or I would carry her. Oh, she did not like to hear that! Having me carry her! And she doesn't even know me! Well, she decided to walk, which, I guess, was a good choice for her."

Susan hugged Katie, who was pouting somewhat while still leaning against her.

Steven noticed that Allison was fairly direct but in a nice way. He wondered if Katie would now give her the silent treatment as she did with him if he asked her to do something that she didn't want to do. Allison quickly shifted gears and made a fuss about Katie's shirt coloring. Katie responded rapidly and positively when Allison brought over a stuffed cat that had the same shade of tan as was on her shirt. Allison let her hold the cat and she told her that the cat could talk for her if she had trouble talking about something. Katie said that she'd like to play with the other stuffed animals and puppets too. Then Allison denied her request and Katie threw down the cat.

"You're mad at the cat because I said no?" Allison asked. "Or are you really mad at me but aren't sure if you want to tell me? No problem with telling me. Why don't you say: 'I'm mad because you won't let me play with the animals. I'm really mad at you.'"

Katie didn't respond and she squeezed Susan's arm.

"Since you don't want to say it, have the cat say it for you," Allison said.

Katie ignored her. Allison then took the cat and she spoke for Katie. This annoyed Katie and she put her fingers in her ears.

Allison turned to Susan. "I see what you mean, Susan. It really is hard for Katie when she can't do what she wants to do. Then she *really* doesn't do what she's told. She just seems to get madder and madder."

Allison then put the cat on Susan's other side and asked her to put her one arm around it just like her other arm was around Katie. Allison then began talking to Susan about Katie's hair. Steven noticed that very quickly Katie was talking with Allison again. Allison seemed to have a way to keep Katie relating positively even after there was a conflict.

After more small talk, Allison switched places with Susan and sat close to Katie.

"Now Katie, I'm going to be talking about some things that are probably hard for you to talk about. It's OK if it's hard for you. If you need to take a deep breath while we're talking let me know by putting up your hand. Let's practice, show me how you'll do it."

Katie smiled and took a deep breath. "Good job, Katie." Allison went on. "Now tell me what was hard about living with your mom and dad, Sally and Mike."

Katie immediately became tense and looked away. Just as suddenly she said, "They were mean to me. Mike hit me and kicked me. He even peed on me!"

"Oh, Katie, that must have hurt you so much! And you were so little! And they were your parents! And parents aren't supposed to hurt their kids that way!"

Katie struggled for something else to say. She was not comfortable with Allison's empathy for her pain. "And they didn't feed me. And they never played with me. They said I was bad."

"They hurt you so much, Katie," Allison said more quietly than before. "I'll bet you were so sad you cried a lot."

"I didn't cry!" Katie exclaimed. "I hit them and was mean to them!"

"I can see why, Katie, since they were mean to you and they were your parents! But you were so little. I'll bet you wanted to cry a little bit once in awhile."

"I didn't cry!" Katie said again.

"Well, it never should have happened Katie. And they never taught you how to live in a good family. They didn't teach you how to play with your parents. They didn't teach you how to help out with the chores. They didn't teach you how to have fun and love your parents. No wonder it's been hard for you to learn how to live in the good homes that you've been in since you moved away from Sally and Mike. They never taught you!"

Katie said nothing. Allison reached over and raised Katie's hand. "I thought that you might need some help remembering to take a deep breath. This talk has been hard for you." Allison then put her hand on Katie's chest and took a deep breath herself. Katie smiled and also breathed deeply. "That should be better now, Katie. Why don't you tell me some of the things that have been hard for you while living with Susan."

Katie hesitated and then said, "Sometimes Susan won't let me have dessert and she makes me sit in the time-out chair."

"But what is hard for *you* to be able to do, Katie? What don't *you* know how to do well?"

Katie again said nothing. She did not get the sympathy for losing her dessert that she had hoped for. She didn't know what Allison wanted her to say.

"You seem stuck, Katie. I'll help you," Allison said. "Is it hard for you to tell the truth when you have done something wrong and Susan asks you about it?"

"Yes," Katie replied quietly.

"Is it hard for you to put away your toys when Susan tells you to?"

Katie again said yes, with a smile now.

"Was it hard for you to be at Jessica's birthday party?"

"No, that wasn't hard," Katie said.

"But you started yelling and you knocked over your soda when you couldn't have the piece of cake that you wanted," Allison suggested.

"But it wasn't hard," Katie maintained.

"It must have been, Katie, or you would have had so much fun that you wouldn't have cared what piece of cake you got."

Katie again was silent. Allison rested her hand on Katie's and slowly said, "Katie, my guess is there are many things that have been hard for you while you're living with Susan because she's a good mom and you don't know how to get along well with a good mom."

Katie seemed somewhat sad. She looked down and was motionless for a moment. Then she saw the cat, suddenly grabbed it and smiled at Allison and said, "I want to play with the other animals now."

Allison put her hand on the cat and said, "Not now, Katie, we need to finish our talk first."

Katie pulled the cat away and yelled, "I want to play with them *now.*"

"*My*, Katie, how you got so mad at me again so quickly," Allison said. "You must not like some of the things I was saying and you want me to stop talking. Why don't you say that? 'Stop talking, Allison!'"

Katie looked out the window and yelled, "Stop talking, Allison."

"Good job saying it, Katie," Allison said, "but you forgot to look at me when you said it."

Katie quickly looked at Allison for a split second and screamed it again, more loudly than before.

"Yes, Katie! I knew you could do it!" Allison said with a smile. "I sure can understand why it is hard for you to live with a mom like Susan when your first mom, Sally, was so different. Susan never hurt you like Sally did. But you probably thought that she did sometimes when you were mad at her."

"Shut up!" Katie screamed.

Allison turned to Susan and said, "Katie has such a hard time talking about these problems. She probably thinks that you hate her when you tell her to stop doing something. She's really mad at me now for not doing what she wants and talking about things that she'd rather not think about. She does get mad! And I think that she's probably kind of sad a lot, too."

"I am not!" Katie yelled at Allison again.

"But Katie, there's nothing wrong with being sad. And I sure can understand why you're sad when you've been hurt as much as you've been."

Katie quietly looked away. They all sat without talking for a moment.

Allison turned to Steven and Susan and said that she'd like to talk with Katie alone for a little while. They went to the waiting room.

"I'm glad that she got to see some of Katie's anger," Susan said. "Often Katie is so charming with adults that people look at me strangely after they meet her. They think that I'm too fussy or too strict."

"Yes," Steven said. "Hopefully Dr. Kaplan will be able to give us some good ideas about helping her."

"She was firm with her and Katie didn't like that," said Susan. "Usually when teachers or doctors first meet her they try to be nice to her so that she is happy and will cooperate. Dr. Kaplan didn't do that and Katie didn't expect it."

They talked quietly for thirty minutes until Dr. Kaplan returned with Katie and brought Susan and Steven back to her office.

"She certainly is a child with a lot of problems and I can see that she'd be very difficult to raise," Allison said. "She really doesn't have any idea of how to become engaged with good parents and depend on them. She is very controlling because she had to depend on herself so much that she just can't trust enough to depend on you, Susan. She won't let herself become attached to you and without an attachment she will never settle into your home, learn from you, accept your authority or begin to enjoy herself, value herself, or feel good about having parents."

"Why won't she, Dr. Kaplan?" asked Steven. "Other foster kids do. She's been in foster care for twenty-one months and she hasn't seemed to change a bit."

"Probably her first few years did not meet her basic needs for a close relationship with her mother. I know that she was abused when she was 5, but I would bet that she was abused long before that, and more importantly, she probably was neglected a great deal. When babies and toddlers are ignored and yelled at all day they never really learn what a wonderful source of comfort and enjoyment their parents can be. They eventually stop asking for any nurturance and enjoyable interaction. And just as importantly, they don't develop in ways that children who are cherished do. They aren't comfortable with physical comfort, which is central in the infant's initial sense of self. Their affective development is poorly regulated and integrated. With rejection, anger, and abuse comes extreme shame that they are not able to integrate. Rather than shame being a vehicle for socialization it destroys their self-worth. Such pervasive shame is such a painful experience that it leads to denial and rage and the resultant behaviors tend to be extreme rather than becoming more moderate and self-regulated. And they really never learn to notice what they feel or think. If they were able to feel anything it would be shame. Their inner life remains ignored and doesn't develop. They don't know how then to engage others with mutual enjoyment and interest. They can only manipulate, make demands, and scream or withdraw when their needs are 'neglected' again. That's why you've been struggling so hard for eight months, Susan, with few, if any, changes in Katie."

"That's so sad," Susan said quietly. "I wish I could say that I'm willing to try again with her, Dr. Kaplan, but I just can't. The rest of the family can't stand her anymore, and that probably includes my husband, too. I don't have the patience anymore for her and she needs a lot of it."

"I certainly understand, Susan," Dr. Kaplan said, "You've been through a lot and you're the only one who can say if you think that you can meet her intense needs or are even able to try again."

"What would you suggest that we do now, Doctor?" Steven asked.

"Well, you first need to be very careful about selecting a new home. If the foster parents have not had successful experiences with children like Katie, they should get some training beforehand so that they're not surprised and discouraged when they get to know her. As I mentioned on the phone, I worked with a foster family and another child similar to Katie. The foster mom's name is Jackie Keller and she might be interested in working with her. Second, you should find a therapist who has some experience providing therapy that will get through to her. The more traditional therapies were really developed for children whose problems are not as severe as Katie's. Most traumatized kids are more able and willing to become attached to their foster parents than Katie is. They also are more able to enter into a therapeutic relationship with their therapist. I work with kids with more severe problems similar to Katie's and I can give you the names of a couple of other therapists who do too. I can send you my report with recommendations. You probably should discuss them with her current therapist, and then decide how you want to proceed."

"Is there much hope that Katie will ever change?" Steven asked.

"Well, I don't know her very well. But her age is a plus. And I was able to elicit some positive engagements, no matter how brief, although I wouldn't make too much of them because right now Katie has such a pervasive manipulative feature to her most basic interactions. Also, there really isn't significant research available since the attachment deficits manifested by many neglected and abused children have not been recognized until fairly recently and are still not well understood. So one should be cautiously hopeful, develop a comprehensive plan, and get to work."

Steven went home that night with more questions that he wished he had asked Dr. Kaplan. She seemed to make sense. She certainly described Katie when she listed the symptoms common to children with attachment deficits. But Steven really didn't have any idea what a parent or therapist would do differently that would make much difference. Two of Katie's foster parents were basically good parents in their previous work with troubled kids. And her therapist, Jan, also had a lot of experience with foster kids. Maybe different parenting would be a little better, but would the difference be that significant? Maybe if therapy pushed her a little harder, she couldn't avoid her problems. But if she really doesn't know anything about love from a parent, how can she learn that?

When Steven arrived home he was greeted by Rebecca, running merrily toward the door, waving her arms, smiling, and shouting "Dada!" He dropped his briefcase, swooped her into his arms and shouted "Becca!" They both giggled and he walked toward the couch in circles, holding her close to him and crying "Weeeee!" until he flopped down with his daughter on top of him. She settled in for a moment and then pulled back and began to get down. She had an idea! She grabbed his finger and began to pull him toward the doorway to the hall, while pointing and saying "Phone!" Knowing her plan, he walked with her to the play area in the corner of the dining room and sat with her on the floor. She reached for her play phone, held it to her ear, and said "Hi, Dada." He picked up a book to cover his face. "Hi, Becca." She paused for a moment as she usually did. Then she said, "Home, Dada." He replied, "I'm almost home, Becca. What's for supper?" She jumped up and ran into the kitchen. He heard Jenny whisper to her. She ran back and again grabbed the phone. "Scetti!" He yelled back, "Spaghetti! Great! I'll be home fast!" Her eyes grew wider as she watched and listened while Steven made loud "car" sounds from behind the book. Then he knocked on the book. She got up and pulled the book out of his hands. He exclaimed, "Becca, I'm home!" She smiled and grabbed him again. He picked her up and they went into the kitchen to greet Jenny.

"Hi, sweety, Becca tells me we're having spaghetti!" Steven and Rebecca both kissed Jenny. She gave them each a piece of celery from the salad she was making.

"What have you and Rebecca been up to today?" Steven asked.

"Well, Steven, we were in the garden and we saw . . . crawling on the ground . . . some tiny, tiny, . . ."

"Ants!" Rebecca said and smiled. As she remembered, she got excited and held out her hand to show her dad how she had held some. Steven then learned about a new library book they had read, Rebecca's bath where the water swooshed over her belly, the banana and peanut butter sandwich, which was still partly hiding under the couch, and their play in which Rebecca wore Mom's jacket and hat and became "Momma."

After supper they checked the garden to see if the ants were still there. It wasn't very long until Rebecca was ready for sleep. After a little washing, finding the p.j.s, two songs, and a story, she was sleeping. By now the dishes were also done and Jenny and Steven had time to talk. Jenny always had many details about Rebecca's day. She needed to tell Steven about each one, and he needed to hear them all.

Later, Steven told Jenny about his meeting with Dr. Kaplan. "She left me more mixed up then ever, yet somehow I think she's right. Katie just doesn't have a relationship with anyone. Not a real relationship. Not like Becca has with us. I never thought about it before. Probably Katie never had as much fun with her parents as we just did with Becca the last couple of hours. It's hard to imagine. It was always obvious to me what abuse would do to a kid. But, it seems now that it would be just as bad if she never got much hugging and laughing and singing and talking."

"From what Dr. Kaplan said, it might even be worse," said Jenny. "Rebecca so much needs for me to be engaged with her for hours each day. I can't imagine what it would do to her if I simply left her alone for long periods and ignored her movements toward me. I know it would hurt her a great deal."

"When you and Becca are together, it's like nothing else exists," said Steven. "You two are so in sync that I almost can't tell where one of you starts and the other ends. Like you're one being."

"I guess that's what bonding is all about," Jenny said. "It's such a unique experience. Different than our bond. I'm so aware of her feelings and thoughts and actions. Sometimes it feels like I experience them at the same time that she does. And I have a feeling of just wanting to help her to bring them out, to express whatever is going on within her, to let her know that whatever she feels, it's special to me and OK with me."

They held hands and thought about their kid some more. Then Steven said, "I'm beginning to think I know what Dr. Kaplan was talking about. To deprive a kid like Katie of thousands of experiences like we've been talking about is nothing if it's not neglect. No wonder she can't live very well in a family. And she's almost 7. All those years! During the first five no one wanted to hold and hug her, and during the last two she hasn't wanted anyone to."

COMMENTARY

Allison's evaluation of Katie consisted of obtaining her distant and recent history as well as in observing and testing her interactions in the office. First she obtained from Steven a summary of her experiences of abuse and neglect as well as her placement history. She would want to know if Katie had any stable and positive relationships during her early years when her attachment history was unfolding. She would want specific details of her past history in order to address them briefly with Katie and observe her response.

Allison also would want to determine Katie's most recent functioning with Susan. She would want to know her symptoms as well as her strengths. She would ask about her response to attunement as well as shame experiences. She also would observe the interactions between Katie and Susan.

Allison related with Katie during the evaluation session in a manner similar to, although somewhat less intensely than, she would in a treatment session. She wanted to observe how Katie would respond to directives and to challenging themes for both diagnostic reasons, but also for an estimate of how she would respond to therapeutic interventions. How easily would she respond to empathy and playfulness? Would she be receptive to Allison's curiosity about her thoughts, feelings, and behaviors and would she be open to reframing her experiences? How would she express her anger and would she resist being led from anger to the likely feelings of sadness, loneliness, and fear that were likely to underlie her rage? Allison would observe and then attempt to develop a composite view of Katie that she could use for the purposes of her evaluation.

During the evaluation Allison saw Katie alone for awhile, something that she seldom did during her psychotherapy with poorly attached children. She wanted to see if Katie responded differently than she did when she was in the presence of her foster mother. Had she used her foster mother's presence for any sense of security? Would she be more or less critical of her foster mother when she was not present? Would she be more able to express various emotions? Would she express any guilt or responsibility for the problems in her foster home or express only excuses and blame the rest of the family? Could she access any sense of sadness over being so alone in the world and any desire to learn how to become attached to her parent? What psychological and physical boundaries would she have when speaking with Allison alone? How would she relate with her?

Steven and Jenny's relationship with their daughter, Rebecca, demonstrates the contrast between how a healthy attachment develops and how Katie was raised. The routine, but magical, experiences between Rebecca and her parents serve as the foundation for the development of both her sense of self and also her present and future attachment relationships. Without them, a child cannot experience herself as being special and worthwhile. Nor will she identify with her parents and make them special to her.

JACKIE KELLER'S THERAPEUTIC PARENTING

Two days later Steven went to meet Jackie Keller. She wanted to talk with him before deciding if she would bring Katie into her home. Jackie lived in the town of Vassalboro, about ten miles north of Augusta. Jackie's husband, Mark, was a science teacher at Gardiner High School. They had two birth children, Matthew and Diane, both in high school, and a foster son, John, who was 16 and had lived with them for two years. John apparently had been physically abused by his father. He maintained a relationship with his parents but probably was not going to return to live with them. They also had a large, graying Black Labrador, who licked and liked anything that moved. His name was Whimsy.

Two months ago, Jackie's 11-year-old foster son, Gabe, was placed in an adoptive home after living with her for two years. She missed Gabe and still had some contact with him.

Steven immediately liked Jackie. She seemed warm and relaxed. Her home had a casual, but organized and active quality. He imagined how it would sound when three teenagers returned from school. But in many ways Jackie reminded him of Susan. Would this be different? Would Jackie be able to give Katie the affection that she needed without being overwhelmed by her rage?

"Tell me about Katie, Steven," Jackie said as she brought him coffee. "You've mentioned that she's now in her third foster home. What's she like?"

"She's an angry and controlling kid. When things are going her way she seems just like any kid, but if things don't go her way she immediately becomes outraged. Dr. Kaplan says that she has significant attachment problems similar to the boy who just left your home. That's probably why she suggested that I call you."

"So I might be getting myself in for quite a lot if I take her," Jackie said. "Though I like the idea of working with Allison again."

"Dr. Kaplan isn't treating her. She just evaluated her a few days ago," Steven said.

"I can't take Katie unless Allison is her therapist, Steven," Jackie said.

"Why is it so important that she see Dr. Kaplan?" asked Steven. "She has a good therapist who could address Katie's attachment difficulties now that we know what they are."

"I don't know her therapist, Steven," Jackie said. "But I do know Allison, and she knows how to connect with kids who don't want to connect. Just knowing that she has an attachment disorder does not guarantee that one is able and ready to treat it. This is very hard work, Steven, and if I can't work with Allison, I'm afraid I'm not ready to commit to start working with Katie. I don't want to become her fourth disrupted home."

"But she has worked with her therapist, Jan, for over a year and a half. It doesn't make sense to me to break her attachment with Jan if we're trying to help her to learn to attach to people," Steven said firmly.

"Steven, if Allison is right and she does have significant attachment problems, she doesn't have an attachment with her therapist," Jackie said. "She may enjoy seeing her in order to get to play or to get snacks or to just get a chance to control someone. But if she has little ability to develop an attachment she really would not miss her therapist. Just like she doesn't miss her previous foster parents and she won't miss her current foster mother. If a child is really unable to attach to a parent, she will definitely not be able to have a secure attachment to anyone else."

"Well, I'll have to think about it and talk with Jan," Steven said.

"That's fine, Steven," said Jackie. "And while we're talking about Katie living with me, I should ask if Allison talked with you about how I would have to be raising her."

"No she didn't," Steven said. "Is it that different?"

"Yes it is. I didn't raise Gabe like I'm raising my own kids, or even like I'm raising John. When I first started working with Allison, I had a hard time following her suggestions. I felt that I was being too hard on him, especially since he had been through so much already. But what Allison said to do did prove to be necessary. Without it, I know that Gabe would never have changed. So I'll need to know that I have your support in the ways that I'll be raising her before I can agree to become her mother and expect her to form an attachment with me."

"Could you give me an example of what you mean?" Steven asked.

"Well, if you stop by to visit you're likely to see that she's getting a lot of supervision. She'll be needing permission for just about everything. She'll be doing a lot of sitting and probably a lot of chores. Also, she has shown some desire to hurt others, Steven. Although I think the other kids can take care of themselves, I do have to be careful about Whimsy. That dog will love her silly and will need my protection or she is likely to be mean to him.

"Also, I'll have to ask you not to take her out and have a lot of fun with her. If she's to have any fun it's going to be with me first, and within my guidelines."

Steven didn't know what to say. No foster mother had ever been so direct with him about the kind of support that she wanted. Jackie seemed to be saying that she would be as tough as she wanted with Katie and Steven would have no say in whether or not she was being too strict. He didn't know if he could agree to this or even if he wanted to agree. He was Katie's guardian. "I don't know, Jackie. What am I supposed to do if I think that you're being too hard on her?"

"What I would want is for you to initially accept my decision. You could then talk with me and Allison about it and we'll tell you why we're doing it. But unless I'm abusing the kid, I would need you to support me, and I would need to have Katie know that you support me," Jackie said with certainty.

"You are her guardian," Jackie added. "I know that you have to do what you think is best for her. By telling you now how I'll probably have to be raising her, I want to avoid hurting Katie again by your removing her from my home because you disagree with what I'm doing. I want you to know as much as possible so that if you disagree, you can simply not consider me for Katie at this time, and save putting her through another disruption. I know that some of the interventions I use are uncommon, and you might have trouble with them. If you do, I want to see if we can resolve them now."

Steven was beginning to sense that Jackie would not be overwhelmed by Katie. There was a strength about her and a confidence about what Katie really needed and what she would be getting from

Jackie. Steven still wasn't sure if he could accept Jackie having this degree of control over her care. It seemed that she was taking some of his responsibilities. He would have to discuss it with Kathy.

"I imagine that you think I'd be running an army boot camp for Katie, Steven," Jackie said. "And you can be sure that she'll think it's a boot camp. But when I'm with her I'll have an attitude toward her that you'll never find in boot camp. Allison calls it 'The Attitude.'"

"What kind of attitude are you talking about?" Steven asked.

"There are five qualities to the attitude. They are *being accepting, curious, empathic, loving,* and *playful.* They will be a part of all of my interactions with a kid like Katie and they'll make all the difference. Without this attitude, the tough behavioral structure and consequences that she needs to have would not really be therapeutic."

Steven thought about what Jackie said. "The Attitude" made "boot camp" a little more understandable.

Before Steven left, Jackie also told him that she would like to talk with Katie's three foster mothers and meet with her before deciding. She also suggested that before he and she made a final decision, they should meet with Dr. Kaplan to discuss more details about their plans for Katie. Steven left feeling that he would be losing some of his authority if he worked with Jackie. It made him feel uncomfortable and somewhat vulnerable.

On May 19, 1994, Steven and Kathy met with Jackie and Dr. Kaplan at her office. Steven had decided that he might be asked to agree to things that would require Kathy's OK, so he had asked her to be present.

"Jackie tells me that she's still interested in Katie becoming her foster child," Steven began. "She made it clear that she would need you to be Katie's therapist, Dr. Kaplan, so I discussed her request with Kathy and Jan Temple and we agreed that if we decide that Jackie will be her foster mom, and you were able to see her, we would transfer her to you."

"Jackie and I work well together and I am able to see Katie," Allison replied. "I'd be more comfortable if you would call me Allison, since we're going to be working closely and since that's what Katie will be calling me."

"That's fine, Allison," said Steven.

"Steven tells me that you and Jackie will probably be working with Katie in ways that he might disagree with," said Kathy. "Is that why this meeting is necessary?"

"Yes," said Allison. "DHS has custody of Katie. It is your call as to what kind of treatment is in her best interest. I don't want to begin working with her if you have any fundamental differences about my approach with her, or Jackie's way of raising her at home. It certainly won't be good for her if six months from now you say that you don't really believe in what Jackie and I will be trying to accomplish."

"That's fair," said Kathy. "Why don't you tell us the general outline of your approach."

"Good," Allison began. "The first thing that I will stress is that if Katie is to ever change and begin to trust her mom and depend on her, she will need to reduce her pervasive need to control every-thing and become comfortable with Jackie being in control of the major realities of her life. As you have seen, waiting for Katie to voluntarily give up control will be a long wait and probably will be too late for her ever to have the opportunity to be parented. She has lived for almost two years in three different homes and not shown any readiness to be parented. By her maintaining such a strong compulsion to be in control, she is avoiding experiences of healthy dependency on her mother, and she is not able to learn that such experiences are pleasant and safe. *And* she is not able to make the developmental changes that require such experiences. Thus, Jackie will be taking control at home and I will be in therapy. But we won't do it in a mean way. We'll give her a great deal of empathy and support for how hard it is for her not to have control. And when she's ready, we'll slowly begin to give her some control back. We don't want this control. We're taking it because she can't manage it well. Her being in control prevents her from attaching and developing in healthy ways."

Allison turned to Jackie. "Why don't you tell Steven and Kathy some of the specific ways that you plan to take charge when Katie moves into your home."

"Sure," Jackie said. "Well, I'm going to begin the moment that she moves in. I'll be letting her know right away what I expect and what the rules and routines are in my home. I'll be telling her that it must be hard for her to have to learn how to live in so many different homes, but I'll be glad to teach her. I'll let her know that I'm aware of some of her past behaviors and I still want her to live with me. She'll be needing help to learn to change those behaviors in my home."

"And if she poops in your hamburger?" Steven asked.

"Good question," Allison said. "In fact, I'll be discussing that with Katie in an early therapy session."

"If she does that in my home," said Jackie, "there probably would be a variety of consequences. She might be cleaning the kitchen and bathroom for awhile. She'd most likely have to do some chores to earn some money to buy new hamburger. She'd go to the store with me and order the meat and pay for it with her money. She'd probably be supervised more closely in the kitchen for quite some time. There might be some other things, too, depending on how she's doing overall at the time. Also, I will actually be treating her as if she did poop in the hamburger in my house, since she only did it a couple of weeks ago and I have no confidence that she would not do it again with me if she were in the mood and the opportunity were presented to her. I might actually tell her that she will be supervised fairly closely around food for now because of my concern that she might decide to poop in our hamburger or soup, too."

"One reason we'd discuss it in therapy is to let her know that we know what she did and to help her to know some of the factors in why she did it," Allison said. "Her knowing why she does her outrageous behaviors is not to give her an excuse, but rather to help her to feel less profound shame for her behaviors so that she can gradually be able to face them."

"Do you really think that she feels shame?" asked Steven. "Her other foster parents say that she never shows any remorse for what she does."

"Shame is not guilt, Steven," said Allison. "Her sense of guilt may well be weak since it is a more complex and developmentally more mature emotion than shame. But she does experience shame, although she seldom allows herself to be conscious of it. She unconsciously feels and thinks that she is worthless and that conviction is experienced as shame. The rejection and humiliation that she must have experienced over and over with Sally and Mike must have left her convinced that she is 'just no good.' Her frequent rage is her effort to not only control others and maintain her precarious sense of safety, but also to block out the painful experience of shame. Her constant lying and denial of her behavior also shows her intense effort to avoid experiencing shame."

After a pause, Allison continued, "In therapy I might be suggesting that family gatherings like the one at Susan's must be hard on her when everyone else is having fun and she doesn't feel that she fits in because she really doesn't know how to have fun. She decided to ruin everyone else's fun too. I'll give her empathy for those feelings and then tell her that it's probably best for now that at Jackie's she either won't be able to participate in family gatherings or she will be supervised the entire time—whatever seems best to Jackie."

"But wouldn't that make her feel that she's not a part of the family?" asked Kathy, "and slow down the development of the attachment that you want?"

"Great question, Kathy, because it goes to the heart of this approach," said Allison. "If we give her enjoyable experiences that she fails at, we will not be helping her to attach. She will just be feeling more of a failure, her shame will increase, and she'll be less receptive to further enjoyable experiences. It's like taking a person who was lost in the desert for three days and giving him a gallon of water to drink. It feels right to give him a lot of water since he is dehydrated and seems to need that much water. But that much water won't help him, it will kill him. He needs it in small, carefully supplied amounts. He cannot receive it more quickly than he can absorb it or it won't help him. The same is true for Katie. If we give her a great amount of experiences that most children would find to be enjoyable, she will sabotage them all. She can't integrate them. They don't fit her self-perception or her view of parents. It's too great a stretch for her and it makes her anxious and uncomfortable and will elicit behaviors that will seek the rejection and anger that is more comfortable for her."

"I'm still lost, Allison," Steven said. "If her early years of deprivation are the source of her problems, how can depriving her of enjoyable experiences now cause the change that you want?"

"Our goals for Katie are the same as they would be for any kid having difficulties. We want her to experience a loving relationship with her parents, we want her to have many opportunities for enjoyment and satisfaction in her life, and we want her to have the freedom to choose, among numerous options, what is in her best interests. However, with Katie, and with other poorly attached children, she has extreme difficulty integrating, and benefiting from, experiences of fun, love, and freedom to choose. She sabotages fun, undermines efforts to love her, and her choices are invariably not in her best interests. Essentially, if she is to benefit from them, she needs training in receiving and accepting experiences of fun and love while learning to make better choices. Also, Katie's pervasive shame has to be reduced. We are not trying to eliminate it since healthy shame is crucial for socialization. But we will remove rejection, humiliation, and contempt from shaming experiences. Most importantly, we will quickly reconnect with her emotionally after her experience of shame so that she will be able to sense her worth and feel secure in her attachment with Jackie, even when she must experience consequences for her poor behavioral choices."

"We want what you want for her. But from her activities over the past twenty-one months, it seems fairly certain that these goals must be long term. We must build up to them slowly, one step at a time, minimizing failure, and gradually showing her how to live well within a good family."

"But how are you going to motivate her if she has nothing to work for?" Steven asked. "If you are that restrictive why should she want to change?"

"Jackie and I really won't be *that* restrictive, Steven," answered Allison. "And we definitely won't be angry and rejecting of her behaviors. More than anything else, we're going to be going back to what she should have received during the first two years of her life. We will be patiently and persistently providing her with the countless experiences of affective attunement that babies and toddlers should receive, but which Katie did not."

"What do you mean by 'affective attunement'?" asked Kathy.

"Affective attunement refers to the early experiences of mutual interests and joy that the mother and her infant have over and over during the first couple of years of life, and which actually will never stop in a good parent–child relationship. It refers to those moments when the mother and her infant are lost in their mutual eye contact, facial gestures, synchronized movements, and shared focus that eliminates every other reality when they are so engaged. The mother and her baby are sharing their affective lives. Katie needs those experiences with Jackie, and she needs to receive them throughout every day, regardless of her behaviors. In fact, if Jackie has some success in engaging her at that level, Katie's behavior is likely to become more oppositional and angry as she tries to get Jackie to stop. Hopefully, most of the time Katie will not be successful and Jackie will continue to give her what she needs—namely, to experience mutual joy and interest with a person who loves her, and who will not reject her regardless of her behaviors."

Steven was now quite interested. Allison was talking about Jenny and Rebecca! But he still couldn't understand how Jackie could provide those experiences to a defiant child almost 7 years of age. "How can Jackie give Katie all of that attunement when Katie is constantly getting herself in trouble?"

Jackie laughed and said, "With difficulty. But also with practice and some rest, and some support from Allison, my husband, Mark, and from you and others. For me, my beliefs in God help too. My discipline is not given in anger. I look on discipline as an opportunity to build the attachment rather than a hindrance to it."

"How is that?" asked Steven.

"I'll give her empathy rather than annoyance when I limit her and give her consequences for her actions. Experiences of mutual acceptance and enjoyment will hopefully precede and immediately follow her misbehaviors that trigger shame. I'll be letting her know that I know it's hard for her to make these changes, and I'll be patient and thorough in teaching her how."

"You're not going to get angry with her! Is that realistic?" asked Steven.

"I won't say that I'll never get angry, but I'm now confident after having raised Gabe for two years, that I'll be angry in order to achieve a goal with Katie rather than because I lost control. When Katie is able to 'make' me angry, I'll know that she's winning, she's in control, so that both of us are losing. It was hard to develop this way of responding, but Allison showed me how important it is, and now it's fairly easy to attain most of the time. Also, if I'm going to help Katie, I don't think I have any choice."

"Are you saying, Allison, that if a parent gets angry at his kid that he is damaging him and hurting their attachment?" asked Steven.

"I'm not talking about healthy kids who have a secure attachment with their parents already," said Allison. "Those kids are able to deal with their parents' anger without undermining their own sense of worth or their trust in their parents' love for them. But with poorly attached kids, routine anger, or even mild annoyance when it is frequent, will damage our efforts to facilitate their ability to attach, because it triggers a pervasive shame response with its related self-contempt and parental mistrust."

"I want to assure you," Jackie said, "that although I will be tough with Katie and my standards for her behavior will be high, I will not be rejecting her and I am not harsh. I was fairly 'easy' with my own kids; it's the way I prefer to raise kids. But Gabe, and I think Katie too, could not handle 'easy,' so I was forced to change my style to meet his needs."

"But Jackie," Kathy said, "how can you have high expectations if you're going to ask Katie to change 'one step at a time'?"

"If my expectations aren't high, she won't change at all. I will, however, be restricting her choices. Within the choices that I give her, my expectations will be high."

"I still don't get it," Kathy said.

"Kathy," Allison said, "Although Katie is almost 7, Jackie will have expectations for her that are more similar to a 2- or 3-year-old child. But she'll be expecting her to do a good job at being a 2- or 3-year-old. If Katie doesn't do a good job, then Jackie will be asking her to do it again until she gets it right, or she might change her immediate goals and began to ask Katie to do a good job at being 18 months old. But she will not accept Katie doing things poorly, no matter what age expectation Jackie has. Katie does need to be socialized if she is to ever live within Jackie's home and our community. For example, Katie might not know how to share a family activity like playing a game together very well as is evidenced by her arguing over the rules, talking loudly, or cheating. Katie will be told clearly how to play the game with the family the acceptable way. If necessary, she'll receive practice doing it and close supervision sitting next to Jackie on the couch. The length of time she can play may be limited. But Jackie will not be correcting her a dozen times. She will not be overlooking any behaviors that are not acceptable. She will not be coaxed to do it right."

"What do you mean by 'coaxed'?" Steven asked.

"Too often parents and other adults work harder to get a child to make the right choice than the child does himself," Allison replied. "The child might be given three chances, which were preceded by two warnings. It must be confusing to the child. His appropriate behavior is of benefit to whom? If the parent is that invested in the child acting well, then the child will become less invested. Once Katie is told what is expected of her in a situation, she will not be given a second chance, and she will not be reminded or coaxed to meet the expectation. Rather we assume that she's smart enough to remember what is expected, and she'll make the choice that she thinks is best for her. We may disagree with her choice, so we may give her a consequence that fits that particular choice, and that might help her to choose differently the next time she's in the situation. But we do not get upset over her choice, we simply encourage her to consider alternatives for the future."

"Allison," Steven said, "Jackie told me the other day about an attitude that she'll have with Katie. How does that fit in with what you're talking about now?"

"'The Attitude' is another way of saying what we just described," Allison replied. "The five qualities of The Attitude provide the emotional context in which Katie will be able to accept attunement experiences. They will enable her to tolerate the stress of our behavioral expectations, supervision, and consequences, all of which trigger shame. They will help her to reconnect with us after shame. In essence, they will help her to see what attachment is all about."

"What Attitude?" Kathy asked.

"Kathy, over the past few years, some therapists, parents, and I have become increasingly aware of how we actually *are* when we relate successfully with poorly attached children. We identified five features, which actually are very similar to the attitude that a parent has when she is attuned with her infant or toddler. The features are *accepting, curious, empathic, loving,* and *playful*. We think that all five are necessary, and that this attitude needs to become the background atmosphere—both in the family and in therapy—if the child is to begin to respond to the interventions provided. When a parent like Jackie has developed this attitude to the extent that it's an easy and natural way of interacting with her child, then it's fairly easy to avoid angry, frustrated, and tense interactions most of the time. Once the parent is good at maintaining this attitude, for both attunement and for reattunement after shame experiences, parenting becomes a lot easier, regardless of how outrageous the child's behavior is."

"Easy for you to say!" Jackie laughed. "No, really, Allison is right. When I lose that attitude, every hour is difficult. When I can maintain it, I actually often feel that raising this very tough kid is fun. I can relax and enjoy her more. I don't try to predict and control her behaviors. I'm curious and accepting about them and I'm free to respond with empathy in ways that can best meet her needs. I can be playful and loving in my responses. She can't control my emotions so I can use them to remain emotionally engaged with her no matter what she does. This attitude does remind me of how I was with my birth kids, Matthew and Diane, when they were babies. It makes raising these tough kids so much easier. It's good for both parent and child."

"Could you summarize for us what happens in your treatment sessions?" Kathy asked.

"Certainly," Allison replied. "I'll meet with her at least weekly and the sessions will last between ninety and 120 minutes. Jackie will always be present during the session. Her presence is needed because my goal is to facilitate an attachment with Jackie, not with me. Also, I do not want to meet with her alone because I will be touching and holding her a lot and because of her history of abuse, both Katie and I will feel safer if Jackie is there.

"At the beginning of each session, I will speak with Jackie about what has been happening at home to develop some ideas for interventions that I might try in the session. I also might give her some suggestions for interventions that she might try at home. I don't want Katie to know what I am recommending until I know if Jackie agrees with me.

"Much of my routine in therapy is based on attachment sequences that occur in daily life in healthy mother–child attachments. I first want to establish a relationship with Katie in each session that has features of affective attunement and the attitude that we discussed earlier. Then I'll bring up a shame-inducing experience from her current life in her foster home or her early life with her birth parents. For that reason, I will want to know everything that you know about her early life of abuse and neglect. Finally, I will work to reestablish affective attunement with her, to help her to gradually begin to reduce and integrate her experience of pervasive shame and also become more receptive to comforting and to discovering that her experiences of shame will not hurt her relationships with Jackie or me."

"That sequence of establishing attunement, experiencing a break in the relationship because of shame, and then re-establishing attunement will probably occur a number of times during each session."

"I'm having trouble picturing how you'll being doing this," Kathy said. "Will you simply be sitting near her, playing with her, and then talk about her problems before playing with her again?"

"The qualities of The Attitude will permeate all aspects of the sequences. Katie will be experiencing acceptance and empathy throughout every interaction. She also will experience my intense curiosity about her inner life—about what she feels and thinks about everything—and she will experience these interactions within a light and gentle, playful quality. While I will not be communicating that her problems are 'funny,' I will be showing confidence in her. I will be communicating that I see a healthy self within her that will not be destroyed, or even compromised, by whatever traumatic or stressful experiences that she has had. When she can smile with us over her difficulties in learning to live in Jackie's home, and even smile with sadness when recalling her life with Sally and Mike while being comforted by Jackie, she will have taken a giant step in forming a secure attachment with Jackie."

"I have heard your therapy called 'holding therapy,'" Steven said. "What does that refer to?"

"Regrettably there are as many types of 'holding therapy' as there are 'holding therapists.' They range from having the therapist only hold the child, to having the parent only holding the child. Some stress eliciting rage, and I believe, increasing shame, and are quite confrontational. Others emphasize the nurturing quality of holding a child. Because of ambiguity of the phrase as well as because of the fact that holding the child is only one aspect of the interventions, I do not use the term 'holding therapy' when referring to this work. I cannot think of a short phrase to describe this therapy." Allison laughed. "The closest that I can come is Attunement-enhancing, Shame-reducing, Attachment Therapy."

"But your question about 'holding therapy' suggests that I should speak about how Katie will be held. During much of the therapy session either Jackie or I will be interacting with Katie in ways that maximize touching her, or we will actually be holding her," Allison replied. "Just as it is with infants and toddlers, touching and holding her is very helpful in efforts to help her to experience affective attunement with us. She will feel closer to us, in spite of her well-established defenses, and she will actually feel safer when she is being held. She will be more receptive to affective memories and current experiences that she habitually guards against. When I am holding her I am confident that she will be more receptive to experiencing both affective attunement as well as the pain of shame."

"Will you hold her against her will?" Kathy asked.

"The answer is 'yes' but with qualifications," Allison said. "She is likely to resist entering into both of the experiences of attunement and shame. She is also likely to very quickly break off the experiences before they can even begin to be integrated. For those reasons, I will hold her in spite of her telling me that she wants me to let her go. In my experience the child invariably comes to accept being held and working on the therapeutic issues in a fairly short time and then accept, and even look forward to, being held even though the therapeutic work remains hard."

"On some occasions being held against his or her will has triggered anxiety that is trauma based. I immediately focus on the anxiety with empathy, explore the possible traumas, and enable the child to gain mastery over the anxiety. On only a few occasions have I had to stop holding the child when he was anxious and allow him to work through the trauma while sitting separate from me or his mother. On each occasion the child did it successfully and was then ready to be held again by one of us. I have never worked with a child who persistently demonstrated that being held in therapy was a negative experience. A few times, a child has not been at all receptive to my holding him, but he was quite responsive to his parent holding him. I accepted that with those children and I touched them, but seldom held them, although the parent held them a lot. If there are any signs that Katie's emotional response to being held is in any way traumatic, we will stop holding her in therapy and discuss her response with you."

After a pause, Kathy said, "I think that we can and should give approval for you to work with Katie, Allison, and for her to move into Jackie's house. I like what you're saying, although I still will want to see how it works from day to day. Would you have any objections to Steven regularly talking with you about how the therapy is going as well as stopping by Jackie's house on a more frequent basis than he otherwise would?"

"None at all," both Allison and Jackie responded. Allison added, "Actually if Steven would like to sit in on some sessions with Katie, Jackie, and me, that would be fine."

"I'd like that," Steven replied.

"Let's try it then," Kathy said. "You can be confident that we won't interfere with what you are doing even if we're not sure about it being helpful. We'll let you call the shots on anything other than abuse or neglect. We would be willing to commit to six months before reviewing your approach with Katie. Is that sufficient?"

"While it may not be sufficient for Katie to make substantial progress," Allison said, "it should give us enough time to show you what we're doing and for you see some initial changes that we'll be building upon."

"What are the rates of success in using this approach in working with kids with significant attachment deficits?" Kathy asked.

"I wish that I could provide you with well-established research findings," Allison replied. "But there is so little research on children with these deficits, and even less on therapeutic and parenting approaches to take with them. I can tell you about my own experiences over the last six years."

"That would be helpful," Kathy said.

"Well, a rough estimate would be that about one third of the children with significant attachment problems that I have worked with have made very significant progress, another third made some progress that proved to be helpful, and a final third made little if any progress. About all I have been able to accomplish in the final third has been to assist their families in learning to live with them in ways that help to preserve the family. My goal then is to keep the consequences of the child's problems within the child, rather than having him or her hurt the other members of the family. And I help the parents explore the painful possibilities involving having the child placed in a group facility if that seems to be necessary."

"I have to say that your results leave me somewhat discouraged," Steven said.

"I understand that," Allison said. "But they are much better than the results that I saw before when I used the traditional approaches of play therapy and cognitive-behavioral child rearing interventions. Back then, I would have had to say that for children with significant attachment problems, my interventions had little or no effects 90 percent of the time. Now I see positive effects two thirds of the time, and in many of those cases the effects have been very significant. For that reason, I'm elated with the results that I now see, although I grieve for the children and families that I cannot reach. We need good research on creative and comprehensive approaches to these children. They have very significant psychological problems that do not respond to treatment easily."

"Are there any other approaches for these children?" asked Kathy.

"None based on research, I'm sorry to say," Allison replied.

The four of them sat quietly for a few moments. They all experienced sadness for every child who had no attachment to good parents, and who lacked the ability to have such an attachment when given the chance. A nightmare life.

"OK," said Kathy, "why don't we set a date for Katie to move to Jackie's home."

COMMENTARY

Allison and Jackie needed to present a detailed account of the way that they would be intervening in Katie's life because it was crucial that their strategies be understood and accepted before she were placed in Jackie's home, with Allison as her therapist. The interventions at home and in therapy often vary from the traditional view of what constitutes appropriate care.

Allison and Jackie repeatedly stress the need to maintain a therapeutic attitude if they are to be able to have an impact on

Katie's development. It is the attitude that make the strategies employed therapeutic. If Katie is restricted from a family party, or if she has to take two hours to clean up the milk spill because she is choosing to do her task slowly, these consequences need to be presented in the manner conveyed by the attitude described previously if they are to be therapeutic. Jackie will say to Katie, "I'm sad that you're not ready to join the party with us. I can't wait until you can handle having fun with us better so that you can be with the rest of us at times like this." Such a statement is therapeutic. Contrast it with, "You're not allowed to be in the living room while we're having the party. Until you learn how to act right, we don't want you with us." Another comment to avoid would be, "You never do what you're told. It's your fault that you can't be with us." Each of the three interventions involved restricting her from the party. The nature of the attitude conveyed to her determined whether or not the intervention was therapeutic.

An equally destructive way of managing the situation would be to allow Katie to attend the party, with five warnings about how she had to behave properly, even though, in the last three similar parties, her behavior was very disruptive and aggressive, and there was no reason to think that this party would be any different.

Too often children like Katie are given dozens of chances to make the appropriate choice, even when they have failed on every occasion. Each failure is responded to with annoyance, a lecture, and a "fresh start," which would be more accurately described as a "stale repetition" of failure. This would be an excellent way to increase Katie's sense of shame and her worthlessness. If a child in the seventh grade can read only at the third-grade level, should that child be given a "fresh start" every day and given a seventh-grade book to read? Is it not much better to recognize that he reads at the third-grade level, give him a third-grade book, expect him to work at his level of ability and encourage his small steps toward further development of his reading skills? Unattached children do not function, emotionally, cognitively, or behaviorally at their chronological age. They need an environment that recognizes that fact, is sensitive to their actual developmental level, and builds an environment and parental care, supervision, and expectations, appropriate to that level. If Katie is functioning more like a toddler, *and she is*, then she needs the same degree of attunement experiences, supervision, parental involvement in her choices, restrictions, and appropriate level of expectations that we would give to a toddler. The attitude of acceptance, empathy, love, curiosity, and playfulness will insure that by treating her as a toddler, the interventions are therapeutic and not punitive or humiliating.

FOSTER HOME #4—JACKIE KELLER

On Thursday, June 9, 1994, Katie moved into the home of Jackie Keller in Vassalboro, Maine. Still 6 years old, she had been in foster care for twenty-one months, and, counting her life with Sally and Mike, she was moving into her fifth home. As he had done in the previous moves, Steven drove her with most of her clothes to Jackie's. Susan had told Katie about a week before that she would be moving to a new home that would be more able to meet her needs. Katie did not show much of a response. She certainly made no efforts to change Susan's mind. Rather, she was interested in what Jackie's home was like. She had met Jackie a few weeks earlier but didn't really remember her.

Jackie and Mark lived on a winding road a mile off the highway. Five years earlier, when they had decided to care for foster children, Mark built a two-bedroom addition on the home. Katie would sleep in one of the two downstairs bedrooms. Jackie and Mark slept in the other one and the three adolescents slept upstairs.

When Steven arrived at 2 P.M., Jackie and Whimsy were waiting for them in their large dining room. No one else was around. Jackie greeted Katie with enthusiasm. Whimsy licked her and immediately wanted to be her best friend. Katie patted Whimsy's neck as she looked around the kitchen. Jackie then helped her with her suitcases and boxes and brought her to her bedroom. Steven and Whimsy waited in the kitchen until they returned for some milk and crackers.

"Well, Katie, I'm pleased that you're here. I'm glad that you're becoming a member of our family. You'll be meeting your new dad, Mark, and your older brothers and sister before dinner. Now we'll have some time for you to get to know me and what it's like living here. You can have some crackers and milk."

"I want some cookies. That's what I eat in the afternoon for snack," said Katie.

"I'm glad that you let me know what you want, Katie. I like cookies too. Here we have crackers or fruit for an afternoon snack. You might be sad about that, but you'll get used to it after awhile."

"I don't like those crackers!" said Katie.

"Well you certainly don't have to eat them, Katie. You can just drink your milk if you want, or you don't even have to drink it, if you don't want," said Jackie.

Katie stared at her milk and crackers in front of her. She seemed to be pouting. She didn't seem to know what to do.

"I can see you don't like only being able to have crackers. You might be thinking that I'm kind of mean. And you just met me! You might even be wondering if this is going to be a rotten home that you won't like at all. Looks like a hard start for you."

"You are mean!" Katie exclaimed and she suddenly moved her arm and sent the glass of milk flying. Most of the milk hit the table and the rest went right to the floor. A fair amount of what hit the table seemed to actually bounce before falling into Steven's lap.

Steven jumped back and up from his chair, grabbing his pants and yelling, "Katie, why did you do that?"

Jackie quickly moved between Steven and Katie, focused all of her attention on Katie and said, "Wow, you really are mad! You don't waste any time showing me how mad you get when I won't let you do something. My guess is you wanted to say, 'I don't want any of your milk!' I'll bet that you wish that you had gotten the milk on me rather than Steven!"

Jackie turned to Steven and suggested that he might use a towel in the bathroom if he wanted to try to dry his pants. She then turned to Katie again and bent down, placing her arm on the back of her chair. She quietly said, "Katie, I can see that this is hard for you. You've had to move so much. So many families! Cookies, crackers, fruit! Always something new to get used to. Wow, it must be hard."

Katie only continued to stare at the table, where her glass of milk had been a moment earlier.

"I'd like to make it as easy as I can for you, sweetie. It's so important for me to show you right from the start how we live here. It wouldn't be fair to trick you into thinking that you can have cookies for snack, when it's crackers or fruit. You probably think that's dumb. 'No cookies for snack.' But that's the way we all live here. Even I don't get cookies for snack."

She leaned over Katie for a few moments while this 6-year-old survivor seemed to weigh her options. Jackie was relaxed and accepting. Katie's behavior might be very understandable if one could watch a videotape of the millions of moments of anger and indifference to her wishes that she may have experienced during those early years of her life. Any refusal to grant her wish might now be felt as another sign of contempt for her and complete apathy about what she felt.

Katie might have sensed Jackie's acceptance. She might have thought that she would take another approach or she might simply have decided to wait for another day. Katie reached for a cracker, and as she raised it to her mouth she quietly asked for some more milk.

"Oh, Katie, I wish you could have milk, but you threw it all over the table, the floor, and Steven's pants. I'll tell you what. While you're cleaning up the milk, I'll get you a glass of water to drink with your crackers."

"I want more milk!" Katie screamed and threw her cracker across the room. It hit a cabinet, broke into a hundred pieces and joined the milk on the floor.

Jackie reached down and removed the two remaining crackers. "I'll save these for me, Katie. You are so mad at me! No cookies, no new milk, and no more crackers to throw! You probably feel like throwing me, but I'm too heavy."

Katie stood up and tried to grab the crackers in Jackie's hand. Jackie took her wrist and held her hand away as she placed the crackers on the counter. "Now, Katie, I'll show you the bucket and sponge that you'll need for wiping up the milk from the floor."

"No I'm not!" Katie screamed and pulled away, trying to free her arm from Jackie's grasp.

Jackie sat down and took Katie's other wrist too. "Oh, this is a hard start for you, Katie. No fun at all. I have to teach you, sweetie, that here, if one of us throws stuff on the floor, that person has to clean it up. You'll probably hear me tell Daddy Mark that a lot." Katie began to struggle to get away.

"You're really mad at me now and I can see you're not ready to clean up the milk. You can sit in the chair for awhile before cleaning it up. But I can't let you run around now. You're so mad you might throw more things and break them or hurt yourself."

Jackie guided Katie to a chair and she sat down with obvious rage. She looked away and slammed her arms on the table. Just then Steven came back into the room.

Katie looked up and screamed, "I don't want to live here! I hate her! Take me back to Susan's!"

Steven was speechless. Jackie quickly filled the silence. "Katie is really mad at me, Steven. First, no cookies. Then I wouldn't let her have more milk. Then I told her that she had to clean up the milk. And finally, after she threw her cracker, I took the other ones from her, and told her to sit there since she's too mad now to clean up the milk and cracker from the floor. And I still haven't even told her yet that she has to tell you that she's sorry for spilling milk on you and then ask you what she can do to make up for it! Katie doesn't like me at all."

"I hate you!" Katie screamed.

"I guess right now she even hates me! No wonder she doesn't want to live here with me," Jackie said. Then she spoke more quietly, directing her words to Katie. "She probably was hoping that she'd finally get a mom that she'd really like. And now she's afraid that I might be the worst mom that she ever had. This must be so hard for her."

Steven sat down and spoke to Katie. "I'm sorry that you're mad at Jackie now, Katie. I'm not taking you back to Susan's though. I know Jackie, and I think that once you get to know her too, you'll like her."

"I don't want to stay here!" Katie screamed again.

"I'm afraid you have to, Katie. This is your new home and I hope that someday you'll like it and Jackie," Steven said, without much confidence in his own words.

"I never will!" Katie screamed.

"Steven, right now Katie is really, really, mad. I don't think that you'll be able to change her mind. Maybe it would be best if you left now and Katie could start to get used to being here."

"No!" Katie screamed and jumped up from her seat.

Jackie went to her quickly and took her wrists again as she reached for Steven. Katie spun and tried to kick Jackie. After two years of caring for Gabe, Jackie anticipated the move and in one easy motion spun Katie in her arms and sat back down in the chair with Katie securely held in her lap.

"Why don't you call tomorrow, Steven, and I'll let you know how Katie is doing. Maybe the next time you come she'll be ready to say that she's sorry for the milk on your pants, " Jackie said.

Steven did not know what he could do besides leaving as gracefully as possible. He could not think of anything to say to Katie that would help the situation so he settled for "goodbye, Katie" as he reached for the door.

As Steven drove down the driveway, Katie continued to scream at Jackie while she tried to scratch, bite, hit, and kick her. Jackie held her securely, with the back of her head against Jackie's chest. If Katie were bigger she'd have to hold her another way. She should be able to keep them both safe this way while Katie expressed her rage.

"Oh, Katie, how hard this must be for you! You don't even know me and now you're all alone in the house with me. Steven left you here with someone you hate and don't know. I know you might not believe me but I can promise you that you'll be safe no matter how mad you get at me. I'll keep you and me safe while you're being so mad at me."

"You're hurting me!" Katie exclaimed.

"You might think I'm going to hurt you, Katie, and it must be scary that you can't move your arms and get away from me but I'm not hurting you," said Jackie matter-of-factly.

"Yes you are!" Katie screamed again.

"Oh, Katie," Jackie said quietly. "How much you've been hurt in your life. I'm sorry that you've been hurt so much."

"Shut up! You are hurting me!" Katie screamed.

"Oh, Katie," Jackie said quietly.

Over the next fifteen minutes, Katie's struggles and screams gradually decreased. Then a car pulled into the driveway. A minute later, Diane, John, and Matt could be heard on the porch and they bounced in through the door. They stopped and stared at their mother, a sweaty, wrinkled little girl, and the milk.

"Kids, I'd like you to meet Katie. She's your new sister and she's living with us now," Jackie said in a casual and relaxed manner.

"Hi, Katie!" Diane said. Her brothers followed with less enthusiasm.

"Katie is having a hard time now, but things are OK," Jackie said. "If you want some milk and crackers you'll have to get your own now. And don't step in the milk."

Diane came over to Katie. "Well, so you're my new sister. I'm glad that I'll no longer be the only girl. Looks like you and Mom are having a disagreement. What does she want you to do?"

"She says I have to clean up the milk!" Katie said with both interest in Diane and annoyance at her situation.

"Too bad, sis. Well, if you get it done soon, I'll show you around the place." Diane left for her room and Katie followed her with her eyes.

"You can let me go now," Katie said firmly. "I'll clean up the milk."

Jackie was surprised by the suddenness of her mood change and her willingness to do what was expected of her. The arrival of three teenagers might have simply broken the atmosphere. Maybe she wanted to impress Diane and did not want to start on the wrong foot with her. Diane and her brothers might be allies against this evil mother.

"It sounds like your anger is gone, Katie. But I don't know you very well. Are you able to handle it if I let you go?" asked Jackie.

"Yes, I won't hit you," Katie said evenly.

"Fine, Katie." She stood up and released her arms. She took a small bucket and sponge from under the sink, filled it partly with water, and gave it to Katie. Katie took it and proceeded to wipe up the milk. Just then Diane came in and got an apple.

"You're doing a good job, Katie," said Diane. "Maybe now Mom won't ask me to help her all the time."

Katie smiled and continued her cleaning. She actually did a good job and gave the bucket to Jackie when she finished.

"Diane, Katie is probably still kinda mad at me. Would you show her the rest of the house and the garage and swing set?"

"Sure, Mom." Diane smiled at Katie. "Come on, sis. We'll start with your bedroom and then I'll show you mine."

Katie walked off with Diane as if she had never been happier. Whimsy followed them. Jackie was a little worn out, but Katie seemed to be full of energy. Jackie would never get used to how kids like Katie could move so abruptly from one mood and activity to another, with no signs of anything remaining from the last event. Jackie wondered if that would make life easier—just move on and have no regrets. It was more likely, however, that one's life would be more fragmented, with less continuity and integration of the various experiences that life brings.

On the way back to his office Steven had his doubts about Jackie and Allison and everything that they had said. It may have sounded good but the real thing seemed to be different than the theory. Didn't Katie need to feel welcomed and relaxed the first day, he wondered. Why couldn't Jackie have given her a damn cookie? What was the big deal? And then she had to make an issue of the spilled milk! And telling me that she was sorry! Couldn't she see that the kid was off to a bad start? Why did she have to push it? She seemed to want Katie to fight with her! She should have known that Katie wouldn't smile and clean up the milk!

Three days later Steven arrived at Allison's office for Katie's first treatment session. He met with Allison and Jackie first while Katie remained in the waiting room.

"How are things going?" Allison asked Jackie.

"Things are pretty much going as I expected. Steven saw her first tantrum, which happened about five minutes after she arrived. She's had a few more since then, but I mostly think that she's biding her time until she has the lay of the land. She's putting much more energy into trying to be nice to the other kids than she is trying to get closer to me. I suspect that she's looking for weaknesses that she could attack at some future opportunity."

"I was wondering why you seemed to want Katie to have a tantrum when she first arrived," Steven said. "You probably could have avoided her tantrum if you had tried."

"Maybe I could have, but I don't think that would have helped her any. She wanted her way and she was checking to see if having a tantrum would help her to take control in our relationship. I had no need for her to have a tantrum."

"With kids like Katie, Steven, it's generally not a good strategy to try to avoid her tantrums. *She* needs to be working to avoid tantrums," Allison suggested. "If she sees us doing the work she's likely to think that either we are afraid of her getting angry or that she is not able to manage routine frustrations. Either message is not what she needs."

"But the first minute she was there? Why not let her choose between cookies or crackers?" Steven asked.

"Then she would have searched for something else to justify a tantrum," Allison responded. "She wanted to find out how easy it would be for her to take charge of this new family. She needed to see that if she wanted to have a tantrum, that was OK. Jackie would not reject her for the tantrum, nor acquiesce to it. If she had chosen to accept what Jackie offered her, that would have been OK too. Actually, Katie probably benefited more from having her tantrum and seeing Jackie's response to it, than if she had chosen to be 'good.'"

Steven was still skeptical, but he decided not to push the issue further.

Jackie continued to describe the first few days. "Katie seems to be sleeping OK so far. Her appetite is OK too. She fussed over her daily chores the first two days, but then she did them. I'm staying pretty close to her. She was annoyed that she couldn't go out with the older kids a few times."

After some additional discussion about Katie's recent behaviors and strategies for the next week, Allison went for Katie in the waiting room. Jackie and Steven heard Katie chat excitedly on the way back.

"What are they doing here?" Katie asked Allison upon entering the treatment room.

"Good question, Katie. You're used to having therapy with Jan and she saw you by herself didn't she? Well in therapy with me, your mom, Jackie, will always be with us and sometimes Steven will be here too," Allison said calmly.

"I don't want them here!" Katie yelled.

"I didn't think you did, Katie," Allison replied. "You sound kinda angry about their being here with us."

"Make them leave!" Katie yelled at Allison.

"You *really* don't like them here! And I can tell that you want to be the boss of what happens here," Allison said. "Well, I'm glad to hear what you want, but I need to decide what's the best way to use therapy to help you with the troubles that you've been having in your life for such a long time. And your mom really needs to be here."

"She's not my mom!" Katie yelled again. She was looking for something else to be in control of since her command that Jackie and Steven leave did not work.

"But she is, Katie. She's not your birth mom, but she is the mom who is taking care of you now."

"She's not my mom!" Katie was not ready to concede to Allison.

"Wow, Katie, you really sound mad at me and at your mom. Things just aren't going the way you want them now, are they?"

Katie did not respond. She was sitting on the corner of the couch looking away from Jackie and Allison. She was not a happy girl! She did not like the idea of therapy, unless she could control what were to happen there. She certainly didn't want Jackie to be present. Allison wasn't going to make Jackie leave, but she certainly couldn't make Katie talk to her. Katie would ignore her!

Allison sat on the couch near Katie and said quietly, "It's too bad that this has gotten off to a hard start for you, Katie. Your mom says that you haven't wanted to talk much with her at home either. It must be rough having to get used to so many moms in six years! No wonder you don't want another mom. No wonder you want to say to moms: 'Leave Me Alone!'" Allison added emphasis on the last phrase to try to let Katie know that she understood her anger at having to have a relationship with Jackie. She went on, quietly and more slowly, "You're so tired of moms. They have hurt you so much. Especially Sally. No wonder at times you'd rather be all alone than to get close to a mom. No wonder you probably often want to say: 'No More Moms.'"

Katie was sitting motionless, withdrawn into a reality that she seldom attended to. She normally didn't let any feelings or thoughts stray into those experiences that had caused her to give up on people. She wasn't aware of where her thoughts were taking her or she would have been yelling about something else by now. Anger was always her favorite distraction.

Allison could tell by her lack of movement and her distant and sad gaze that she was responding somewhere within herself to Allison's words and to her empathy. She continued with her comments, even more slowly and deliberately than before, watching Katie for any clue of her emotional response. "You probably wish that you didn't need any mom. You might wonder why someone else can't give you food, and clothes, and a place to stay. Someone who isn't a mom! Someone who doesn't try to get you to like her and be close to her." Allison gently rested her hand on Katie's hand, and then removed it before Katie could protest. She allowed a moment of silence before she continued.

"Let's talk about something else for now, Katie," Allison said, changing her tone of voice and posture. "I hear that Diane is taking you swimming after therapy today!"

"Yeah! We're going to a big lake. And we're going to bring some food!" Katie replied with enthusiasm.

"She sounds like she's going to be a neat big sister!" said Allison.

"Yeah!" Katie smiled.

"So I guess that you'd like it if we got this therapy over with for today so you can get to the lake with Diane," Allison suggested. Katie looked at her, waiting for what was next.

"Well, Katie. I know that you've had some hard times and probably not been real happy with Sally and Mike and then in the three other homes that you lived in before your mom, Jackie. Is that right?"

"Yeah," Katie replied.

"Do you think that you probably did some things that made it harder for you in those foster homes? Do you think that it might be a good idea for me to be able to help you to be happier in this home than you were in your other homes?" Allison asked.

"Yeah."

"Well OK, Katie, but it probably means that you'll have to work pretty hard because you've had a lot of problems for a long time. Is that OK with you?"

"Yeah."

"Is that all you can say, 'Yeah'?" Allison smiled and took Katie's arms in her hands. With a big smile she went on, "Well, cut it out! No more 'Yeah.' Give me a few of those 'No I won't!' that I know you can say."

Katie paused, smiled and hesitated further, not sure what to say.

"I said to say, 'No I won't!,' and say it now!" Allison held her closer and smiled even more.

"Yeah!" said Katie with her biggest grin yet.

"No!" screamed Allison and she quickly took her in her arms. She lightly tickled her side for a moment and Katie laughed loudly.

"I said to say, 'No I won't,'" Allison yelled again.

"Yeah!" yelled Katie in reply.

Allison tickled her again, and this time added a quick hair rub. "No I won't!"

"Yeah!"

"No I won't!"

"Yeah!"

"Katie, if you don't say, 'No I won't' you'll be in big trouble!" Allison said with a forced frown on her face.

"Yeah!"

Allison wrapped her arms around her and gave her a tight hug. "You say that one more time and I'll give you two more hugs!"

"Yeah!"

Allison again hugged her tightly as she said "one" forcefully. She released her, smiled into her eyes, and said "two" as she hugged her again. "I thought you said that you wanted my help," Allison said in the same tone of voice.

"Yeah!"

"Well, Katie if I'm to help you you'll have to agree to do what I say. OK?" asked Allison.

"Yeah!"

"Great, Katie! I know that I'll be able to help you when you work hard doing what I tell you to do. You get a big hug for that!" Allison squeezed her again.

"No!" Katie yelled while she laughed.

Allison then bent over and whispered, "I can be a tricky therapist. You better watch what you say or you'll be getting a million hugs."

Katie looked at Allison, smiled and said, "No I won't!"

Allison smiled and again bent over and whispered, "You can be tricky too. That's neat, we must be twins!" She hugged her again.

"No we're not!" Katie continued to laugh and yell. Her smile was genuine, spontaneous, and unexpected.

Allison then released Katie from her arms, sat back, and breathed deeply. "Wow, this kid is smart. She knows what's going on. It's going to be fun working with her."

Katie watched Allison without knowing what to say or do next. She was much more receptive to Allison than she had been initially. She had some fun in spite of herself. She had fun in spite of Jackie sitting nearby and smiling at her working. Did she do any work? If she did, she hadn't intended to. Maybe she would have to watch that tricky Allison more carefully.

Allison alternated between small talk and playful interactions involving gentle pushing, touching, tickling, and one screaming hug. She seemed to establish an interaction with Katie and then leave it, over and over again. Katie followed her lead each time and Allison did not want to maintain the connection beyond what Katie would accept. She broke it before Katie did, making it easier for her to remain in charge of the interactions and the overall affective tone to the session. She was pacing Katie's ability to tolerate reciprocal communication and enjoyment. Such interactions—so basic for healthy children—were a stretch for Katie. Allison recognized this and paced the session accordingly.

Allison decided that Katie must now begin to benefit from being led into an area of her self that had not yet received attention. She knew that central features of Katie's personhood were buried under shame. As long as these areas were untouched and unexplored, they would effectively maintain the barrier that separated her from others, especially from Jackie.

Shame! Shame would descend over Katie whenever she did anything that met with the slightest question or criticism. Shame would equate her with "bad," "worthless," and "unimportant." Shame would prevent her from accepting the reality of discipline as central for socialization into the human community. Shame would make her unable to understand how her behaviors were connected to the consequences that followed. And if shame were to remain entangled throughout her sense of self, she would never . . . could never . . . believe that she was special to someone. Such shame would not leave room for attachment; it would not allow a self whose features and sense of worth emerged from attachment.

As she would throughout therapy, Allison approached the realm of shame in a calm, caring, and matter-of-fact manner. She wanted Katie to know that this area of her self and her life would be explored like every other. Her attitude and her emotional tone would not change. She accepted and did not judge this area of Katie just as she accepted and did not judge every other area.

"Well, Katie, our meeting will be over soon. I do want to talk briefly about one more thing. But this will probably be hard for you." Allison leaned forward and said very quietly near Katie's ear, "When I talk about this you might get mad at me and want me to shut up. You might think that I'm being very mean to talk about it. If you think or feel that, it's OK. Just let me know if you want to." Then she gently patted her hand a few times.

"Katie, I hear that you had a hard time when you first got to your new home. You really didn't like those crackers. You wanted cookies. And you thought that your mom was being mean to you for not giving you any! So you knocked over your glass of milk! Wow were you mad! And it went all over Steven's pants! And he got upset! And you thought that it was all your mom's fault."

Katie did not respond nor look at Allison. Neither were necessary now. Allison thought that this would be too difficult for Katie to hear and still maintain some active emotional connection to Allison. She hoped that her empathy for what Katie had probably been thinking and feeling would enable her to remain passively responsive.

"There are two things that I'd like you to do, Katie. I know that this might be hard." Allison paused, and again gently touched Katie's hand. "First, I'd like you to look at Steven and tell him that you're sorry for getting the milk on him."

Allison left her hand on Katie's and calmly waited. If Katie would not apologize she would accept the decision and "help" her by doing it for her, by pretending to be Katie. Since she didn't need to have Katie respond she was able to remain accepting and nonjudgmental. This attitude would make it easier for Katie to choose to do it.

After some delay, Katie looked up, looked out the window, and said that she was sorry for spilling milk on Steven.

"Your words came out fine, Katie, but your eyes missed. Steven is not standing in the window. Try again." Allison smiled and gently encouraged her.

"I'm sorry that I spilled the milk on you," Katie said quietly, while looking at Steven.

"Thanks for telling me, Katie," Steven replied. "That was the coldest milk in Maine!"

"Way to go, kiddo," Allison said casually. "Now I'd like you to tell Steven that the next time he comes to your home to visit, you'll serve him milk and crackers without spilling one drop."

Katie smiled and looked at Steven again. "The next time you come to my house I'll get you milk and crackers and I won't spill any."

"That would be great, Katie," Steven responded affectionately.

Allison smiled and grabbed Katie again. She held her close and said, "Guess what happens if you spill one drop on Steven?"

"I don't know," Katie responded with some confusion and interest.

"Steven will tell me and the next time I see you, you'll get seven hugs, four tickles, two nose squeezes, and three hair mess-ups. So you better be careful!"

Katie laughed and Allison released her. She turned to Jackie and said, "I think that Katie worked hard today."

Jackie agreed. "It seemed that it didn't bother her that I was here and know what she worked on. That should help me to help her better at home."

"Yeah," Allison said. "And she sure needs mom-help, although right now she doesn't like it very much."

After the first session Steven was again uncertain about Allison and Jackie. What they did made sense. But didn't they ever give her a break? He knew that Allison hadn't pushed her too hard. But at the same time it seemed that she did. Was it really necessary to bring up the milk again after they had a pretty good session? Was it worth the risk? Why rub it in? She's had such a hard life. Why make a fuss about something so small, that only happened once in Jackie's home? Also, didn't Katie have the right to ask that Steven and Jackie leave her session? If she's more comfortable seeing

Allison alone at first, shouldn't her wishes be granted? Steven didn't know what to think. In such situations he talked to his colleague Betty Norton back at the office. Betty always had a gut reaction to things and, more often than not, her response made the most sense. He told her about the milk and crackers episode as well as the first treatment session.

"Let me get this right," Betty said with interest although she seemed to enjoy Steven's struggles. "This kid threw a glass of milk on you and you wanted to wring her neck. Then you got mad at her foster mother, argued with her therapist, and felt sorry for her. Then the kid had a lot of fun with the therapist, did what she was told, and told you that she was sorry. Am I right so far?"

Steven was both uncomfortable with where Betty was going with this story, while at the same time, enjoying her pleasure over his doubts.

"And finally you get a promise from this kid to serve you crackers and milk, *without spilling any*, and you think that maybe things should be different. Right?"

Steven smiled and replied with difficulty, "Right."

"Well, Steven," Betty said seriously, "You have a good point. You should have held out for milk and *cookies* served by Jackie and Allison. How dare they get her to face behaviors that have gotten her moved from three foster homes!"

Steven laughed.

"I think that they're doing great so far. I don't know if it's going to help Katie, but I think that they're on target so far. This kid has major problems. We can't simply have business as usual."

The next few days were fairly uneventful at Jackie's. Katie wanted to spend her time with Diane, and whenever Diane was around, Katie was helpful and charming. However, when Diane was gone with friends or wanted to be alone in her room, Katie's mood was more variable. When Jackie spoke to her, she might or might not respond. When Jackie showed her how to do something, she might or might not do it as she was told. Sometimes she seemed cheerful and friendly, sometimes indifferent and irritable. When Katie wanted something from Jackie she was more friendly and "giving," but not nearly to the degree that she turned on her charm for Diane. Katie might be looking for an edge, for a way to establish some control over Jackie. When she found it, Jackie would know who was actually in charge!

On June 20, Katie was eating her breakfast slowly. Jackie already knew her well enough to guess that this might be one of her "might not" days. Katie finished her cereal and juice, got up, and headed for her room, probably to see if Diane were up yet.

"Not feeling like doing your work today, I see. Well, sweetie, I can help you if you need some help," Jackie said with a smile.

"What?" Katie asked angrily.

"*What?* You want to pretend that you don't know what to do after you finish your breakfast. You *really* don't feel like doing your work." Jackie continued to smile.

"What am I supposed to do?" Katie demanded.

"Sweetie, if I thought that you forgot, I'd certainly tell you if you asked in a nice and friendly way. But I know that you know. And you would have to ask me differently than you just did." Jackie paused as Katie stared toward the table. "Why not ask in a friendly way and I'll pretend that you don't know and I'll tell you."

"What do I have to do?" Katie demanded again, with almost as much rage as her last statement.

"That's not what I'd call 'friendly,' sweetie. Do you want to try it again?" Jackie asked, continuing with her caring and accepting tone.

Katie decided that being friendly to Jackie now was the last thing in the world she wanted to do. She rushed to the table, grabbed the bowl and glass, brought them to the counter and roughly placed them down. She turned to leave.

"Slow down, Katie. Good job of remembering what your job was. Now I want you to tell me something before you leave the room."

"What!" Katie yelled.

"Ask me more quietly," Jackie said in a relaxed manner.

"What?" Katie asked quietly, though her facial expression could have scared a cat.

Jackie walked over to her, smiled again, and said quietly, "I want you to say"—then she suddenly raised her voice—"I HATE YOU TELLING ME WHAT TO DO!"

Katie was startled for a second but then quickly screamed, "I HATE YOU TELLING ME WHAT TO DO!"

Jackie maintained her relaxed and accepting attitude. She gave Katie one last look and said, "You have a great grouchy yell!" She then turned back to the counter. Katie seemed to be confused and she wasted no time leaving the kitchen.

Later that morning, after Diane had left to babysit for a neighbor down the road, Katie turned on the TV in the family room. Jackie had told her twice during the first couple of days that she needed to ask before turning on the TV. Jackie needed to know what she intended to watch. Katie was also told that she'd usually only be able to watch one hour a day. She was told that TV was not something that the family watched much. Jackie explained that kids were better off doing active things rather than just staring at the TV.

Jackie made a point to know where Katie was all the time so she was immediately aware that the TV was on. She walked calmly into the room. "Katie, are you pretending that you forgot another rule?"

"I didn't turn it on!" Katie yelled.

"It is hard for you to tell the truth, isn't it. Well, turn it off please."

"Why? Diane turned it on before she left." Katie was almost convincing.

"Then Diane will be grateful that you turned it off for her," Jackie replied.

"I didn't do it!" Katie screamed.

"It sure is hard today to do what I tell you, sweetie."

"I didn't do it!"

"I'm willing to turn it off for you, honey, but then you won't get to watch it at all today." Jackie remained calm. Her attitude indicated that she really didn't care if Katie turned it off or not. Jackie didn't mind doing it for her. Katie stared at the TV, as angry as ever. Jackie waited a moment and then reached for the TV.

"I'll do it!" Katie yelled.

"Too late, sweetie," Jackie pressed the knob, turned, and left.

On the way back to the living room Jackie heard the TV again. She stopped, chuckled to herself, and returned to the family room.

"Well, I guess it REALLY, REALLY is hard to do what I tell you. And you're SO MAD AT ME!" Jackie turned off the TV and walked over to Katie. She sat down on the couch next to her.

"Katie, I want you to tell me how mad you are at me," Jackie said.

"Shut up and leave me alone!" Katie yelled.

"That's the idea. Say it again, SHUT UP AND LEAVE ME ALONE!" Jackie said.

"Shut up!" Katie replied.

"AND LEAVE ME ALONE!" Jackie added.

"SHUT UP!" Katie said more loudly.

"Way to go, Katie, you said that real loud!" Jackie said.

"SHUT UP!" Katie screamed.

"That's it, kiddo. Now I know how mad you are at my telling you what to do. You're so mad now that I think you might get yourself into some trouble and not do things that are good for you unless you stay close to me for awhile. I'm doing some work in the living room, you can play on the floor there. Let's go and get the Legos."

"No, I want to go to my room!" Katie yelled.

"I know that you probably don't want to be near me very much, but you need to be for awhile. I'll let you know when you can go to your room."

"No!" Katie screamed and stomped her foot.

"Yes, sweetie. I'll take your hand or you can walk in front of me," Jackie said.

"No!" Katie yelled again.

"I'll hold your hand then, Katie," Jackie calmly said.

As Jackie reached for her hand Katie kicked her arm and yelled, "Leave me alone!"

In one easy motion, Jackie pushed down her leg, wrapped her arm around her shoulder, took her other wrist, and pulled Katie to her on the couch.

Katie screamed and tried frantically to release herself.

"I'll just hold you here and keep us both safe until you're ready to come into the living room with me." Jackie was clear and firm but her matter-of-fact, accepting attitude had not varied in spite of Katie's physical outburst.

"I know it's hard for you to do what I say. So hard. That's OK. I don't mind helping you and I certainly don't mind holding you when you need me to," Jackie added.

"Let me go! You're hurting me!" Katie screamed.

"I imagine that you're afraid that I might hurt you, Katie. But I won't. You're safe," Jackie said.

"You *are* hurting me!" Katie screamed again.

"I've held a lot of kids, Katie, and I know I'm not hurting you. But it must still be scary for you."

"You're hurting me! You're hurting me! You're hurting me!" she continued.

"Oh, Katie, this must be so hard for you. You probably were hurt when you were little. Well, you're safe now." Jackie was sure that Katie was not being hurt, but she also knew that Katie might almost believe that she was. Arguing would not do any good. She'd just keep affirming that she was safe.

After about ten minutes Katie's intense rage began to lessen. After another ten minutes, she was quiet and still. She seemed worn out and resigned—not resentful.

"Well, Katie, are you ready to walk with me to the living room?"

"Yeah," Katie replied with a touch of annoyance.

"It's sure been a hard day for you so far. I'll bet it's not your idea of a fun summer day," Jackie said.

Jackie stood up and took her hand. Katie quietly walked with her into the living room. "You sit there and I'll get the Legos." Katie complied, again with a subdued manner. Jackie found the Legos. She gave them to Katie and then turned to her paperwork at the desk near the dining room. She spent the next thirty minutes at her work, commenting on Katie's construction, chatting about lunch possibilities, and singing quietly to herself. She wanted Katie to be aware of her calm and accepting presence. Their conflict would not damage their relationship. Jackie would be communicating that to her more times than she would care to count.

At the second therapy session, Jackie informed Allison that Katie was relating with her in an unpredictable, moment-to-moment manner. She might be friendly, helpful, and seemingly content. Or she might be tense, withdrawn, and irritable. There seemed to be little connection with what was happening at the time. Katie appeared to be resigned about Jackie's behavioral expectations. She would have a number of verbal outbursts each day, but she had been held only five times for aggressive behavior. Generally she would complain, then comply when Jackie told her to express her anger more directly, and finally follow the directive.

Steven asked if there was anything that she could do differently to be able to avoid having to hold her.

"I don't mind holding her if that's what she needs," Jackie said.

"But for Katie's sake, isn't it better to find an alternative?" Steven asked.

"She always has alternatives, Steven. If she wants to be held, that's OK with me." Jackie remained firm, not being willing to follow Steven's way of approaching Katie. Steven saw restraints as a failure that must be damaging Katie; Jackie didn't.

"Steven, I know that it takes some getting used to that we believe Katie being held is perfectly acceptable and even beneficial for her," Allison commented. "But when it is done with a loving attitude, she is learning some very important things. First, she will not be rejected when she is enraged and aggressive. Second, she will be kept safe. And finally, that Jackie is so committed to her that she will get sweaty, tired, and possibly bruised, to give her what she needs. If Katie were held three times every day I wouldn't be concerned about it as long as Jackie can remain loving and accepting. I might worry about Jackie's health and stamina, but I won't be worrying about Katie! She may really need to be held when she is angry now. We can't avoid holding her if she needs to be held."

Allison paused and then added, "Actually, Jackie is probably helping Katie to avoid being held, if that's what she wants, by her own calm and accepting attitude. Unnecessary restraints occur most often when the caregiver is tense and angry herself and her attitude is felt by the child. That's not happening with Jackie."

"You're right. It does take some getting used to. I've spent a lot of time talking with parents and foster parents about avoiding conflicts, especially those that get physical," Steven said.

"And in many families that's probably the safest course. Jackie is good at dealing with these conflicts in a way that facilitates the relationship and does not hurt it. With Katie, I really don't think that she'll learn to attach if she doesn't lose control of her affect and behavior at times, and then experience Jackie as accepting the rage and keeping her safe. These are shame experiences for her and she needs to be able to experience them without being rejected or humiliated, and she needs to sense that Jackie's emotional support and empathy remain available to her. If Jackie couldn't deal well with Katie in these situations, we'd have to try to avoid them. But that would not help Katie as much as what Jackie is doing now," Allison said.

"Anything else we should discuss before I get Katie?" Allison asked.

"I've noticed that she doesn't sleep well at night. It takes her awhile to get to sleep and she's restless. I never had that trouble with Gabe."

"You might try tucking her sheet in on three sides," Allison said. "That will keep some gentle pressure on her body and may help her to feel more contained and secure. Let me know if that doesn't help and we'll explore some other ideas."

When Katie entered the therapy room she was friendly and expressive. She told Allison that she was going swimming with Diane that afternoon. Then she began talking about how much she liked her new home. Then she asked if she could play with the stuffed bears in the corner of the room. Allison could see that Katie had decided to try to maintain control of the session through her chatter and questions. If she could direct them toward playing with the toys, so much the better. Her angry orders at the onset of the first session had not led to controlling the situation; maybe her charm would be more effective.

"Well, Katie, you sure seem to feel like talking today. That's what I'd like to continue doing now rather than playing with the bears," Allison said cheerfully. "I'm interested in knowing more about why you like your new home."

"Diane is my new sister. I like her," Katie quickly replied.

"I'm glad that you have such a nice big sister, Katie," Allison replied. "What do you think about your new dad, Mark?"

"He's nice. He pushed me on the swings."

"Great, Katie. Your dad does seem nice. How about your mom?"

"She's OK," Katie replied evenly.

"Is she a good cook?" Allison asked.

"Yeah, we had pizza!"

"Pizza!" Allison exclaimed. "No wonder you like your new home and your mom.

"Did you bring any with you?" Allison asked with a smile. "I'm hungry."

"No!" Katie replied, grinning.

"No!" Allison looked shocked. She reached over and put her finger in Katie's shirt pocket. "Maybe you're hiding some. I have to find it."

Katie laughed and pulled back. "It's all gone!"

"All gone, and you didn't save me any! Katie, how could you do that?" Allison laughed too.

"She ate some, too!" Katie pointed toward Jackie.

"Who did?" Allison asked.

"She did!" Katie pointed again.

"Who did?" Allison moved closer to Katie and took her hand.

"Jackie!" Katie replied.

"Who?" Allison asked.

"Jackie!"

"Who is Jackie?" Allison persisted.

"My foster mom," Katie finally answered.

"Oh, your mom! Well, that's OK, since she made it," Allison said.

"She didn't make it. We got it at Pizza Hut," Katie replied and smiled.

"I thought that you said that she was a good cook? And she bought it? Are you sure she's a good cook?" Allison smiled.

"Yeah, she made a chocolate cake!" Katie said.

"Well, Katie, I guess she is then. For a second I thought that she really wasn't a good cook. I thought that you just made it up so your mom wouldn't get into trouble for being a bad cook. Sometimes daughters are that way in defending their moms," Allison said reasonably. Then she moved closer and lowered her voice. "Now I have a big question for you. I heard that Steven stopped in to see you yesterday. What about the crackers and milk?"

"I gave them to him and I didn't spill any," Katie said with a smile.

"You didn't spill any!" Allison seemed surprised.

"Not any!" Katie was definite.

Allison turned to Steven. "Is she telling the truth, Steven?"

"She sure is. And they tasted good too."

"More proof that Jackie is a good cook!" Allison replied. Then she looked at Katie with a look of utter annoyance. "And you didn't spill any! So I can't pick on you like I said I would if you spilled some. Darn it. I wanted to pick on you and I can't!"

"No you can't!" Katie seemed pleased and excited.

"Well, then I'll just have to show you how happy I am for you that you didn't spill any." Allison reached down and removed Katie's shoes. She took one foot in her hand and said with a large smile, "This little piggy went to the market. . . ."

Katie was taken by surprise. She seemed to be trying to remember something from her past, but she wasn't sure what Allison was doing. Allison was going to do something unexpected and Katie became alert.

When Allison began "Wee, wee, wee, all the way home!" Katie screeched with laughter. Then Allison took the other foot and repeated the game. Katie screeched even louder.

"Well, Katie, you must wonder why this lady is teasing you and tickling you and playing silly games," Allison said.

"Yeah," Katie replied.

"Well, I guess it's time to tell you," Allison said as she smiled and squeezed Katie's big toe. "You see I want to be able to find ways to help you live a regular life as a kid in your new family. I know that you've been in THREE other foster homes and I've been thinking that FOUR is TOO many for a girl. Moving is TOO hard—new parents, new bedroom, new rules, new school, new friends. It's just TOO much. NO MORE MOVING!"

Katie nodded yes.

"So I thought that I might be able to find ways to help you to learn to live in a good family." Allison then leaned forward and said slowly and quietly, "I know that when you were very little you didn't live in a good family. Sally and Mike did not take good care of you. They didn't know that babies and little kids need to laugh, . . . and be held, . . . and be warm and fed, . . . and be smiled at, . . . and tickled, ..." Allison smiled, lightly touched Katie's toe until she smiled in return, and then went on, "So you never learned what living with a good mom and dad was like. Well, . . . Katie, . . . Jackie is a good mom, . . . and Mark is a good dad, . . . but it's hard, . . . so hard, . . . for you to know that they are. How would you know that? It's hard to tell a good mom from a not-good mom when you did not have a good mom when you were a baby."

Allison leaned back again, smiled in a gentle way, and then squeezed Katie's toe again. Katie was very quiet and attentive. She lay motionless on the couch with her legs folded and Allison at her feet. Her eyes were locked on Allison's eyes. Allison took a deep breath and quietly said, "It's hard, . . . so hard."

Then Allison leaned forward and with a twinkle in her eye whispered loudly, "Look at Jackie, Katie. Can tell you that she's a good mom by her black pony tail? No? How about that little dot on her cheek? How about those white sneakers with the red line on the side? No? There must be something about her that will show you that she's a good mom. Let's stare at her for awhile."

Katie began to giggle and Allison joined in. Soon Jackie and Steven began laughing too. Finally Jackie groaned, "Oh cut it out, you two. You're making me feel embarrassed!"

"Well, Katie, I guess there's no way of telling that Jackie's a good mom by looking at her. So I'm going to have to teach you how to know for yourself that she's a good mom. Once you know that, it will be so much easier to live with her. You'll begin to . . . feel happier . . . and not mind it when she teaches you stuff . . . and want to make cookies with her . . . and pick corn in the garden with her . . . and even hug her when she helps you to find your special doll that you lost. OK with you?"

Katie nodded yes.

"So, kiddo. Katie Kiddo. What a neat name! I'll be telling you to say and do stuff here. And I'll be suggesting that you and your new mom do stuff at home. I'd like you and your mom to agree to do the stuff that I tell you. If you both do, then you'll be able to learn if Jackie is a good mom. If she is, your life should be a lot better than it has been for so long. Do you agree to do what I tell you to do here and at home, Katie Kiddo?" Allison asked.

"Yeah," Katie replied.

"Great, kiddo. Your work here is to do what I tell you to do. That's all. When you do your work here, therapy generally is able to help you more and it goes faster. But sometimes you won't want to do your work here. No big deal. No kid wants to do her work all the time. It's OK for therapy to go slower too. Fast, slow. Slow, fast. Sometimes work, sometimes no work. Either way you get some hugs." Allison smiled.

"So, kiddo. Ready to work?"

"Yeah," Katie said.

"There's that 'yeah' again. Is that all you ever say?" Allison asked as she squeezed her toe.

"No!" Katie yelled and laughed.

Allison turned to Jackie. "Will you help Katie to learn whether or not you're a good mom, Jackie?"

"I *will* help Katie to learn that," Jackie replied. "And I'll work hard too."

"Great. With both of you trying so hard, my job will be easy," Allison said. "Now we need to do something to find out what Katie is going to learn." Allison sat quietly, put her hand to her face, said "hmmm, hmmm," looked around the room, and suddenly yelled "Yes!," looked at Katie, and smiled mischievously.

Katie's eyes got wide, she smiled broadly, and she said, "What!?"

"Jackie, I want you to take Katie's left big toe. I'm going to take her right big toe. If my little piggy gets home first then that means that you're a good mom. If your little piggy gets home first, that means that you're a great mom!" Allison said cheerfully.

Katie screeched and yelled, "Noooo!"

Jackie came over to the couch, grabbed Katie's left foot, and shortly thereafter the piggy race began.

"She's a great mom!" Allison yelled at the end of the race. She could barely be heard over Katie's laughter, wiggling, and yelling. Jackie went back to her chair and Allison continued, "What a great start, Katie Kiddo! There's going to be so much that you'll be learning about your new home and new parents. I'm happy that after all those years you now have a chance to really know . . . what a great mom . . . is really like."

Allison paused, took a deep breath again, and then continued. "Now I'd like you to practice doing some things that I tell you. Get up."

Katie smiled and quickly got up.

"Now jump up and down three times." Katie did so.

"Good job. Now walk around your mom's chair two times." Katie did, with a big smile.

"Way to go. Now go over and shake Steven's hand." Again, Katie did as she was told.

"Three in a row. Now, Katie, stand in front of your mom and look at her. That's it. Now say to her, 'My name is Katie.'"

"My name is Katie," Katie said while controlling her laughter.

"I'm now living with you." Katie repeated what Allison said.

"Sometimes, I don't like what you tell me." Katie again complied.

"Sometimes, I get mad at you." Katie repeated it, more seriously now.

"Your eyes are missing your mom's," Allison said. Here, I'll put my hand on your chin to help you to aim your eyes better."

"Sometimes I don't think that you're a good mom." Katie said what Allison directed, more quietly than before. She made eye contact for only a second.

Then Allison said, with her head behind Katie's ear, almost in a whisper, "And sometimes I think that you don't like me." Katie quietly said what she was told, without looking at Jackie. She said it again, with fleeting eye contact that Allison accepted.

"Now Katie, look at your mom as she tells you what she thinks about what you just said," Allison said.

Katie stood quite still as Jackie said slowly and calmly, "I'm glad that you're now living with me and the rest of the family, Katie. I know that sometimes you don't like what I tell you to do. And that you get mad at me. I know that sometimes you think that I'm a bad mom. It's OK being mad at me and thinking that I'm a bad mom. I know that it's hard at times getting used to living with me and following my rules. That's OK. I'm happy to keep teaching you. And finally, Katie, I do like you, I like you a lot. Even when you get mad at me and think that I'm a bad mom. I still like you then."

Katie seemed to become anxious as Jackie spoke to her. Allison noticed this and said, "Tell your mom, Katie, 'It's hard hearing you say that, mom.'" Katie quietly complied.

"Now tell her, 'I'm not sure if I want you to like me, Mom.'" Again, Katie complied. She stood motionless, seemingly confused and not knowing what to feel, or think, or do. Allison reached over and pulled Katie up into her lap. "Good job, Katie Kiddo. You're learning good." She gave her a quick hug and sat her on the couch close to her.

"Now," Allison continued, "I want to show you how I'll often be working with you here. Sometimes I'll be holding you and sometimes your mom will. One of us will be holding you a lot. Now, I want you to lay across my lap with your head resting on these pillows and your arm behind my back. That way it will be a lot easier for us to look at each other as we talk. It will also be easier for me to help you to yell or laugh or be sad. And if you get scared I can help you to feel safe again. Here, let me show you." Allison helped Katie to get in the position across her lap that she described. Katie seemed cooperative, but somewhat uncertain. She seemed to want to say something, but she remained silent.

"That's it, Katie. See how easy it is for me to bop your nose . . . and fuss with your hair . . . and tickle your side . . . and give you a quick hug . . . and just talk and smile together. Are you comfortable?"

"Yeah," Katie replied.

"Good. I'd like to do a little work then to help you to get used to it," Allison said casually. "First, kick your feet on the couch till I tell you to stop."

Katie was surprised but readily did it, with a lot of force.

"Stop, Katie, good job. Now tell me how many elbows you have."

"Two!" Katie hollered and laughed.

"Now tell me how many fingers you have."

"Ten!" she yelled.

"Now, tell me how many freckles you have," Allison said.

Katie paused, surprised. "I don't know!" she exclaimed.

"You don't know!" Allison seemed shocked. "Well we just have to find out." Allison proceeded to touch the freckles on Katie's face and count quietly as she did. Katie initially laughed, but then became quiet and eventually peaceful.

"Seventy-two! Wow, Katie, that's a great number of freckles to have. That means that you are going to learn how to be a regular kid in a good family! If you forget that, just look in the mirror and see your seventy-two freckles. They'll remind you what you're going to learn. Isn't that great?"

Katie did not reply.

"Isn't that great?" Allison persisted.

Katie laughed and said "NO!"

"No!" Allison screamed. "Say yes, kiddo!"

"No!" Katie continued.

Allison seemed horrified and tickled her side, "Say 'Yes,' Katie!"

"No!" Katie laughed and yelled. She continued to yell "No!" as Allison poked her cheek, messed her hair, gave her a hug, and rocked her on the couch. When she tickled her neck briefly Katie yelled "Yeah!" Allison joined her yell and gave her a quick hug.

"Well, Katie, you do know how to do this work! Way to go." Allison leaned back and took a deep breath. Often when she changed the tone from one of active excitement to one of quiet and relaxation, she made it obvious. Katie so far followed the change in tone quite readily without being aware of it.

"Now, Katie, I want to talk with you about something that is going to be harder for you." Katie immediately appeared tense. The muscles in her face and body tightened up. Allison stroked her hair and rubbed her shoulder and arm until Katie began to relax again.

"Your mom told me how you got mad at her at home the other day because she turned off the TV. Tell me, Katie. Say, 'I got mad at my mom!'"

"I got mad at my mom!" Katie yelled, matching Allison's loudness.

"I didn't want her to turn off the TV!" Allison yelled and Katie repeated it.

"I wanted to watch TV!" They continued.

"You're being mean to me!"

"You won't let me do anything!"

"I think that you're a mean mom!"

"And then you hit your mom, Katie, and she held you," Allison continued quietly. "Say to your mom, 'Leave me alone!'" Katie complied. "Louder, Katie!" She again complied. "Louder!"

Katie screamed, "LEAVE ME ALONE!"

"Now look at your mom, Katie, and yell it as loud as you can," Allison said quickly.

Katie looked at Jackie and screamed, "LEAVE ME ALONE!"

Allison leaned over and calmly said, "That's it, Katie, good job of telling your mom what you were thinking and feeling. I know that was hard for you. When your mom holds you when you're really mad, you probably really don't like it. You might think that she's going to hurt you. No wonder you don't like it."

Katie became calmer fairly quickly. She was listening intently to Allison.

Allison turned to Jackie, "Would you move your chair over here, Jackie?"

When her chair was near the couch she said, "Would you hold Katie's hand? There's something I want her to say to you."

Jackie took Katie's hand.

"Now look at your mom, Katie, and say, 'I don't like your holding me when I'm mad.'" Katie said what Allison said to her, while looking into Jackie's eyes.

"Now say, 'It's scary when you hold me when I'm mad, Mom.'" Katie complied.

"Say, 'I'm afraid you might get mad at me and hurt me.'" Katie repeated it.

"Say, 'Will you get mad and hurt me, Mom?'" Katie did.

"No, sweetie, no matter how mad you get at me, I won't get mad and hurt you," Jackie replied gently.

"Say, 'Thanks, Mom. But it's hard to believe you.'" Katie did.

"I know it's hard, sweetie. I hope that it will get easier for you," Jackie said.

"Say, 'I hope so too, Mom,'" Allison said, and Katie repeated it.

"Now ask your mom for a quick hug, Katie," Allison directed her.

"Can I have a hug, Mom?" Katie asked quickly. Allison let Katie go and Jackie reached over and gave her a big hug. She then sat back and Katie again reclined on Allison's lap.

"Good work, you two!" Allison said cheerfully. "What a mom and daughter you two are going to be! You two are really something together!" She smiled at them both.

For the remaining minutes of the session Allison directed the discussion toward Jackie's thoughts about Katie's swimming abilities. She ended the discussion by saying to them both, "I'd like it if you would both do something before the next session. Katie, I want you to draw a picture of a time when you think that your new mom is being mean to you and another picture of a time when you think that she's being nice to you. Jackie, I'd like you to draw two pictures too. I want you to guess what pictures you think Katie drew and draw those. Then during the next session we'll look at all four pictures. OK with you both?"

Jackie and Katie both agreed and the session ended. Allison heard Katie talking excitedly to Jackie as they left the building. Steven waited for a chance to talk with Allison for a few minutes.

"That seemed great, Allison," said Steven. "But did Katie really mean what you told her to say?"

"What does 'really mean' mean, Steven? Would Katie have said that on her own? No. Does she feel what I had her say? Not that much. But did those words resonate with a small, deeply hidden aspect of herself that needs to develop if she's going to make it? Yes. Did those words hopefully raise a doubt and a possibility within her awareness that there might be something special in a child's relationship with her mother? I truly hope so," Allison said calmly.

"You mean that if you tell her often enough about healthy parent-child relationships, she'll begin to believe it?" Steven asked.

"Not simply 'telling' her. As you noticed, the words were always embedded in an interaction that was emotionally meaningful to her. She was alert, receptive, and curious. Just giving her a 'lecture' will have no effect. The words that she receives must naturally arise from a playful, nurturing attitude from me and Jackie. That's the way language develops in healthy infants and toddlers, and that's the way it has to be if it's going to stay with her and affect her. Also, Jackie's behavior toward her at home, hour after hour, day after day, will have to make those words real to her if she's to begin to 'feel' what they mean and truly believe them. Jackie's goal will be to maintain that playful and nurturing attitude throughout as many interactions with Katie as is possible. Again, that's how babies form an attachment with their mothers. Have you seen the special way that a mother interacts with her 6-month-old infant?"

"Now that you mention it," Steven smiled, "my wife Jenny and I have an 18-month-old daughter, Rebecca. And yes, I know what you mean, although I think you should include fathers in your description of the way parents interact with their babies."

"Wonderful, Steven, and yes, I'm sorry for not including fathers," Allison said. "So when you are with Rebecca, imagine that that's the way Jackie will be trying to relate to Katie. And that's the way I'm trying to relate to her here too."

"Sounds easy, Allison," Steven said.

"I wish it were. The problem is that Katie now does not want that way of being with her parents the way Rebecca does. She has so much that she needs to unlearn. Also, her behaviors are tough and they make it a lot harder for Jackie to maintain that attitude toward her. I promise you, this will not be easy."

"I know that you're right," Steven said quietly. "I just worry a lot about that kid and I want her to make it."

"We'll just have to keep working at it then," Allison said calmly.

When she and Katie arrived home after the session, Jackie anticipated that Katie might not do well. Katie had relaxed her degree of needing to be in control during the session and Jackie expected that she might quickly do something to establish her idea of how their relationship should be. Katie would try to negate anything that she may have said or done during the session.

When they got out of the car, Jackie stood on the walk toward the kitchen door, waiting for Katie. She looked back and saw Katie on the other side of the car. Katie bent over, seemingly to pick up something. She didn't get back up.

"Katie, come on in the house," Jackie said. There was no reply or movement.

"Katie!" Jackie said more loudly.

"What?" Katie yelled back, with an edge of anger in her voice.

"Come here, Katie," Jackie said. She saw Katie stand up straight and walk quickly around the car. Something wasn't right.

"What were you doing?" Jackie asked.

"Nothing!" Katie was now more annoyed.

"What were you doing behind the car?" Jackie asked.

"I said nothing!" Katie yelled.

Jackie took her arm and said, "I need to check, sweetie. The way you're talking makes me think that you did something that you shouldn't. Maybe I'm wrong. We'll see," Jackie was matter-of-fact.

"Leave me alone, I didn't do anything!" Katie was becoming upset but she came along with Jackie.

Jackie went around the car and looked at the ground. Nothing was there. Nothing was wrong. "Well, Katie, I guess you were right and I was wrong. Oh, well. Someday I'll be able to know that you're telling me the truth and I won't have to check. But now I do."

As Jackie turned toward the house again she glanced at the car. She immediately noticed a scratch, about six inches long, on the passenger door. She knew that it was new, and she knew now why Katie knelt down after getting out of the car.

"Well, it looks like I was right after all. It's sad that after you and I had a good time together at Allison's you needed to do something wrong. I guess you really wanted to get me mad at you. Well, sweetie, it didn't work. Let's go into the kitchen," Jackie said.

"I didn't do anything!" Katie screamed. She struggled to get her arm loose but Jackie held her tight. "Let me go!"

"I need to have you near me now. I can see that you're getting all worked up. I'm afraid you'll get into even more trouble if you don't stay near me." Jackie was clear. Katie was going with her.

They came up the walk. Katie was resigned, still yelling that she didn't do 'it,' but without much confidence that she was going to get her way. Jackie opened the door and brought her to the table.

"Sit here for now, Katie," Jackie said calmly. Katie sat. Jackie went to the counter to begin preparing lunch. "I'll be checking with Dad to see how much it's going to cost to get that door fixed. I'm afraid that you're going to have a lot of work to do to pay for it."

"I didn't do it!" Katie screamed.

"I'm fixing some tomato soup. We'll have cheese sandwiches, too."

"I don't want cheese!"

"No problem, sweetie, soup is a good lunch." Jackie didn't mind.

"I want baloney!"

"Only have tomato soup and cheese sandwiches today. But you don't have to eat it." Jackie said. She continued to prepare their meal when Diane and John came running in. They were dressed for swimming.

"Better hurry with your lunch, Katie," Diane said, "My friend, Susan, will be here in fifteen minutes to take us to the lake."

"I'm afraid that Katie won't be going with you, Diane. She scratched the car door with a stone and she's going to have to start her work this afternoon to pay for it," Jackie said with disappointment.

"I'm going swimming!" Katie screamed. It never had occurred to her that her scratching the door would prevent her from going swimming. This made no sense to her. She had been told at break-fast by Diane that she would take her! How could Jackie stop her from going? "I'm going swimming!"

"I wish that you could go. It would have been fun, it's such a nice warm day. But when you ruin something like the car door, you have to work to pay for it to be fixed. I'm sure you'll have your work done before the summer is over. You'll have more chances to go swim-ming." Jackie showed empathy for her rage and confusion.

"I'm sorry that you can't go, Katie," Diane said. "I'll take you again when Mom says that you're ready."

"No!" Katie screamed and she lifted the soup spoon to throw it. Jackie was standing near and she knew to expect something like this. She reached over quickly and grabbed the spoon from Katie's hand.

"I hate you!" Katie screamed at Jackie and she jumped up to try to run from the room.

Jackie stopped her. "You need to sit at the table during lunch, sweetie. I know you're mad at me! That's OK. But you do have to sit here now."

"No, let me go! I hate you!" Katie screamed again. When she took a swing at Jackie, her mom took her arm, pulled her to her, and sat down on the chair with Katie on her lap.

"Would you check the soup, Diane, please? And would you put the cheese away? Katie needs me to hold her now."

"Let me go! Let me go!" Katie struggled to get loose. But she needed to remain in Jackie's lap for awhile after Diane and John left for the lake. Finally, when she calmed down, Jackie sat her in another chair. She then got her soup and sandwich and sat near her. "Do you want your soup or cheese sandwich now, Katie?" Katie ignored her. "This sure has been a difficult day for you so far and it's only 1:00."

That afternoon Katie spent her time with her new mom. Jackie had beans to pick in the garden and Katie helped, reluctantly. Jackie estimated that she worked for about thirty minutes of the time that they were in the garden. Then they did the laundry together with Katie sorting the clothes. Jackie chatted away like they were on the best of terms. Katie said little, and that with effort. Jackie was pleased with herself. She was quite calm and engaged. Her patience was there, as was her empathy. But she thought to herself that it might be a really long summer. This kid was not going to give up her way of living easily!

COMMENTARY

From the moment that Katie entered her home, Jackie related with her as if she had lived with her for months. Jackie did not want to be "nice" to Katie during the first day and ignore her mis-behaviors. She needed to demonstrate quickly what life would be like in her home. She did not do that in an authoritarian, harsh manner. She simply commented on what was expected and she presented various consequences to Katie's choices depending on whether or not she met Jackie's behavioral expectations. She also was quick to express empathy for Katie's anger and distress, to remain accepting of her and in charge of her own emotional re-sponse to the "milk and crackers" incident. Jackie wanted Katie to know what she might expect in the months to come. If she "gave in" to Katie because it was her first day, Katie would expect her to "give in" forever. When Jackie finally began to assert the regu-lar routines and expectations, Katie would think that Jackie was getting more strict. She would conclude that as Jackie got to know her more, she liked her less, and therefore Jackie became more mean to her.

Often when poorly attached children are held, at home or in therapy, they complain that they are being hurt. Assuming that Katie was not being hurt, there were various reasons for her to make that statement. First, she might have been trying to manipu-late Jackie into letting her go. Second, she might have been fright-ened by Jackie's complete control of her, and she might be expe-riencing her vulnerability to being hurt. Third, she might be experiencing a reenactment of a time when she was hurt by some-one. When Katie said that she was being hurt, Jackie needed to first check to be certain that she was not accidentally hurting her. When she was certain that Katie was physically OK, she needed to express empathy for how frightening it must be to be held and not to be able to go. She then might imagine some of Katie's fears and reassure her that she was going to keep her safe and not hurt her. In order to help Katie recognize that the present situation is different and not abusive, Jackie might also recall some possible acts of abuse from her past.

There are various brief courses that instruct parents and child-care workers in techniques for safely holding children who need to be restrained. Many therapeutic foster care programs, residential facilities, and group homes for children and adolescents train their parents and staff in using those techniques.

During the first therapy session, Allison established the general framework of the treatment, and during the second session she verbalized for Katie what she could expect to occur in therapy and what she would be asked to do. She made it clear from the onset that Jackie would be present during the sessions. The reasons for Jackie's presence are numerous. Jackie would be providing Katie with emotional support, and she would be having opportunities for mutual enjoyment with her. Her presence would also help Katie to differentiate her from her birth parents and to carry over therapeutic experiences into the home. Jackie would also be available to challenge Katie's lies and excuses and to share her own thoughts and feelings about her. Allison would also use Jackie's presence to reinforce her parental authority to Katie and to communicate her confidence in her parenting abilities and in Jackie's commitment to Katie. Finally, her presence serves to provide safety to both Allison and Katie, while they are engaged in these very intimate and stressful emotional and physical interactions.

During the first two sessions, Allison demonstrated that therapy would provide the setting for affective experiences for facilitating attunement and for decreasing shame. She would initially establish a supportive atmosphere characterized by playful, empathic, and accepting interactions. Later she would explore shame-inducing themes in a way that would reduce Katie's sense of shame and make her more able to address and integrate these experiences. Allison initially spoke for Katie a great deal because it was most unlikely that Katie had the ability or motivation to speak for herself. In the first session, Allison focused most of the interactions on Katie's response to her. In the second session she was beginning to direct Katie's attention and responses to Jackie more often.

As she would do throughout the course of therapy, Allison accepted Katie's resistance whenever it arose. When she asked for a specific response and Katie refused to give it, Allison gave it for her or she accepted and developed Katie's resistance. She wanted to communicate to Katie that she would remain engaged with her, doing this very difficult work, regardless of what Katie did to avoid engagement, elicit anger and frustration, or resist a therapeutic theme. Allison would not become angry with Katie nor allow her to avoid exploring these important themes. Throughout the sessions, she would be maintaining the same attitude in therapy that Jackie was maintaining at home.

4

A
New
Start

LIFE WITH JACKIE

By July 20, Katie had managed to pay off her responsibility for the car door and she had some limited privileges again. She even had her first day of swimming with Diane. Of course she was supervised a great deal of the time. When Jackie or Mark was not actually watching her, they knew exactly where she was and what she was doing. They remained alert for any strange sounds or movements from Katie's direction. Katie's mood was unpredictable. If she wanted something, she was cheerful and helpful. Most of the time she was simply planning what to do next, while complaining about what she was doing now. She wanted to know everything that was going on. If Mark and Jackie were talking, she would be nearby until directed to wait in a specific chair. When the teenagers were around, she would constantly interrupt them or ask to be involved in their plans. She didn't want to be alone, but she could not relax and enjoy herself when she was with any family member. Rather, her energy seemed entirely taken with scheming and manipulating to get something. When redirected, she would sulk and complain.

By now the teenagers were losing patience with her. Diane had given her some of her old dolls and Katie quickly destroyed them. She also had taken some money from Matthew's wallet and she had broken John's watch. They had begun avoiding her, which meant that they spent less time with Jackie, and more time in their rooms or out with their friends. Jackie had seen this happen before, just after Gabe had come to their home. His negative attitude soon affected the whole family. The atmosphere at home had become tense and angry and even she and Mark had begun to quarrel over numerous small things. They also had disagreed a lot over Gabe. Mark had thought that she was too strict with him because his misbehavior had led to days of little other than consequences. Jackie wanted to be sure that Katie was not able to ruin their family atmosphere, too. If she could maintain her empathy, acceptance, and playfulness, be loving and curious, then Katie's effect on the other family members would be less. Katie needed to become like their family at its best: friendly and helpful, relaxed, and supportive. Each one in the family had his or her own space and interests. They also cared a lot for each other and that was the context in which everything else occurred. They did not need to become like Katie. There was too much rage, fear, and despair in the world already.

On August 4, 1994, Katie became 7 years old. Allison and Jackie had discussed her birthday in the last therapy session. They knew that Katie would find a way to ruin it. There had not been one happy and fun activity since she had been in Jackie's home that had not left her tense, irritable, and in need of sabotaging. She would find something destructive or defiant to do either during the activity or immediately afterward. Should she be given the opportunity to do the same to her birthday? Would the brief "pleasure" of having a big party with nice presents be more beneficial than the shame that was sure to follow when she did something to ruin the day for her and the family? Would the message conveyed by receiving the nice presents outweigh the shame that she would feel after she destroyed them? Should she be given the chance to learn from the "natural consequences" of ruining her special day?

Jackie and Allison decided that she probably had experienced the "natural consequences" of destroying happy experiences and nice gifts and possessions dozens of times in her short life without showing any signs of learning from those compulsive acts. The odds that she would respond differently this time were extremely poor. Why set her up for failure at what should be a happy celebration of her life? It was hard to imagine that she could "celebrate" her life, given her self-contempt and her mistrust of everyone around her. Thus, Jackie and Allison decided to have only a small acknowledgment of Katie's birthday. Possibly that would not be too great a stretch for her and she would be able to successfully integrate it. Steven was not convinced of the wisdom of their plan. But as usual, he deferred to their judgment. It was left to Jackie to tell Katie.

At breakfast on the morning of August 4, Jackie had some time alone with Katie. Katie had not mentioned her birthday to her. Diane said that she had told her about it a few days before.

"Well, Katie, today is your birthday. You are 7 years old! I hope that you have a happy day!" Jackie said cheerfully.

"Am I going to have a party?" Katie said with her innocent, lovely facial expression that could even melt the heart of someone who hates kids.

"Not a very big one, honey. You get to pick the dessert tonight and your dad and I bought you a small gift. I thought that we'd sing 'Happy Birthday' to you, but we'll have to sing quietly so you don't get too mixed up about it."

"Why can't I have a big party?" Katie asked. She seemed to be confused. Not really angry and certainly not sad. Just confused.

"Well, honey, your dad and I decided that you're not ready for a big party yet. I wish you were. We'd love to give you one and we're sad that we can't. It's just that when you have too much fun you do get all mixed up inside and then you do things to mess it up. We decided that it wasn't fair to you now to give you too much fun, and we decided that what we're going to do would be just right for you now." Jackie was clear and calm and very receptive to Katie's mood.

"But it's not fair! Every kid gets a party! I did last year!" Katie was becoming upset.

"I know you did, honey. And Ruth said that you screamed and threw things after the party and had to be held. And the next day you broke all of the presents! You must have been so sad when you did that. We think that it would happen again if we gave you too many presents and you had too much fun." She believed what she was saying, but desperately wished that she could be saying something else.

"You don't like me at all!" Katie screamed.

"I do like you, sweetie. And now that I've gotten to know you, I'm beginning to love you. I want to give you a big party and I'm really sad that I can't. I sure understand why you're mad at me and think I don't like you. It must be hard for you to know that you're not ready for a big party and a lot of presents."

"I am ready!" Katie screamed.

"I wish you were, honey. It's sad that you're not ready yet," Jackie said quietly.

"I am ready," Katie said. Her anger seemed less. She seemed to withdraw into her thoughts. She did not seem to be planning to try to change her mind or to strike out at her. As Jackie watched her she wondered if this were the closest thing to sadness that Katie could feel or show. She thought that if Katie were to begin to cry now, her resolve not to give her a party might evaporate. She'd be tempted to rush out and fill the car with presents and the biggest cake in Augusta. But it didn't happen. Katie didn't cry. She never did. And the car stayed in the driveway.

After their discussion, Katie acted as if nothing had been said and it were a regular day. As she usually did, she complained about restrictions and also about her chores, but she wasn't unusually upset. She had picked chocolate cake for dessert and she ate her piece as rapidly as ever. Katie could devour sweets faster than she could be served them. She smiled at everyone when the family quietly sang "Happy Birthday" to her. After she opened her gift to find a jump rope and a bright blue swimming suit, she thanked everyone and seemed content. That night at bedtime Jackie sat on the edge of her bed as she always did and talked quietly about the day.

"I enjoyed spending your birthday with you, Katie. I'm glad that you picked chocolate cake. That's one of my favorites too."

"Can I have some more tomorrow?" Katie asked.

"Well, Katie, I know that there's some left so I'll make sure some is saved for you so that you'll have some if you eat your dinner," Jackie replied. Then she added quietly, "You might feel mixed up about that jump rope and swimming suit, Katie. I know that it's hard for you to accept presents, even if they are small. I'll be happy for you if you don't have to destroy them. That would probably make you sad. But they are yours and it's up to you if you keep them safe or wreck them."

"Can I wear my swimming suit at the lake?" Katie asked.

"Sure, sweetie, if you want. The next time you go swimming," Jackie replied.

Katie did not have anything else to say. She again seemed more distant and thoughtful than usual, but Jackie had no idea what she might be thinking or feeling. She did wear the swimming suit the rest of the summer. The jump rope disappeared. It would be a long time before Jackie would know whether or not it survived as a present that Katie could accept.

Jackie saw no signs of progress in Katie's functioning during the rest of the summer. She knew that she had to be careful not to expect much, but it was hard not to hope for signs of change each day. She had already made that mistake with Gabe early in the placement. When he did not show signs of improvement, she became discouraged and she began doubting her ability as a foster mother. Every day she found herself judging her own success as a parent on whether or not he "behaved." Allison had been able to help her to focus more on her own attitude and behavior, not Gabe's. She began to review how she had related with him and responded to crises and conflict. When she judged that she had cared for him in the way that he most needed for her to care for him, she was content regardless of his behaviors. By maintaining this outlook, she was able to be more accepting of him, and this was central to the progress that he eventually made. It also enabled Jackie to avoid following the mood and behavioral extremes that Gabe manifested. By remaining more stable herself, she was able to help him to reduce his extremes. This also prevented him from gaining control of her emotional life. She hoped to maintain this attitude with Katie and she generally was able to do so more often than she had with Gabe.

Early in the third treatment session Allison focused easily with Katie on her daily routines as well as her moment-to-moment comments, facial expressions, gestures, sighs, and even the color of her socks. Without making demands on Katie, while at the same time relating with her in a light, gently teasing and relaxed manner, Katie became fully engaged in the immediate interaction.

Allison led Katie and Jackie to her desk and said that she wanted them to show their drawing abilities. She placed a large white paper on the desk and asked Jackie to sit down and then place her cheek on the paper. Katie was asked to trace Jackie's profile with a long pencil. On a second sheet of paper she traced a second profile. She then cut out the two silhouettes and pasted one of them on a blue paper and the other on a red one. On the first silhouette she filled in Jackie's face, with a large smile. On the second, she gave Jackie an angry look. Then it was Jackie's turn to trace Katie's profile twice, cut them out and fill them in with happy and angry expressions. Allison then taped the four profiles on the back of the rocking chair and she asked Jackie to hold Katie on the couch.

"There you both are—and there are TWO of each of you," Allison said. "Since BOTH of you can be BOTH happy and upset, I thought that we should be able to see what you look like both ways."

Jackie briefly "complained" that her nose was not as large as Katie had drawn it.

"Now I'd like to look at the homework that I gave you both last week. Katie was to draw a time when her mom seemed to be mean to her and another of a time that she seemed to be nice. Jackie was to guess what Katie drew and then draw her guesses."

When they were comfortably resting on the couch, Allison showed them the picture that Katie drew of a time when Jackie was being "nice" to her. The picture was of Jackie giving Katie some paper and crayons. Both figures were smiling, but there was little detail. They discussed the picture and Katie acknowledged that she liked Jackie when she gave her something. They turned to the second picture in which Jackie was seen as being "mean" to her. In this picture, Jackie was taking a game away from her. Jackie was drawn as a very large and menacing figure, with large eyes and hands. Katie was small and lying on the floor. In spite of Jackie's frightening posture, Katie appeared to be very angry, rather than scared. Katie told Allison that she does not like Jackie when she will not let her have something.

Allison handed Jackie some markers to give to Katie. They both smiled as Jackie placed them in Katie's hand. Allison directed Katie to thank her mother for the markers.

"Here, Katie, these are for you," Jackie said.

"Thanks, Mom."

"Do it again," Allison said. They repeated it three times, laughing at this activity which seemed quite silly to Katie.

"Now, Jackie. Tell Katie to give you the markers." Jackie did and Katie relinquished them to her, with less humor than was present during the first script. They repeated it again.

"Katie, tell your mom to give you the markers."

"Give them to me."

"Look her in the eyes and yell at her to give you the markers."

"Give them to me!"

"Again, Katie!"

"Give them to me!"

"Louder!"

"GIVE THEM TO ME!"

"Say, 'You never let me have anything!'"

"You never let me have anything!"

"You're mean to me!"

"You're mean to me!"

"You never give me anything!"

Katie repeated what Allison said, becoming more animated with each phrase.

"Why are you always mean to me?"

"You think I'm bad!"

"You think I'm the baddest girl in the world!"

"I am bad!"

"Why am I so bad?"

"WHY AM I SO BAD?"

Allison repeated the phrase again, this time with less intensity. She noticed a few tears in Katie's eyes and she whispered it twice more. Each time Katie responded. After a short pause, Allison quietly said, "Say 'Am I really bad, Mom?'"

Katie asked Jackie if she were really bad. Jackie softly embraced her and whispered "No" in her ear.

Katie immediately became uncomfortable and her body became rigid and she yelled "Let me go!"

Jackie continued to hold her but she pulled back somewhat and said, "I guess you've had enough of this for today."

"I guess she has," Allison said. Then she turned to Katie and added, "I think you were kinda surprised at what you ended up saying. I can understand why you want to stop now. What you just did must have been hard."

"Let me go!" Katie exclaimed again.

"Soon, Katie," Allison replied. "First, I'd like you to do one more thing with Jackie that's a little different and not so hard." Katie stared at her, not struggling to get up, but waiting to hear what Allison was going to say.

Allison did not comment on Katie's few tears. The experience of intense affect was stressful for her, and Allison did not want to push her into having an experience beyond what she thought that she could integrate. Attempting to go too far in the early sessions would prevent her from integrating important, though incomplete, glimpses into her inner life and not remain available to her as something to build on. Pushing her too hard would elicit a more global denial of the experience, which would make it harder to remain accessible to her in later sessions.

Allison took a marker and asked each of them to hold one of its ends. She suggested that they take a deep breath and smile before they began. Katie waited for a moment but smiled when Jackie did. Allison knew that she was ready to become engaged in a new activity.

"Now you two, I want you to pull the marker back and forth without letting it go." Allison said, "When the marker is close to you, Katie, you and I will yell, 'Thanks, Mom!' and when it is close to you, Jackie, Katie and I will yell, 'No!'"

Allison leaned over behind Katie's head, put her hand on her hand, and they pulled the marker toward them.

"Thanks, Mom!" they both yelled.

When Jackie pulled the marker back toward her, "No!" they screamed.

Back and forth the marker was being pulled, faster and faster. The first five or six times their yells were in time with the movement of the marker. After that, they became less and less synchronized with the movement and their cries seemed to emerge randomly. Trying to get back the rhythm, Katie yelled "No!" three times in a row, while Allison was continuing to alternate her cry. With that, they finally all exploded in laughter.

As Allison sat back, they continued to laugh, with the three of them truly feeling merry all at the same time. This did not happen often with Katie.

Casually, Allison said as they came to rest, "You know, Katie, having a mom can get a kid ALL MIXED UP. First she gives her something, then she takes something away. Then she gives, then takes away. Yes, no. Yes, no. What's a kid to think! It's almost like she has two moms, but there's only ONE! One, two, two, one, how confusing! You must have a Yes-and-No-Mom!"

"A Yes-and-No-Mom!" Katie chuckled.

"That's me!" Jackie exclaimed. "Your yes, no, yes, no, yes, no, Mom!"

"Makes it hard for a kid to figure out, doesn't it, Katie Kiddo?" Allison asked.

"Yeah."

"Well, kiddo, that's why we drew those two pictures of you both," Allison said. "You see, you are both Yes-and-No-People. When your mom says 'yes' she probably looks happy to you and 'good.' When she says 'no' she looks mean to you and 'bad.' And you, kiddo, when you feel happy, you have that smile and think you're 'good.' When you feel angry, you have that look, and you think that you're 'bad.'"

Allison allowed Katie to look at the pictures for awhile. She then added, "You both did a great job with those pictures. We're going to be looking at them a lot so that some day, Katie, you won't be so MIXED UP about who you and your mom are."

During sessions four through nine in therapy, Allison continued to engage Katie in a playful, accepting, and curious way. She explored current experiences and wondered what Katie thought and felt about them. She frequently raised other possibilities about what she might have thought or felt, while showing empathy that a girl with her early experiences would most likely think and feel as she did. She elicited rage toward her and toward Jackie by discussing some shameful experiences that Katie wanted to deny. She returned a number of times to how mixed up she must feel, having a "Yes-and-No-Mom." She suggested that Katie might also have feelings of sadness and fear, but Katie usually rejected those ideas. Throughout the sessions, Allison held Katie a lot. She hugged her, played with her hair, tickled her, and made circles on her face. On a number of occasions Jackie held and hugged her too. Katie was clearly more tense with that than with Allison holding her. But it was a beginning. At the end of a few of the sessions, Jackie read her a story. On some occasions Allison played quiet music that helped to set a relaxed, mutually enjoyable mood. In general, Katie followed the directives set by Allison and tolerated a bit more easily the exploration of shame-inducing experiences.

Allison also discussed Katie's birth parents, Sally and Mike, more in the therapeutic sessions. She spent some time covering what the DHS records said about Katie's first five years of life.

Katie listened closely to what had been written in the records and she even asked Jackie to read over again some of the reported incidents. But, apart from the incident that actually brought her into custody, Katie seemed to remember very little about these crucial formative years. Allison, however, would be covering this period of her life again and again in treatment. Katie would most likely gradually remember more about her years with Sally and Mike.

COMMENTARY

When Jackie informed Katie that she would not be having a party but only a small acknowledgement of her birthday, Katie's response took her by surprise. Katie showed more sadness than rage over this restriction. Since Katie's habitual response was to be outraged at the source of her frustration rather than to allow herself to feel sadness, Jackie rightly saw this as a step toward Katie learning to become aware of more of her inner life than her anger. If Katie could begin to notice her sadness or fear, she might be expected to gradually come to accept those feelings as well as her profound vulnerabilities. She might also begin to allow herself to feel the shame that permeated much of her waking life. If she could confront such painful work, she would be likely to turn to Jackie for aid and comfort. Jackie would not be solely her antagonist, she also would be her guardian. But, one incident does not make a pattern. One pattern does not create a self. Jackie would have to be patient, and continue with her therapeutic attitude, as Katie continued being whoever she was.

During the third treatment session, Allison wanted Katie to begin to be aware of the inherent nature of ambivalence in healthy parent-child relationships. Jackie was a yes-and-no mom because she gave Katie both nurturance and discipline, acceptance and socialization expectations. Given that, it was not surprising that Katie would like her sometimes and dislike her at other times. It was almost as if Katie had two moms, a good mom and a bad mom. This psychological reality is present often in the world of the toddler who has not yet integrated these opposing experiences and internalized a coherent relationship with her one mom.

THE EPISODE OF THE QUILT

In mid-September, about two weeks after school had begun, an incident occurred that made it clear to Jackie how far Katie still had to go. It was Saturday morning, which meant that everyone was doing a few chores. Since Katie's readiness to do her work independently was still not evident to anyone, including Jackie, she, therefore, did her work wherever Jackie happened to be in the house. Movable jobs, such as sorting laundry, dusting, and tidying up were ideal now. Jackie also might have her practice some school work or organize her bureau drawers. Katie's complaints about the need for her to share space with Jackie were less. Jackie was starting to imagine that she might be accepting it.

About 10 A.M., Whimsy started to bark and Jackie heard a car coming up the drive way. Judy Morris was stopping by. Judy was active on the Vassalboro School committee and one of her kids was a classmate of Matthew. She had spent much of her spare time that summer working on a quilt that the School Committee planned to raffle off at the Fall Festival that would be held early in October. She was now bringing it to Jackie who would be responsible for making sure that it would be displayed at various community gatherings over the next month before the actual raffle.

Jackie brought Judy into the living room where she and Katie were working. She admired the quilt and showed it to Katie. They discussed the raffle and Jackie's plans to show it. Judy could not stay long and Jackie walked her to her car. They stood outside for a few moments to discuss a new afterschool program and they planned to see each other the next week.

When Jackie returned to the living room she wanted to admire the quilt again. Fear struck her immediately when she saw that it was not on the table. Isn't that where she left it? Of course it was. Katie! She looked over at Katie who was sorting socks on the living room floor. "Katie, where is the quilt?"

"I don't know," Katie replied—her standard response to most any question.

As she was about to address her again she saw the quilt on the couch, folded neatly as it had been on the table. Katie must have just wanted to look at it! She went to the couch and picked it up. Something was wrong! It was wet! Fear returned. Jackie was horrified. She knew what she had to do, but she was afraid. She raised it to her face and smelled it. Urine! It was urine! Katie had peed on it!

Jackie was in shock. She couldn't move. Tears came to her eyes. She wanted to scream and cry and erase the last 10 minutes from her life. How could she have done it? How could she have left Katie alone with this quilt? What could she say to Judy? What could she do?

First she needed to clean the quilt before the urine really sank in. She knew that it had been made for "rough wear." She ran to the kitchen sink and she soaked it in warm water. She held it with the water running through the fabric. She squeezed the water out and did it over again and again. Her own tears mixed with the water running through the quilt. Finally, not knowing what else to do, she laid it out on towels spread out on the kitchen table. She would wait to tell Judy until after it had dried and they would know if there was any permanent damage.

She finally returned to the living room. Katie was still sorting socks although she could have been done long ago. She looked up at Jackie as if nothing had happened. "Can I have lunch now?" Katie said, without any hint of something being wrong.

Jackie got down on the floor, kneeling in front of Katie. She took her arms in her hands and leaned closer to her.

"Katie!" Jackie yelled. She was angry and Katie would know it. "I am very, very angry with you for peeing on that lovely quilt. That was a very mean thing to do to Mrs. Morris after all the work she did to make it. That was not fair to all the kids at your school who will not be able to do some special things if the quilt is ruined. And it was not right to do that to me since I'm responsible for it. I am angry with you. Members of this family do not treat other people that way! You are a member of our family. I am angry that you have done this to Mrs. Morris and to our family."

Jackie was watching Katie's response. She saw her usual guarded, resentful look that she often had when being confronted with her behaviors. But she also saw another look. Katie seemed to be both somewhat afraid of Jackie's anger, but also pleased that Jackie was mad at her. Katie finally got Jackie mad! She was in control! And Jackie was finally telling her that she *was* a bad girl.

Jackie kept staring into Katie's eyes. She took a deep breath. This would be hard for Jackie to do but she needed to continue talking to her.

"Katie," Jackie said in a much quieter voice tone, "I love you, sweetie. I love you a lot and it's very important that I continue to teach you how important it is *not* to do things like this to people. I know that it's hard for you to learn this stuff, but since I love you, I'm going to keep teaching you until you get it." Jackie continued to stare into Katie's eyes. Katie now seemed to be more frightened than she was when Jackie was yelling at her. Katie seemed lost and afraid. Jackie reached over and gave her a hug. She continued to embrace her while her own tears came. She pulled back, staring into Katie's startled eyes. Katie was bewildered. She could not begin to understand or express the affect that now enveloped her. Jackie was crying just like her other foster mothers had done. But this felt different and she did not know why. Katie sensed that she was not in control and she was frightened. Jackie gave her one last hug. Then she got up and went into the kitchen.

Telling her that she loved her then was the hardest thing that Jackie had done since Katie came into her home three months before. It would have been so easy to keep yelling at her. And threatening her with having to move to another foster home if she ever did anything like that again. It would have been easy to look at her with disgust and either not touch her or else grab her arms tightly and squeeze them. If she did that to Katie, she would become like her birth mother, Sally. She would be telling her that Sally was right—she's not special, she's just a bad kid and nobody should bother with her. If she did that, she would be telling her that Katie's self-hatred was right, too. She *was* no good and there was *no* reason for her to try to learn how to live like the Keller family. She *never* would belong in their family or any other good family. Jackie would not do that. She knew that Katie had enormous amounts of shame for her behavior. She had to reestablish a connection with her, not reject her. Katie would learn. It was a question of when. Jackie would keep working. And crying.

That evening Jackie sat close to Mark on the couch. "I was so close to shaking her and screaming how bad she was for what she did. Gabe had never gotten me to feel so much anger. I kept thinking, 'What am I going to tell Judy?' I kept picturing the quilt having a big brown stain, and a smell that would make it unfit to put over a horse in the winter."

Mark never did talk much about his feelings, but he was interested in Jackie's thoughts and feelings, listened well, and thought a lot about his family and his life. He was strong for Jackie when she needed him to be. At times, Jackie was not sure what he felt about things since he tended to understate what was on his mind. But she had learned to read him much better over the years. She knew that he chose his words with care; they represented what was most important, and thus most private, to him.

"I'm sorry that this happened, honey. But you seemed to have handled it about as good as anyone could."

"If only I hadn't left her alone with it. What was I thinking?"

"You were thinking about Judy for a second. Is the quilt OK?" asked Mark.

"So far I think so." Jackie replied. "I'll be able to tell better when it's dry."

"You sure did a good job dealing with your anger at her," Mark said.

"Maybe, but I sure felt like rolling her up in that quilt and shipping her back to Steven."

After a moment Mark added, "If we're really keeping the kid, I want to be able to help in any way I can."

"Thanks, honey," Jackie replied, "I know you do and believe me, you'll be the first to know if there's something else that you can do. Just promise never to take her side if she's complaining about me."

In therapy that week Jackie told Allison about the quilt incident and her response. Steven was present, although he now attended only one out of every three or four sessions. Allison felt sad for Jackie. She knew how difficult it must have been for Jackie to tell Judy about Katie's urinating on the quilt that she had worked on for weeks. And it had happened within only 10 minutes after Judy had given it to Jackie! Allison focused on Jackie's feelings now, to see if she were able to maintain her therapeutic attitude toward Katie at this time. Allison knew that without that attitude, Jackie would be in no position to continue to raise Katie well, and certainly in no position to be able to facilitate Katie's attachment.

Allison's first task each session was to focus on Jackie and her needs. Nothing that she could do with Katie would have any beneficial effect if Katie went home to a mom who wanted little to do with her.

"Jackie, I'm so sorry that happened. I know how hard it must have been for you."

"I was not a happy camper!" Jackie replied.

"No, I imagine that you were not a happy foster mother," Allison said quietly.

"Sure, I was mad at Katie," Jackie said, "but I was even more angry with myself. How could I have left the quilt alone with her? What was I thinking?"

"For a minute, Jackie, you were just being a regular mom in a regular home," Allison suggested. "It's so hard to be a therapeutic mom with a kid with Katie's troubles every second of every day."

Jackie seemed discouraged. Allison had not seen her this worn out since Gabe was in one of his very difficult periods.

"You're right, but it doesn't feel any better. With Katie I can't afford to 'forget' or she could really hurt someone or herself. If it were just more predictable! If I knew that she was upset about something, I would have known not to let her out of my sight. But she seemed OK. I can't think of anything that she might have been upset about!" Jackie was so frustrated.

"And there probably wasn't one specific thing upsetting her then. With kids like Katie, simply living makes her angry. Being who she is makes her ashamed. Being with people like you and not being attached to them makes her feel lonely and scared. She's sitting with nothing particular in her mind. Something special, like the quilt, is left near her. No adults around. Feelings burst from within her! Impulses follow that make them concrete. There's no healthy *self* to be aware of, monitor, and integrate those feelings and impulses. They have a life of their own. The excitement of getting even with you and everyone else in her life! The satisfaction of expressing her deep sense of being evil and worthless! The anticipated thrill of seeing you scream, or cry, or possibly even hit her. Those feelings exploded from within her when she saw that quilt, left alone with her."

"Why can't I remember that?" Jackie asked.

"Jackie, why aren't you a saint? Or a robot we could program to be 'correct' 100 percent of the time? You're a real person! You've probably given more to this kid in the past three months than anyone else has in the past seven years. She doesn't need a saint or a robot. She needs a mom who loves her. Who sweats for her. Who cries for her. And, at times, who gets angry with her. She doesn't need you to be perfect, Jackie. She simply needs for you to remain committed to her, find ways to enjoy her and teach her. And that's probably often harder than being perfect. I couldn't do what you're doing for her," Allison said with compassion and admiration for this woman.

Jackie took a deep breath. There were tears in her eyes. "Thanks. I need to hear that once in awhile." She blew her nose and laughed. "That little kid sure knows how to get to me. I could hug her one minute and strangle her the next. I know that you're right about what is going on under that angry mood and mean behavior of hers. If I didn't know that, I could never live with her for more than 1 day."

The three of them sat quietly for a moment. Then Allison suggested that she get 'the kid' from the waiting room.

With Katie lying across her lap, Allison began exploring with her some recent events in her life in the Keller home. It was immediately obvious to everyone present that Katie was not thinking about the quilt at all. It could have happened a year ago. It was as if someone else had been involved in peeing on it, not her.

Allison fairly easily got into her usual relaxed and playful manner of relating with her. At first Steven had some trouble getting used to her approach with Katie. No matter what Katie had done, Allison always spent a good part of her interactions with Katie laughing with her, poking and tickling her, teasing her about something she said or did, challenging her to do something and then enjoying Katie's resistance, or doing something unpredictable and surprising that would leave Steven as confused as Katie as to what Allison was up to. Today was no exception. The quilt would obviously wait.

Steven noted Katie's response to Allison. As usual, she quickly fell in with Allison's playful, friendly, and interested manner. Katie was alert to Allison's every move and statement. She clearly enjoyed teasing Allison about her graying hair and she roared with laughter while screaming "I will!" when Allison warned her not to tell anyone how many gray hairs she has. She would shriek when Allison would start searching for fuzz between her toes. She would squirm and moan at first when Allison would tell her that it was time for the "friend circle." With her finger, Allison would trace a large circle around Katie's face five times. Then she would gently tap her nose five times and finally kiss her forehead five times. Although she usually would express annoyance about that practice, Katie often found a way to "remind" Allison about it near the end of the session if she had not given her one. She would say, "I'm glad that you're not doing the 'friend circle' today." She then expressed great annoyance when Allison thanked her for reminding her of the need to demonstrate their friendship. Initially, Katie would wipe the circle and kisses off her face. Then Allison told her that "everyone'" could see the "friend circle" and that it would remain on her face for one week if she did not wipe it off within three seconds after the last kiss was planted on her forehead. Allison then held her hands while she counted to three and she asked Jackie and Steven if they liked the circle. Both agreed that it was lovely and Katie expressed her usual annoyance. Jackie reported that later that day she noticed Katie staring at herself in the mirror, searching for the circle.

As she sometimes did, Allison began discussing one of Katie's "behaviors" without a pause. She simply moved from the playful and light content into the difficult area without any change in voice tone or general expression of enjoyment of Katie.

"Oh, Katie, your mom mentioned about your peeing on the quilt. I was a little mixed up. What made you decide to do that?"

Katie immediately tensed up and became annoyed. "Don't talk about it!"

"But sweetie, it's something we need to talk about because I know that you and your mom have had a lot of feelings about it this week, and that makes it important to both of you."

"It's not important to me!" Katie declared.

"Oh, I think it is. But I know it's hard for you to talk about. No problem. I can help," Allison said in a matter-of-fact tone.

"I don't want your help!" Katie screamed.

"Great, Katie, say that again!" Allison raised her voice.

"I don't want your help!"

"Again, Katie!"

"I don't want your help!"

"One more time, Katie!"

"I don't want your help!"

"Great job, Katie!" Allison's words matched Katie's in intensity and cadence. Allison then leaned closer to her and spoke quietly and slowly near her ear. "I know that taking our help is hard for you, sweetie. But you need it so much. And your mom loves you and I like you a lot, so we're going to keep helping you to have a happier life."

Katie screamed "No!" She arched her back and began struggling with Allison to get out of her arms. She quickly kicked upward with her left foot, almost hitting Allison on the side of the head.

"Oh, you're mad at me!" Allison yelled, again matching the intensity of Katie's "No!" "You want to kick me and hit me. You want to get away from me and never see me again! You really are mad at me now!"

"Shut up! Shut up! Shut up!" Katie screamed as she continued to try to find some way to escape Allison's hold.

"You want me to shut up!" Allison continued to yell with Katie. "You want me to stop talking to you about how mad you are at me, and at your mom, Jackie." Allison waited for a pause in Katie's thrashing and she continued, now much more quietly, "But I need to keep talking, sweetie, because I know that you're a sad and scared little girl, and you don't like yourself very much."

Allison's quiet tone, and her moving the focus toward her vulnerabilities, mobilized Katie's rage again. "I do like myself!" she screamed as she renewed her efforts to kick Allison.

"Say it again!" yelled Allison.

"I do like myself!"

"Again!"

"I DO LIKE MYSELF!"

"Louder!"

"I DO LIKE MYSELF!"

"Louder!" Allison said, although her voice was now quieter than the last time, as she noticed that Katie had peaked and could not maintain her intensity.

"I do like myself!" Katie now had tears running down her cheeks.

"One more time," Allison said more quietly again.

"I do like myself."

Katie was barely moving. She was not looking at Allison. She was lost somewhere in the despair of her past.

Allison leaned forward and whispered into Katie's ear. "I wish you did, sweetie. I want to help you to really like yourself." Katie began to shake as the tears continued to flow down her cheeks and onto Allison. Allison hugged her tighter and Katie squeezed her in return. Allison began to rock slowly, while holding her closely.

Jackie and Steven sat motionless, watching Katie and Allison, not wanting to disturb the mood. They had never seen Katie cry before this moment. Jackie now knew that what had happened around the quilt was important to Katie after all. Her empathy for Katie became strong again.

After a few more minutes, Allison motioned to Jackie to hold Katie. They traded places with Jackie holding her on the couch. Katie cried some more and gave no resistance to this first strong embrace with Jackie. "Katie, Katie, Katie," Jackie said quietly as she rocked slowly in her arms.

Allison waited until she became quiet and then she told Katie to open her eyes and look at her mom.

When Katie did, she immediately noticed that Jackie had been crying too. She stared at her for a moment, and then Allison said, "Now, Katie, say to your mom, 'Mom, I'm sorry for peeing on the quilt.'"

Immediately Katie said to Jackie, "Mom, I'm sorry for peeing on the quilt." She began crying again, and Jackie embraced her again. "I'm glad for you that you're sorry, Katie. I'm glad for you," Jackie said quietly.

Moments of silence supported their continuing embrace and affirmed what had just occurred.

Allison spoke quietly. "This kid is a hard worker, Jackie. I can see why you love her a lot."

"Yes she is," Jackie replied. She then took some tissue and began wiping the tears from Katie's face and from her own. Katie watched her without moving.

"I need a tissue too. I guess all three of us had a lot of tears that needed to come out," Allison said.

Katie looked over at Steven. "He did, too. Steven cried, too."

"Yes he did, Katie. We all know how hard this is for you. We all get sad when we see how hard you have to work to have a happier life," Allison said.

All of them, including Katie, were enjoying the quiet of the moment.

Allison gently asked Katie, "What is your consequence, sweetie, for peeing on the quilt?"

"Mom said that I have to help clean the house. I even have to wash the kitchen floor." She then turned to Jackie, seeming to have a new thought. "Do I still have to do it, Mom?"

Jackie smiled, "Yes you do, honey. But don't worry. I'll make sure to show you how to do it right."

Allison smiled and said to Katie. "Say, thanks, Mom!"

Katie smiled and thanked Jackie and they all laughed. They then spent some time checking to see who had the stickiest tears. They agreed that Steven's were the stickiest, which meant that he had to get glasses of water for the other three.

At the end of the session, Steven waited a few minutes to talk with Allison, a habit that he found to be very helpful in understanding Katie. "I think you really got somewhere with her today, Allison."

"Important experiences did occur for her. But they will not stick unless we are able to create for her hundreds of similar experiences, in therapy and at home, in the months ahead. She needs to share many, many such intense affective experiences with Jackie before she will begin to believe that she is a good kid, and that her mother's love is a wonderfully important, pleasurable, and healing reality for her."

"Before we started with Katie, you spoke with Jackie a lot about her feelings toward Katie after the quilt incident. Did you think that she was going to ask her to leave?" Steven asked.

"No, but I wanted to be sure she was able to get back the therapeutic attitude that she needs if she is going to be able to help Katie's attachment."

"I see what you mean. I know what you're talking about," Steven said. "You were able to show the attitude in therapy today."

"I try to, Steven, or I don't think that I would be able to help her. She needs to have adults relate to her in that way, as much, or even more than your daughter, Rebecca does. Without those attunement experiences, she never will attach to Jackie and she never will begin to have a healthy 'self' that she likes. It's easier to keep that attitude in therapy than it is at home, hour after hour," Allison said.

"Well, I better get going. I'm glad you spent the time supporting Jackie. She seemed to need it."

"She did. And because she did, Katie needed to have me help Jackie before trying to help her," Allison replied.

"Makes sense to me," Steven replied.

As Steven headed toward the door Allison said, "I saw some ancient wisdom on a T-shirt once."

"What's that?" Steven replied.

"It said 'If Mom ain't happy, ain't nobody happy,'" Allison said.

Steven smiled. He might just stop on the way home and get Jenny some flowers.

On the way home from therapy, Katie asked Jackie if they could stop at McDonald's for a snack. Since they never had gone there after therapy and because Katie had long since stopped asking, Jackie assumed that Katie wanted a reward for her work in therapy. Katie knew that the adults liked what happened in therapy so she might use it to her advantage.

"No, sweetie," Jackie said. "I'd like to get on home like we usually do."

"I want some french fries," Katie yelled.

"I'll bet you do, Katie, you worked hard in therapy and I imagine you might be hungry."

"Then get me some."

"I'll find you an apple or orange when we get home."

"No, I want french fries."

"It sure is hard for you sometimes when I won't give you what you want."

"Get me some french fries!" For emphasis, Katie slammed her foot against the dash board. Jackie immediately pulled the car over to the side of the road.

"Katie, I sure understand why you're mad at me for not stopping at McDonald's. You can tell me about your anger, but you can't kick the car."

"I don't care. I hate you."

"That's the idea."

"I'm glad that I peed on that quilt!"

"I'm sure that part of you is glad, sweetie."

"You're not my mom! I hate you!"

Jackie was silent. The kid certainly was using words to express her rage over being deprived of her french fries. She probably was also telling her that everything that she felt and said in Allison's office was a lie. Katie didn't want hugs, she wasn't sorry, and she didn't want anyone to help her, especially Jackie. Katie was frightened, she had revealed a lot in therapy, to Jackie and to herself. She now was trying to minimize or deny her earlier expressions. Jackie thought about conveying empathy for how confused and scared that Katie must be now, but she decided that this was not the place to do it. She did not want to have to search for Katie in the woods. Nor did she want to spend the next few hours sitting in the car with a snotty kid. She decided that silence would be in her own best interest.

After about five minutes of quiet, Jackie decided to continue on her journey home. She guessed right. Katie did not have the energy to fight further. She pouted the rest of the way home.

The next day Steven called Jackie to see how Katie was doing. He expected that the therapy session would have brought about some changes for the better. He was surprised to hear about the car ride home. He was further disappointed to hear that when he called Katie was kneeling on the stairs, washing off the pee. Early that morning she had stood at the top of the steps and peed down them.

"It must have been quite a waterfall," Jackie said with her dry sense of humor.

Steven was frustrated. Would Katie ever change? Why would she do that?

"Steven, she has a long way to go," Jackie said calmly. "I knew what I was in for. She can't take giant steps. Yesterday's session was important, but I imagine only a small part of it will stick. She needs many experiences like that, with me and with Allison, before we can hope to see real change. I am hoping that washing down the stairs after peeing on them will be another experience that will also help the process."

"How will that help?" Steven asked, wondering how Jackie could consider it to be similar to yesterday's therapy session.

"Katie is saying that the therapy session was all a lie and that she's no different. I'm going to accept her action and accept this part of her, too. If I get angry and discouraged now, she will be able to minimize the session. She'll convince herself that even I don't believe that what she showed yesterday is real! It's as if she is searching for shaming experiences to convince herself that she's still bad. By responding with soap and water, along with The Attitude, I'm showing her that I do think therapy was real, just as the part of her that peed down the stairs is real. I am still connected to her. I'm going to be the same, in responding to both parts. Hopefully, someday the part of her that we saw in therapy will be a lot stronger and she'll be able to bring both parts together."

"I'm glad that she didn't pee on my stairs, Jackie. I don't think that I'd be so understanding," Steven said with admiration for her.

"Once you got used to trying to raise a kid like Katie, you would. Or else you couldn't keep doing it. And I'm not a martyr. I do get a lot of satisfaction when I see that frightened and sad little girl inside of her take a few steps into the sunlight."

Steven told Barbara and Al at work about Katie's behaviors in therapy and afterward. He needed to sort out his thoughts about her. He concluded that he really did not know Katie. That "part" of her that was so angry and destructive, and . . . *mean*, seemed to have a life of its own. Would they get through to her? A larger question was who was the *her* that they were trying to find? When they found *her* would they be pleased or frightened? Did this *her* even exist?

Steven decided that if he thought about Katie anymore right now he would only worry more. He turned to his paperwork. That would calm him down. He could lose himself in the words and rules. He could avoid experiencing the profound terror, rage, and despair that many of his foster kids faced every moment of their lives. For him, paperwork did the trick. For Katie, it was kicking dashboards, peeing down stairs and on quilts, and eating french fries.

That weekend Steven and Jenny decided to work outside. They had been busy canning the tomatoes and beets the previous few weeks and it was time to put the garden to bed. Rebecca was now

20 months old! What a free spirit! She walked fast and she ran faster. Which means that she fell as often as she saw something new to explore. Certainly the task of cleaning the garden held endless opportunities for adventure. Dirt and stones, plants and weeds. Things to grab and break open, taste and throw. She found the cherry tomatoes, which were a favorite of hers when she spotted them in her salad. And now there seemed to be millions of them! Just hanging from the branches waiting for her fingers and lips. Her face was soon red, her parents were busy deciding how many she could safely consume without creating havoc in her sensitive stomach, and Jenny decided to get the camera to record one of the many moments of Rebecca's life that Alice had insisted should not be lost to future generations.

Steven hauled more plants to the wheelbarrow and turned to see if Rebecca had reached her limit. His red-faced child was careening through the garden toward him with a giant smile on her face and the trowel in her hand. Without thought his heart stopped and his voice shouted, "Rebecca, stop!" while he visualized her falling and striking her face with the trowel. A heartbeat later he leaped toward her, her smile disappeared, her legs stopped, and a startled expression covered her face. By now, Steven was next to her and he reached down and quickly removed the trowel from her hand. Her eyes met the tension and fear in his face. Her mouth quivered, she sat heavily on the ground, and her face turned away from him and down toward the ground. A cry erupted from her lips.

Steven tried to console her as he picked her up but she arched her back and looked and turned her shoulders and face away from him. Just then Jenny came running up with her camera and Rebecca heard her and turned in her direction. She reached up her arms and almost flung herself out of Steven's arms. She wanted Jenny with as much force and need as she had ever shown. Jenny took Rebecca and held her tightly. She spoke in her calming and reassuring voice as her daughter shook and sobbed in her arms.

Steven watched them. He was relieved that Rebecca had not gotten hurt. He could understand that he had frightened her and that she now needed her mother. He needed to have her understand that he had not been mad at her. He had yelled and scared her because he was frightened for her. Maybe he could have managed it differently but his motive was to keep her safe.

Jenny quietly told Rebecca how Steven had been frightened because she was running with the trowel. She explained that he had not been angry with her, just frightened for her. Rebecca seemed to peek out from over Jenny's shoulder at her dad. Jenny walked slowly toward Steven. He reached out toward his daughter and, after a moment's hesitation, she came into his arms. He hugged her, reassured her, and found her eyes. She smiled and pointed toward the cherry tomatoes. He carried her to the nearest plant and they sat on the ground. She pulled one ripe tomato off the plant and fed Steven. He fed her. Now Jenny had another photo opportunity.

Rebecca lost interest in the tomatoes and Steven and wandered off toward the cucumber vines. Steven sat there watching her. Just a routine event in a routine day with the two most important beings in his life. She often got upset with him or Jenny. She wanted to touch and hold so many things wherever she found herself. She did not take "No" lightly. She seemed surprised whenever her parents thwarted her desires. Especially when they got upset over something that she had done.

He sat for a few minutes more. Rebecca had felt shame! Of course—that was an example of what Allison and Jackie had been talking about. Certainly, Rebecca had experienced shame on numerous other occasions, but this was the first time that Steven actually connected her distress to what Allison had so often talked about. And Rebecca's shame was brief and left suddenly as she was comforted by her parents. That is what Katie experienced every moment of her life. Shame defined Katie's existence. For Rebecca, shame was simply integrated into her developing sense of self and her relationships with her parents. It was a vehicle for learning limits to self-expression, the need to integrate one's own wishes with the desires of others, and the necessity of considering the consequences of one's acts. For Katie, shame was not such a vehicle. Shame proved her worthlessness. She could not learn from it; she wanted to destroy it through her rage. She needed to conceal what it said, for it said that she was unwanted on this earth.

COMMENTARY

Katie's urination on the quilt created the first crisis in her placement. Such incidents are certain to happen in any placement with
an unattached child, because such children are experts at sensing
what will infuriate their parents. With that awareness, they do not
avoid those behaviors, rather they embrace them. They have a
compulsion to recreate their early experiences of rejection, abuse,
and disgust directed at them from their parents. They need to reexperience that sense of being worthless that such shaming experiences create within them. Feeling worthless affirms the reality
of the "hated self" and destroys any reason for trying to form a
relationship with Jackie. There could be no way that Jackie could
love her. Or, if she had loved her, there could be no way that she
would continue to do so once she really saw how bad she was. Katie
would put a stop to the placement herself, on her terms, rather
than wait for Jackie to do it. That it would end, either through
rejecting Jackie or being rejected by her, was inevitable.

Therapy began, as it always did, with Allison talking with Jackie
about how Katie was functioning at home. This enabled Allison to
know how both Katie and Jackie were doing. After the incident
with the quilt it was crucial for Allison to focus on Jackie and her
immediate emotional response to what had occurred, as well as
her current thoughts and feelings about it. If Jackie was not able
to maintain her therapeutic attitude toward Katie, progress would
stop and the placement would be in jeopardy. Allison needed to
attend to Jackie's needs if they both were to be able to address
Katie's needs. Allison also valued Jackie for herself, not simply as
Katie's foster parent. She needed to communicate that Jackie's well-
being was important to her and her distress would receive her full
attention, before turning to Katie. In working to facilitate the
attachment between Jackie and Katie, Allison needed to communicate that they were both important to her. Jackie would not be
forgotten.

The therapy session at least temporarily derailed Katie's quest
to terminate the placement. Allison had led her, through pacing
her affective experiences, from her rage and her resistance to
being helped, to her self-rejection and despair. She cried, something that she had not done in years, and she became receptive to

the healing and caressing words and touch from Jackie and Allison. In spite of her self-loathing and her distrust of feeling close to others, she felt their comfort and warmth and she could not deny or refuse the experience. But, of course it had to end, and her habitual mode of experiencing herself and others quickly returned. She now felt a compulsion to invalidate what had occurred in therapy and she quickly did so in the car after therapy, and by peeing on the stairs the next morning at home. Jackie's response of accepting her attempts to sabotage the therapeutic experience, was crucial in preventing Katie from minimizing its validity. Jackie was maintaining her affective connection with Katie in therapy, but also in the car and while she supervised her washing the stairs. The soap and water, applied with Jackie's therapeutic attitude, maintained the validity of Katie's tears.

Jackie's response to Katie for peeing on the quilt raises the important question of what a therapeutic parent needs to do with her anger at her unattached child. For good reasons, the *attitude* that these children need if they are to learn to trust their new parent does not include anger. Katie's early life with Sally and Mike was permeated with rage directed toward her. Such rage contained rejection, contempt, and disgust and served as the cement for the foundation of her self-contempt. That rage had nothing to do with her behavior or with healthy socialization experiences. How can a therapeutic parent express anger without triggering a cognitive and affective response that lies within that old template for defining self and other?

Jackie's anger was expressed without calling Katie names, threatening her, or expressing contempt for her. It was expressed while Jackie maintained eye contact with her as well as physical contact. Jackie used "I-messages," connected her anger toward the specific behavior, and explained why the behavior was not acceptable to her. She went further, to combine her anger with her love for her and with her commitment to teach her how to live well in her family. Jackie's tears conveyed both her anger at the behavior, but also her fear for Katie's future, a fear based on her love for her. Jackie was communicating her continuing commitment to Katie. Through this interaction, Katie was not able to simply interpret the experience as proof that she was bad and that Jackie was disgusted with her. Katie became more engaged in their relationship and in what her action and Jackie's response said both about her worth and the meaning of Jackie's love for her. The experience was unsettling to her and made her more receptive to her underlying terror and self-contempt when Allison explored the incident in therapy.

Jackie's expression of anger was similar to that suggested by Nelson and Lewak (1985), which they call the "60-second scolding." It also is similar to the way that Martha Welch (1989) suggests for parents to express their anger for their child's behavior. Dr. Welch states that parents should express their anger when physically and psychologically close to their child rather than from a distance. Their anger is communicated along with feelings of fear or sadness that are part of their love for their child. This love, not rejection, drives the anger. Dr. Welch also suggests that if these experiences are to be of greatest benefit to the attachment, the child will need to express his affect, with equal intensity and openness. Through their mutual expressions, their relationship becomes stronger and the incident has been integrated into their secure attachment. Jackie decided that at that early stage of their relationship, she would not place such expectations on Katie.

At times, every parent, including therapeutic parents will have an especially hard day. They will be irritable and impatient and will have difficulty maintaining "the attitude" consistently throughout the day. Even their usual methods of self-motivation that get them through such days and enable them to still respond quite well to the attachment needs of their child are ineffective. On those days, the parent needs to face the truth, accept the reality that she has little empathy for others, especially her unattached child, and take care of herself. If possible, she might ask another adult to assume the primary role of caring for her child. If not possible, she might structure the day so that less interaction is required and the routines in place are likely to reduce the probable conflicts.

Parents also need to "own" their affect and not project it on their child. Rather than saying, or even thinking, "You're making me mad!" they need to be able to say to themselves and their child, "I don't have much patience today. I'm in a grouchy mood. It has nothing to do with you, but I thought that you should know it so that if I get angry, you'll know where it's coming from." Or the parent might say, "I'm kinda angry and grumpy today, so I need to spend some time alone. It has nothing to do with you, and don't worry, I'll get over it. But you might give some thought as to whether or not it would be smart for you to make a lot of bad choices today."

Steven's experience in the garden with Rebecca serves to contrast the normal and healthy shame experience that occurs repeatedly in a secure attachment, with the pervasive shame that Katie had constantly experienced. When Rebecca ran to Steven with the trowel, she experienced much excitement and she anticipated a response from Steven closely attuned with her own affective state. His response was clearly misattuned from hers and she immediately felt shame. Her sense of self was not being validated. It felt smaller and less special. She immediately withdrew into herself, physically and psychologically. Jenny and Steven immediately provided her with reassurance that she is special. They were attuned with her distress and they enabled her to experience the security of the attachment from which she could again know that her self had value. Through reattunement, her parents were able to convey to her the meaning of the experience. Its purpose was to socialize, to show the danger of running with a sharp object. Her parents' motives did not indicate that they hated her or that she was bad. Rather, their motives indicated how truly special she was to them.

RESISTING AND REGRESSING

At the start of the next therapy session Jackie told Allison about how intense Katie's resistance had become. "She is looking for every chance that she can to have a fight with me. Her arguing is more intense. She's doing a lot of sitting since she does not want to follow the most basic expectations. Yesterday I asked her to hand me the paper that was next to her and she refused. She even yelled at Diane—something that she rarely does."

"My guess is that our last session really bothered her," Allison said. "She cried and she let you support her. She also felt her self-hatred. Now she might be looking for a way to make the statement that she is bad and that she doesn't want your support. Besides, she believes that you wouldn't want to give it to her anyway. She wants to wear you down."

"Her comment that she was glad that she peed on the quilt did not endear her to me," Jackie said.

"No, I imagine it didn't," Allison smiled. "Well, if she's making a statement to us, I guess that we have to make a statement to her."

"What's that?" Steven asked.

"She's got to hear that we are going to help her because she *is* a kid whom we care for. She's going to hear that we understand and accept her decision to fight our help. She's also going to hear that we're not agreeing with her sense of worthlessness," Allison replied.

"How can you accept her decision and still disagree with her?" Steven asked.

"We have empathy for her fear and resistance. We'll actively communicate our empathy—we'll share her distress—by letting her know that we understand how hard this is for her, given her past. In fact, we'll be trying to show her that her actively fighting us now is a measure of how hard she is actually working to make some sense of her life. She's fighting to maintain the view of the world that she learned from Sally and Mike. We'll understand her need to do this, but we'll keep making it harder for her by continuing to show her another world. This world is based on maternal love for her, enjoyment of her, commitment to continue to reach out to her when she is covered with shame, and confidence in her ability to eventually agree with us as to what is in her best interests."

Allison stopped, knowing that it was easier to talk about this than actually do it. "Well, why don't I get the kid."

"Well, Katie Kiddo, you look kinda perky today," Allison said as Katie crawled into her lap and was soon lying across her with her head on the pillows. "Your hair looks extra curly, your nose looks kinda bouncy, and your freckles look kinda bossy. Is that right?"

Katie smiled in response to Allison's smile and friendly tone of voice. "My nose isn't bouncy!" She laughed.

"Oh no! Let's see." Allison took her forefinger and lightly bopped her nose twice. "Yes it is! I knew you were extra perky today."

"No it isn't!" Katie yelled, now smiling even wider.

"Oh, Katie, I can tell by how much you want to disagree with me that you're extra perky," Allison said, running her hand over Katie's hair.

"No I don't!" Katie said.

"You are so great at arguing, Katie. You do it without thinking," Allison replied.

"No I don't!" Katie laughed.

"You're so good at it I'm going to give you a hug." Allison pulled her into her arms as Katie shrieked. They were both laughing now. Katie smiled and looked into Allison's eyes. Allison was often surprised how easy it was to engage most of the poorly attached children that she saw. She would set a playful, accepting, and curious tone and most kids most of the time would spontaneously follow wherever she led. She knew that it was much more difficult to do at home, hour after hour, with Mom, the woman she most resisted. She also knew that therapy with these kids needed to begin with those playful attunement experiences, but it needed to go far beyond those. It needed to address her negativity and distress if she were to be able to integrate this aspect of herself with the part that was easy to elicit in therapy. Without such integration, whatever experiences she had in therapy, no matter how enjoyable, would not continue beyond the moment when Jackie limited her or told her to do something.

As she often did, Allison related with Katie in a quieter, less joking manner that also was mutually enjoyable. She told Katie of a recent adventure that her cat had with a raccoon. It was usually easy to maintain her interest in stories. Jackie joined in with a tale of how Diane and Katie raked the leaves around the house and eventually had a pile of leaves so high that they buried themselves in them and Jackie and Mark had the hardest time finding them.

"Sounds like you had some fun this week, Katie. Jackie told me that you had a lot of hard times, too. She said that you were unhappy most of the time." Allison maintained her accepting and curious tone while noting Katie's suddenly tension and withdrawal. "I felt sad when I heard what a hard week you were having. It seems like just about everything at home has been bothering you. Anything we could do to help?"

"Nothing's bothering me," Katie said firmly.

"I wish that were so, honey. But when you decide to sit a lot rather than have a chance to play, I think that you must feel kinda grumpy."

"I do not!" Katie replied. Just as her playful and friendly manner of engagement had been total, now she was completely
annoyed, without any sign that she had been laughing a minute
earlier.

"Say it loudly then, Katie," Allison said. "Say, 'I do not feel
grumpy!'"

"I do not feel grumpy!"

"Louder!"

"I do not feel grumpy!"

"Good job, Katie. Now say to your mom, 'Leave me alone!'"

Katie looked at Jackie and said, "Leave me alone!"

"Again!"

"Leave me alone!"

"Now say, 'I don't want your help!'," Allison said quickly and
loudly.

"I don't want your help!"

"Again!"

"I don't want your help!" Katie yelled.

"You don't love me anyway!"

"You don't love me anyway!"

"Again!"

"You don't love me anyway!"

"Katie, say, 'You're just like Sally!'," Allison said rapidly.

"You're just like Sally!" Katie followed Allison's lead, but was
now more tense.

"You're just like Sally!"

"You're just like Sally!" Katie screamed.

"I don't want any mom!"

"I don't want any mom!"

"I'm too scared to love a mom," Allison said, quickly, but much
more quietly.

"I'm too scared to love a mom," Katie responded, equally quiet,
and slower.

"I'm afraid that you'll hurt me," Allison was almost whispering.

"I'm afraid that you'll hurt me," Katie was very subdued.

Allison hugged her. "Good job, Katie. I know that those are some
of your feelings and they are hard to talk about. Or even think
about."

Katie was quiet. Allison continued. "It must be hard to think that every mom won't care for you. . . . No wonder that you have a hard time . . . letting yourself get close to this mom." Allison spoke slowly and quietly. She stroked Katie's face and hair in time with her words.

"Tell Jackie, Katie, that it's hard to get close to her," Allison said.

"No!" Katie screamed.

"Then say, 'I don't want to tell her that!'," Allison said quickly.

"I don't want to tell her that!" Katie responded.

"I don't want to get close to her!"

"I don't want to get close to her!"

"Good job, Katie. I know that . . . most of the time . . . . you don't want to be close to Jackie. It's so hard . . . after the way Sally treated you . . . for . . . so . . . long." Allison spoke slowly and quietly again. Katie barely moved. Allison could generally tell when a child was being receptive to what she was saying. She knew from Katie's relaxed muscle tone and good eye contact that she was listening.

"I don't know why Sally did not love you in ways that you needed, Katie. Maybe she has lots of problems that make it hard for her to be a mom. But I know that . . . it . . . hurt you . . . a lot. Sally hardly ever showed you . . . how special . . . you are . . . how lovely . . . you are. She hardly ever . . . played with you . . . and touched . . . your face . . . and ran her fingers over your arms . . . and fingers. . . . No wonder that you don't want a mom. When you were a baby . . . you needed a mom . . . so much! . . . You needed your mom and she didn't act like a mom should act. You must have been . . . so sad!" Allison continued to run her hand over Katie's face, arms, fingers, and hair. Katie continued to listen.

Without changing her voice tone and pace she continued to touch Katie while talking with Jackie. "I know . . . that you know, Jackie, . . . how hard it was for Katie when she was a baby. Sally did not hold her . . . and play with her . . . and rock her the way she needed. No wonder she gets mad at you a lot, Jackie. She's still mad at Sally for not being a very good mom for her."

"I agree. I know that it's hard for Katie to let herself like me and trust me. I know that she often really does not want me to be her mom."

"Are you mad at her for her anger at you?"

"No. I know why she gets mad at me a lot. I can handle it OK."

"Are you going to stop loving her?"

"No, I do love Katie and I don't plan to stop."

Katie remained motionless. She was listening to Allison and Jackie.

Allison looked at Katie again. She said quietly, "Katie, while you lie there, I'm going to draw a picture. Jackie would you get that paper and pen from the desk, please."

Allison began drawing a series of pictures of Katie beginning with when she was a baby with Sally and Mike and ending with her at 7 years of age and living with Jackie. "In this first picture, you were a happy and loving baby. See, there's your heart. It was working well and hearts are for loving. Then in this picture you can see that your heart was starting to get cracks in it. It was loving but not getting much love back so it was being hurt every day. In this third picture, you can see that you're older and bigger. Here you can see how you built a wall around your heart to protect it from being hurt more. See, none of the hurt can get through the wall. It was a really great way to protect your heart and try to keep yourself safe." Allison paused and watched Katie study the pictures.

Then she continued. "The problem with your plan to use the wall to keep your heart safe is that the wall also keeps out love. See, when you went into your foster homes, you weren't being hurt anymore so you really didn't need your wall. But it is hard to take it down now. So when your foster parents tried to love you, you didn't feel it! The wall caused the love to bounce away from your heart. No wonder that you often don't feel that Jackie really loves you. No wonder you don't trust her!"

"Now, Katie," Allison could see that Katie was very attentive. "We have to figure out ways to help you to take the wall down. You don't need it anymore, but it's very hard to take down."

After a considerable pause, with Katie remaining responsive and quiet, Allison said, "Do you want our help to take down the wall, Katie?"

"Yes," Katie replied quietly.

"Great, sweetie, with you wanting our help it will be a lot easier for it to really be helpful." Allison rocked her gently.

"Now Katie, there's some more hard work to do. Are you ready?"

Katie replied that she was.

"Good, then look at that mark on the wall by the lamp. Pretend that you're looking at Sally. Good. Now say to her really loudly, 'I'm mad at you Sally!'"

"I'm mad at you Sally!"

"You didn't take care of me!"

"You didn't take care of me!"

"You hit me and called me names!"

"You hit me and called me names!"

"You let Mike hurt me!"

"You let Mike hurt me!"

"I'm mad at you, Sally!"

"I'm mad at you, Sally!"

"Louder!"

"I'M MAD AT YOU, SALLY!"

"Louder!"

"I'M MAD AT YOU, SALLY!"

"Good job, Katie, I could feel how mad you are." Allison was silent as she watched Katie. The fight seemed to be leaving her. She seemed worn out.

"I can see, Katie, how hard this is for you. You wanted Sally to be a good mom for you. You wanted her to hold you . . . and rock you . . . and play with your toes. . . . When you were a baby . . . you must have been so sad that she didn't show you that she loved you." Allison spoke almost in a whisper. "Say, 'Sally, I wanted you to love me better.'"

"Sally, I wanted you to love me better."

"Why didn't you love me?"

"Why didn't you love me?"

"I was a good baby."

"I was a good baby." Tears were now in Katie's eyes.

"Why wasn't I special to you?" Allison whispered.

"Why wasn't I special to you?"

"Say it again, Katie."

"Why wasn't I special to you?"

Allison held her closely again as her tears rolled down her cheeks. Allison put her lips near her ear and whispered, "I don't know why you weren't more special to Sally, Katie. You were a baby and babies need so much to feel special. . . . Jackie and I are going to be looking for ways . . . to help you . . . to feel special." Allison rocked her. Then she added, "I want Jackie to hold you now, Katie."

Katie did not object and Allison stood up with Katie in her arms and carried her to Jackie. Jackie immediately held her in her arms and began rocking and humming softly. Katie did not resist her. She continued to cry. Jackie began to cry.

After a time, Allison began quietly talking with Jackie and Steven about how hard Katie had worked again. She added that she had worked a lot at home that week too. Allison said that she thought that Katie was trying to figure out if she wanted Jackie's help and if she was an OK kid. They then chatted about the recent boat ride that Allison had taken searching for finback whales. The boat, which was doing research for The College of the Atlantic, had found a number of whales, many of which they had seen often that season. Katie was interested and asked Jackie if they could go looking for whales too. Allison indicated that the season was now over and Jackie said that she might take her the next summer.

"Jackie, I have just the book for you to read to Katie," Allison said as she walked to the bookcase. Jackie gave Katie another hug. Katie sat up in Jackie's lap as she gave them a book of drawings of various animals and their babies. The next to the last page had a whale and her baby. The final page had a mom like Jackie in bed with her baby. They both smiled and chatted while Jackie read the book and they hugged again after the last drawing.

"We're going to be stopping now, Katie. I know that this was another hard meeting for you. And it probably has you more mixed up than ever. I wish that it was easier for you. But you're getting it. One of these days it won't be so hard as it is now," Allison indicated in her matter-of-fact, accepting tone. "After today's meeting you might decide to fight with your mom again, like last week. If you do, that's OK. Your mom will be able to handle things and she'll still love you."

Of course Katie fought with Jackie that week. And the weeks after. Katie knew no other way to live and her strength and persistence in trying to take control of the Keller home were incredible. She seemed to live from event to event, each time looking for what she wanted from it. She would decide how best to get what she wanted—whether by charming and manipulating or by lying and stealing—and then try to get it. Generally Jackie would notice her strategies and interfere with her plans. Inevitably Katie would rage at Jackie for being so "abusive" and "cruel." Just as inevitably Katie would receive some sort of consequence either for her original act—such as stealing—or for her response—such as throwing a cup—to Jackie's intervention.

As night follows day, a consequence from Jackie followed Katie's behaviors. Jackie was often amazed that Katie seemed to fail to see the connection. Each time Jackie would give Katie a chore in restitution for taking or breaking something from someone in the family, Katie seemed shocked at how unfair it was. It was as if Katie was thinking: "I wanted it, what's wrong with my taking it? You're mean for not letting me have what I want. And you're even meaner for giving me a chore for simply trying to get what I want!" Sensitivity to the rights and wishes of the others in the family was not Katie's strength. The others were there to serve her! Empathy for others! What a strange concept! Considering what others wanted before deciding whether or not to do something made no sense to Katie. Everyone was out for herself. Why should she worry about what others thought or felt? She could not imagine that anyone would really care about what was best for her. She had to conclude that Jackie only wanted to control her, just as Katie wanted to control Jackie.

What wasn't fair was that Jackie was bigger and had the power to make the rules. Someday Katie would be bigger and then she'd be happy! Being a kid was awful! First Mike and Sally hit her and said mean things to her. Now Jackie tries to trick her and say she loves her, but she never lets her do what she wants! Some love! She really just wants to boss her around and make her unhappy! Katie couldn't wait to grow up and live by herself!

When unattached kids enter one of their incredible spells of negative thought, affect, and behavior, it tests the strength and commitment of therapeutic moms like Jackie to continue to maintain "the attitude." It is hard to avoid creating a negative family atmosphere as well as a "vicious circle" of behaviors and punishments. Specific consequences given repeatedly in response to negative behaviors create a sense of punishment, no matter what attitude the parent tries to maintain. As a result, many parents have found that they need to change the overall structure of the home environment for the child. The added structure does not assume that the child will act in a friendly and cooperative manner. The child does not have the opportunity to ruin the tone of each day. Rather, the parent assumes that the child is now not able to tolerate fun, freedom, and many expressions of affection. The parent now meets the needs of the child by removing most choices, greatly reducing free time, restricting opportunities for fun that will be sabotaged, and limiting demonstrations of love. Jackie informed Katie that her recent behaviors indicated that she needed to spend more time with Jackie, and she needed to be asking Jackie for permission to do just about everything. She also told her that she'd be giving her a lot to do, but that it wouldn't be too hard because Jackie would be at her side.

Along with the added structure and supervision, Jackie made sure to keep her sense of humor in her interactions with Katie. When Katie screamed at Jackie for five minutes one afternoon, Jackie assembled the three teenagers and they were asked to participate in the Katie-scream-alike contest. The one whose scream was the most similar to Katie's would win a pack of lifesavers. Katie was asked to be the judge but she refused. John won, although Matthew insisted that Whimsy, who was now howling, should have been the winner. Once Katie was especially angry and instead of slamming her door once as she usually did, she slammed it three times. Jackie went to her room and insisted that if she was going to slam the door more than once she had to do it five times. She indicated that Katie owed her two more "slams." Another time Katie put water in Jackie's rubber boot. At dinner that night Katie's glass was empty. She immediately asked for milk. Jackie said that the milk was gone but she would get her water. She then quietly poured the water from her boot into Katie's glass. She set the boot on the corner of the table and indicated that there was some left if Katie wanted some more. Katie waited until after the meal to get her own drink.

For the remainder of September, October, and into November, Katie was receiving a high level of supervision, practice on her personal and social skills and choice selection, and chores that benefited her and, at times, the rest of the family. Jackie often worked with her in performing the chores since Katie had extremely little ability to work independently. Jackie anticipated that it would most likely be at least six months before Katie was likely to do the most basic chore alone.

When Katie awoke in the morning, she found the clothes that Jackie had selected for her to wear that day. At breakfast, she found the food that Jackie had chosen for her to eat. After breakfast, Jackie went with her and chatted about the day as Katie washed her face and brushed her teeth. Jackie continued to talk with her as they waited for the school bus. When Katie returned from school, Jackie was waiting at the door with a greeting and with milk and crackers. Following that, Katie changed from her school clothes to her work clothes and then she and Jackie had a few chores to do together. When Jackie began to prepare dinner, Katie sat at the kitchen table and did some homework, regardless of whether or not the teacher had given her any. At times, Jackie would tell her to do something to help with dinner. Katie always set the table.

After dinner, Mark would supervise Katie for an hour or so while Jackie took a break and the teenagers managed the dishes. "Mom time" then followed, with Jackie and Katie spending some special time together prior to bedtime. Jackie might give Katie a back rub, shampoo her hair, play with baby dolls with her, tell stories, read books with her, sing, and show her how to play the recorder. When Katie was in a pouting and complaining mood, Jackie would still remain with her and refuse to be rejected or to reject Katie. Jackie then might read out loud, listen to music, or quietly sit and rock while watching Katie. At those times her message for Katie was that she was there for her. If Katie did not want to engage her with pleasure, Jackie would accept her wishes but not withdraw from her physically. She would remain available for her during their special time together. Finally, Jackie would monitor Katie's preparations for bed and they would have a short bedtime ritual involving opportunities for quiet conversation and physical contact.

At times, Katie was receptive to Jackie rocking her during their time together. On a few occasions she even asked to have Jackie give her a bottle as she was being rocked. Jackie gave the bottle to her only when Katie requested it and only when she was able to lie quietly in her arms, make some efforts at eye contact, and follow Jackie's leads. If Katie used the bottle in a demanding way with Jackie, it was removed.

Initially, Katie did not welcome these changes in her day-to-day living with open arms. She became more resistant and more complaining. Jackie could wait. Katie would simply sit near Jackie while she decided to engage in the activity that had been chosen for her. A few times Jackie had to hold her before she would agree to remain in the chair. Once in awhile as she sat, Jackie would give her a hug, a snack, a book to read, or a coloring book. She might also put on some music that she knew Katie enjoyed. At times she caught Katie singing quietly to the music, only to stop when she became aware of what she was doing.

Throughout the days and weeks, opportunities for fun and free play were very structured. Jackie supplied them, but they were not given in response to Katie "being good." Rather, they were given in small measure and at unexpected times. They simply reflected Jackie's decision that she needed a specific fun experience at that time. Since Jackie decided that such an experience would benefit her, Katie would get it. That simply reflected Jackie's love for her. A few times she had casually told Katie how that process worked since Katie was struggling to convince herself that she somehow controlled when she got the "reward." It was hard for her to accept that Jackie controlled when she would have "fun" experiences, and that Jackie presented them to her because she loved her. She thought of sabotaging the fun, but gave up that idea when it was quite obvious that Jackie would only be sad for her that she wasn't ready for even that limited amount of fun. Jackie would not get upset, so why do it?

As the weeks passed, Katie became calmer and less distressed by the tight supervision and nonexistent freedom. She seemed to feel content about not having to make the routine daily choices that invariably had led her into so many difficulties. She seemed to feel content about being close to Jackie whenever she was not at school. She did not have to choose to be near Jackie, which would have suggested that Jackie was becoming special to her. Since she "had" to be near Jackie, she could allow herself to accept her presence without resistance. Jackie would chat with her as they both worked separately in the kitchen or living room. At times she would walk past and run her hands through Katie's hair, rub her shoulders, or give her a "Mom circle." She was not evaluating Katie, she was just enjoying her.

On October 24, Katie and Jackie had their weekly session with Allison. As she usually did early in each session, Allison was demonstrating considerable interest in Katie's daily life. Her comments included the following:

"You mean that you and your mom were together all day! Without one break?

"Your mom says that she kissed the top of your head seven times yesterday and four of those times you didn't know she was going to! Is that right?

"I hear that you were really mad at your mom on Sunday when she told you to rake the leaves with her when you wanted to go for a walk with Diane! Tell your mom that you didn't like raking those dumb old leaves.

"She brought you breakfast in bed and read you a story while you ate? Lucky! Is there an empty bedroom in your house for me?"

Allison asked Jackie to hold her and then she directed Katie toward being more aware of her ambivalence about spending so much time with Jackie.

"Tell your mom, 'I don't want to be with you all the time!'" Katie did.

"Now say, 'I want you to leave me alone!'"

"Leave me alone!"

"Again!"

"Leave me alone!"

"Louder!"

"LEAVE ME ALONE!"

"Why can't I be alone?" Katie was now responding immediately to her leads.

"I want to be alone!"

"I'm used to being alone!"

"When I was little I was always alone!"

"I liked being alone!"

"I was always so alone!" Allison now changed her voice tone.

"I felt so lonely!"

"Nobody was with me."

"Nobody wanted to be with me."

"Where are you, Mom?"

"Please come here."

"I'm a little girl and I need you."

"Why don't you hold me?"

"Little girls need to be held."

"And played with."

"And smiled at."

"Please hold me."

"Please hug me."

Jackie embraced Katie and Allison sat back and waited for a few minutes. Katie's emotions had followed the words. For a few moments, Katie responded and was aware of her longing to be nurtured and played with by her mother. That was all Allison wanted now. A few moments at a time. Slowly building a new way of living for a 7-year-old girl. Sculpturing a life based on trust and relatedness. A few moments at a time.

"OK, Katie Kiddo, I'd like you to sit in that chair. I want to show you something." Katie got out of Jackie's lap and sat in a chair by the desk. This was an unusual spot for her during therapy. She was uncertain about what to expect.

Allison went to the closet and brought out a multicolored shawl and handed it to Katie. This fabric must have contained every color of the rainbow and a few more. Allison opened it up fully and draped it over Katie's shoulders.

"Did you ever see so many bright and lovely colors?"

"No. Can I have this?"

"No, Katie. It's a gift to me from a special friend. But I wanted you to see the colors." She let Katie feel and squeeze it for a time and they identified some of the incredible colors. Allison then took the shawl and placed it over the back of the rocking chair. She then went to the windows and pulled the drapes closed. It was an overcast Maine day and the colors of the shawl lost some of their brilliance. She directed Katie to look at the shawl while she turned out the lights. The colors were gone! She turned on the lights and the colors returned. She repeated the sequence twice more. Then, leaving the lights off she sat near Katie and said,

"In the dark, the world loses its colors. Even the parts of our life that are the most colorful become gray." Allison paused for a moment before continuing.

"Katie, when you were little, your world was like it is now in my office. It was dark, and you were alone, and there were no colors." Again she paused, in the darkened space.

"Even in your life now, when you are really feeling alone and sad or scared or mad, you probably cannot see any colors. Even . . . if . . . they . . . are . . . there."

Allison turned on the lights and the colors in the shawl returned. She opened the drapes and they were again radiant.

"Now, Katie, I'd like you to try something. Get in your mom's lap again."

Katie got back on the couch and settled into Jackie's lap. Allison directed her to look at the shawl again, and really stare at it while Jackie held her. With the light still on, Allison said,

"Now Katie, with your mom holding you, I want you to stare extra hard at the shawl. I'm going to ask you to close your eyes and see if you can still see the colors."

"Close your eyes." Allison waited a moment. "Can you still see the colors?"

"Yes!" Katie exclaimed with surprise.

"Good, now open them again." Allison said. "Now I want you to try something even harder. I want you to keep your eyes open. I'm going to close the drapes again and turn off the lights. I want to see if you can still see the colors with Jackie holding you. Remember to stare real hard."

Allison closed the drapes, turned off the lights, and the room was again dark.

"I can!" Katie shouted. "I can still see the colors!"

Before the after-image went away, Allison congratulated Katie and turned on the lights. She took the shawl and playfully covered Jackie's and Katie's heads with it.

"Well, you two. You've found another special thing that happens when you two are together. Colors in the dark. Colors in the sun. Colors that go away. And colors that come back. Katie, you're going to be noticing a new world of colors and I'm happy for you." Allison reclaimed her shawl and ended the session.

On October 15, Steven had stopped by unexpectedly after school.

"I was in the area visiting another kid and thought I might stop in, chat with Katie and see how she's doing."

"Fine, Steven," Jackie said at the kitchen door. "As you can see, Katie is sitting now. She just got home from school and had her snack. I've found that for now she does best when she sits for awhile without anything to do. After a bit, I'll give her something to do. I'm not sure yet what is best to give her. It depends on how she's doing after a full day at school."

"When will she be done, Jackie?" Steven asked. "I thought that I might take her for a ride and stop for a snack if she wasn't getting a consequence for anything."

"I'm not sure when she'll be done, Steven," Jackie replied. "Maybe in a week or two, but maybe not for a month or two. She's been having a real hard time and she really needs to be close to me now."

Steven was puzzled. He could not think of what to say. He wanted to question Jackie but thought that he probably had better not do it in front of Katie. He engaged in small talk and then made an appointment to stop by and talk with Jackie when Katie was in school.

When Steven arrived two days later, Jackie greeted him with coffee and muffins and they sat at the table.

"I really don't understand what was happening the other day," Steven said after some discussion of practical matters that are always present in the foster care system. "I presumed that Katie was having a 'time out' for doing something, and then you said that she was just 'sitting' and that she was sitting for an indefinite period of time. Why? What does that accomplish?"

"Katie needs to be closer to me," Jackie said. "Like I said the other day, she's having a hard time and needs my presence if she's going to be able to turn it around. Sitting is not a consequence. It simply is a means for enabling her to stay near me without getting herself in a lot of difficulty. She's come to accept it and actually is more relaxed sitting under my direction than if she had freedom to do things and get herself into trouble."

"How long has she been sitting?" Steven asked.

"Not every moment, but for significant amounts of time for about two weeks," Jackie said.

"Two weeks!" Steven said, as if he really didn't believe it. "That really sounds harsh. What does she have to look forward to? Why should she work to get anything if there is nothing to get?"

"Steven," Jackie replied, "I don't want her to work to get something. Achieving external rewards will not get her to change in the way she needs to change. I want her to learn how to live well in my home. To do that, she has got to get the idea that it is best for her to be near me and to accept the decisions that I make for her. She also needs to see that I do enjoy her and to become comfortable with my enjoyment of her, rather than becoming anxious and then trying to get me to stop enjoying her."

"How is she going to enjoy you by sitting?" Steven asked.

"She's accepting my decision that she sit, she's near me, and she's calmer and more receptive when she is not fussing so much about having to be in control all the time. I am in control so much that she almost doesn't notice it. There is simply no control issue, but only as long as she has no choices right now. She simply does what I say; there are no choices to mix her up."

"But she's over 7 years old, Jackie. You're treating her like a baby."

"Good point. There are similarities with how I'm treating her and how a parent would treat a 1- or 2-year-old," Jackie said. "I need to be aware of her and to direct her. She helps me with a number of chores and when she resists my directions for her, she sits. Often she will then sit without anything to do until she chooses to do the chore. But I also need to spend a lot of time enjoying her, having fun with her, and keeping her central in my life, as a mother would do with her toddler. While she's sitting, she might be working or playing quietly. Also, I'm often engaging her with songs, patty-cake, touching, and laughing. We might sit quietly together, and we might dance around the room. But we're together. "

"That doesn't sound so bad. I was afraid it was more punitive than it seems to be," Steven said.

"It's not punitive at all, Steven," Jackie said. "It's nurturing and protective and it's meeting her most basic needs. In many ways she is not nearly mature enough to be treated like a 7-year-old.

Emotionally, she is a toddler and she needs this degree of my taking charge of her life."

"What is punitive, Steven," Jackie continued, "is when parents are encouraged to give a consequence that minimizes the child's problems in order to avoid being 'negative.' A child might engage in destructive or disruptive behaviors over and over for days, and the consequence each time is a five-minute time out, or losing a TV show or a dessert. Then the child engages in the same behaviors again and again. What a set up for repeated failure! And that's supposed to be positive? The child doesn't control his behaviors and the parents aren't encouraged to either. The child is left with the conviction that his parents are not strong enough to help him to change. Or with the sense that his parents think that he's not strong enough to cope with serious consequences for serious misbehaviors. When we minimize the implications of these behaviors that occur over and over, we are supporting the child's efforts to minimize his behaviors too. He thinks that he does not have to be responsible for his behaviors and we support his assumptions!"

"But by having the consequence occur fast and be over with quickly, aren't we giving the kid a second chance?"

"What kind of a chance are we giving her when she just fails again to do what is asked of her? The parent has to make a judgment: 'Is the kid likely to make a good choice or isn't she?' If I'm fairly certain she's going to make a poor choice, I won't give her the option. I'll provide her with a lot of supervision or practice or chores, or whatever, until I have some confidence that she is now more likely to make a choice that really is in her best interest."

"Well," Steven said, "I need to hear you say that after another two or three weeks, Katie will be able to start making good choices so she'll be given more freedom again."

"I wish I could, Steven," Jackie said. "Believe me, this is not a picnic for me. It takes a lot of work to be with Katie all the time. I do know that if she can get the basic message that I'm communicating now, she's going to be in a lot better shape when I gradually turn her loose."

"And what is the basic message?" Steven asked.

"That being with Mom brings security, love, and even some fun, and those things feel good. Once that becomes a fact to her, she'll be ready to make me a part of her, and then she'll feel secure and want to have fun and love with or without me."

"What you're saying is making more sense to me, Jackie," Steven said. "But it would help me in explaining this to my supervisor if you could give me actual examples of some typical days for Katie."

"Sure, Steven," Jackie said. "I keep a record of each day that I can bring with me to therapy. I'll expand on it somewhat and give you a copy."

Jackie's Journal:

10/16/94. As usual, I stepped out of the kitchen for 1 minute to talk with Mark. Whimsy howled and barked. By the time I got back Katie was calmly sitting at the table. Whimsy was in the corner staring at her and then me. He came toward me, with a slight limp. She had hurt his leg! She got my anger again. Every living being in my house was going to be safe! I thought I would gag when I told her of my love for her and my commitment to teaching her how to treat Whimsy right. Whimsy is totally off limits to her. If she's doing something nice in the family room and Whimsy comes in, she has to leave. She will not be in the same room with him unless someone is willing to supervise her 100 percent of the time. Whimsy's wishes have priority over hers now. Of course she also has to clean his poop from the yard and wash out his food and water bowls. I don't trust her with feeding him.

10/18/94. Left the kitchen for a moment and the Cheerios were all over the floor. Katie "didn't know" how they got there. I told her that since she was alone with them it was her responsibility to keep them from jumping out of the box. Thus, she needed to return them all to the box. After 2 hours, half were in the box. I scooped up some from the floor and dropped them down her shirt. Rage followed. In fairness, I told her to drop some down my shirt. She most certainly did. I put some in her hair; she reciprocated. We shared a glass of apple juice. She picked up remaining Cheerios in 30 minutes. Took her to school 2 hours late. After school, she sorted the laundry to reimburse me for the car ride to school. She complained and threw some meat at the dinner table. Left the table. Before bedtime I painted her face with erasable markers and she did mine. Mark got the Polaroid. She accepted snuggling at bedtime.

10/19/94. Home from school in cheerful and helpful mood. Soon asks to have girl from school visit this Saturday. No. She drops cheerful mood. Refuses to sweep floor. Throws broom. Sits in chair holding broom and dust pan until given permission to sweep. Whines when I say she's not ready to sweep yet. She has to ask to sweep while smiling a specific way. She eventually does. Her favorite meal—pizza. Complains about number of pepperonis on her piece. Grabs a pepperoni from Matthew. Has to give him three pepperonis from hers. Throws pizza. Leaves table—I am sad for her. Before bedtime we play "Mother, may I?" She laughs whenever I call her 'Mother.' She accepts back rub and quiet lullaby.

10/20/94. Home from school, dropping school bag and papers on porch. Snack delayed until her school bag comes all the way home too. She makes valiant effort to get older kids to bring it in. Finally throws it in corner of kitchen. It needs to be on table by closet. Eventually gets there, but too close to dinner for snack. Angry at that. Eventually has cold dinner alone. Eats only small part, seemingly to punish me. I tell her that I enjoy being full and am surprised that she doesn't. At bedtime she's not very verbal but does engage me in a friendly tug of war with old sheet. Calms down with rocking. Continually amazing how one emotional state often has no connection with prior one only minutes earlier.

10/22/94. Saturday chores fairly uneventful. "Misplace" her for 5 minutes after she uses bathroom. She steals Diane's teen magazine. I find parts of it under her bed. She doesn't know who put it there. She makes a picture book of five jobs that she will do for Diane. Whenever Diane gives her the picture of the particular job, she has to drop whatever she's doing and do it for her. I draw pictures that Katie can use of a bowl of ice cream, an hour TV credit, and a coloring book, and give them to her. This took her by surprise, but she recovered fast and ate her ice-cream while watching TV and coloring. Steps on crayons in carpet and spills some ice cream on couch. I give her bucket of soapy water and then vacuum. I hug her and the soapy water on her shirt gets on me. I fuss about that, put some more soapy water on my shirt and hug her again. We laugh and the sound seemed strange. She sits in kitchen, listening to me chatter with Diane until mealtime. Actually completes meal with family—first time in 10 days.

10/23/94. Leaves church in middle of service—yawning and burping during sermon. Spends Sunday afternoon taking nap and writing letter of apology to Pastor. Has cold Sunday dinner, after burping ("I didn't mean to") at table, but eats it all. Quiet time before bedtime. She and I play with two of Diane's old baby dolls. She actually makes one of the dolls sit for hitting the other doll. I rock one doll and she does not object when I rock her the same way.

10/24/94. After therapy this afternoon she is more withdrawn. Focus on Mike's abuse of her seemed hard. At home while making muffins with me actually asked why Sally didn't keep her safe. No eye contact. Then drops beans that I had her snapping. Able to laugh when she found two old Cheerios under counter while picking up beans. After dinner I catch her trying to take Mark's school papers that he had out to correct. Unusual that she would go after something of Mark's. Relate to anger at Mike? Letter of apology to Mark and then quiet time. Accepts a bottle for fourth time.

10/25/94. Discovers at school that Halloween is next week. Shocked that she will not be getting a costume and not be "trick or treating." Finds an excuse to attack me and is held for over 40 minutes before she calms down. Actually has a few tears in response to my empathy for not having Halloween like the other kids do. After dinner does a lot of laughing as we sing "Old McDonald had a farm" and "The wheels on the bus."

10/26/94. Angry at breakfast—she screams for pancakes and she gets oatmeal. She won't get dressed for school and misses the bus. Wants me to drive her. I say that I'm too busy so she has chores and homework during the time that she should be in school. Very resistant so they continue until bedtime with breaks for meals and a brief game with me in which I pretend that she is a ginger-bread cookie that I made and ate.

10/27/94. Goes to school quietly. I welcome her home, give her snack, and then lead her to finishing the chores that she had yesterday. Thirty minutes of anger, but the chores were done before dinner. Ate most of her meal, but had to leave when she screamed at John for telling us a story about his day. I guess he needed her permission. Bedtime fine. We mimicked each other in a mirror. I traced her face while she watched in the mirror. She seemed fascinated with seeing my finger causing those sensations on her skin.

10/28/94. My light jacket was missing. I found it in her closet and while I was there I found some soiled and wet underwear. She did not know how they got there. She washed them twice, she removed everything from her closet to air it out. It would remain empty to make it easier for me to search. Clothing and toys were stored in the attic. She screamed over my "stealing" her stuff. I suggested that I was protecting them from being ruined by pee. Since I carried them to the attic she owed me a letter of thanks. The first sentence took 90 minutes. I wrote her a brief letter, thanking her for working so hard on the first sentence to get it perfect just for little old lovable me. At bedtime, I sang to her and then snuggled with her and read a book.

10/29/94. Saturday morning chores are not going well for Katie. While I do the dishes she is sweeping the kitchen floor. When I direct her to sweep it for the third time because of the debris that is still there she screams that it wasn't there a minute before. I ignore her but a minute later I start screaming that someone snuck another dirty bowl into my dishwater. I run into the living room and yell at Diane and then I run outside and yell at Mark. When I get back I scream that another bowl has been snuck into the water. I stomp on the floor and go to my bedroom and slam the door. Katie actually was quiet for a time and finished sweeping the floor. Diane suggested that one of them bring me a glass of water. Katie wants Diane to do it. Diane and I have a good laugh and at lunch I complain about having a sore throat from yelling so much.

COMMENTARY

During the first therapy session in this chapter, Allison managed to build on the prior one in which Katie had been able to cry for the first time, in response to being able to let herself be aware of feeling worthless after peeing on the quilt. In this session she worked to lead Katie into her past and to enable her to feel similar tears of worthlessness in response to her rejection by Sally. The very appropriate and visual wall-around-the-heart story elicited some empathy for "baby Katie," which served to enable her to tolerate reexperiencing, however briefly, her early years of despair.

By directing her anger and her subsequent sense of abandonment toward Sally, Katie was receptive to experiencing Jackie as being different from her first mother. She then was more able to allow Jackie to comfort her while she experienced the pain of her past. The act of being comforted, and accepting comfort, when experiencing distress is one of the most central interactions for facilitating attachment.

In the other treatment session, Allison focused on increasing Katie's awareness of the ambivalent feelings that she had over being with Jackie most of the day. She wanted to help Katie to sense that her "freedom" when she lived with Sally and Mike was actually abandonment and the experience was very painful. She wanted Katie to have some initial awareness of the comfort and security that she might be able to experience through Jackie's continued presence and to contrast that reality with her daily life of isolation with Sally. The use of the colorful shawl served to give Katie a very visual and "magical" experience that might symbolize what might exist for her within her reach.

The days and weeks that Jackie structured for Katie to be able to regress to her actual affective age were crucial for her eventual progress, just as they are for many unattached children. By taking charge of Katie's life to that degree, she was able to raise her as if she were a toddler. She provided her with almost constant supervision and physical proximity, which Katie needed if she were to eventually look upon Jackie as being a figure of trust. Jackie made almost every choice for her, since her own ability to choose what was best for herself was so poorly developed. Eventually, Katie was able to accept her need to have Jackie decide for her. Jackie structured the day closely to ensure that Katie had the variety of active and quiet, fun and work experiences that she needed.

For Katie, the "mom time" or the nurturing and fun experiences with Jackie that were available every day were a crucial part of the therapeutic benefit of regression. For that reason, it was necessary that Katie *not have to earn* her "mom time." To make them conditional on acceptable behavior would undermine their value in affirming Katie's unconditional worth. Regardless of her behavior, Katie was given fun and love experiences with Jackie, just as a toddler in a good home is always given those experiences.

The affective self of the unattached child is poorly integrated. She can move from rage, to pleasure, to feeling frightened, to feeling calm, in an instant. Thus, it often happened that Katie might be very angry with and oppositional to Jackie for much of the day, and then be very engaging and receptive to the nurturing experiences of "mom time" before bedtime. This reality does not make her "mom time" expressions and behaviors manipulative or less genuine. Her functioning during those times are as real as her functioning during her oppositional times. During the "mom time" Katie is able to manifest the "self" that is attuned with a nurturing and playful mother. At almost all other times, she is manifesting the "self" that is misattuned, alone and resentful, and permeated with shame. Lacking integration, Katie is not able to maintain the "good self" when she is not experiencing attunement with Jackie. When Jackie is gone, her small and weakened "good self" quickly disappears under the intensity of the "bad self." Only through forming an attachment with Jackie—both the "good" and the "bad" Jackie—the nurturing and the structuring Jackie, will Katie be able to integrate the "good" and "bad" self. When she can eventually internalize this complete Jackie, she will then be able to maintain her sense of self as whole and worthwhile, and not require Jackie's continuing physical and psychological presence. If Jackie and Allison are going to be able to facilitate Katie's ability to form an attachment with Jackie, it is crucial that they be able, regardless of Katie's barriers, to elicit her full engagement in those experiences of attunement, where the healthy self can begin to blossom.

THE THANKSGIVING DEBACLE

By Thanksgiving, Katie had been in the Keller home for five-and-a-half months. It seemed to Jackie like five years. The only thing predictable about Katie was that she always wanted to be in control of every situation. She would do whatever she thought might achieve control over Jackie and the others in the family. At times she seemed to be more peaceful because of Jackie taking charge of every moment of her life. But her desire to resume control was never far from the surface. She still resisted, became enraged, destructive, and irritable. She might be cooperative and compliant with Jackie for a number of days. The second that Jackie gave her a bit of freedom, Katie would take the opportunity to try to be in control again and sabotage her efforts. Still, there was some progress, and Jackie decided that she would take the chance to bring Katie with the rest of the family to the traditional Thanksgiving dinner. Besides, during the holidays respite opportunities were nonexistent and Jackie did not intend to stay home for Thanksgiving with Katie while the rest of the family went to her mother's.

On Thanksgiving day, the Keller family traveled to Brunswick to have the traditional dinner with Jackie's mother, Ruth. Jackie's siblings, Jane and John, and their families were also coming, just as they had all done for years. She did not see much of Jane, who lived with her family in Connecticut. John worked at the University of Maine in Farmington so she visited with him much more often. As a result, John had gotten to know Gabe, and now Katie, fairly well, and although he did not understand them, he knew how much work it was caring for foster children and how they often required a different way of child rearing. Ruth tried to understand, but of course she had her opinions, which she freely gave to her daughter. Jane had her own life and never really understood what her sister was up to with her foster kids. Jackie did not expect to have the most relaxing Thanksgiving dinner with her family. Still, she felt ready to deal with Katie's probable increase in oppositional behaviors. With an audience, Katie tended to experiment with new ways to irritate Jackie, seemingly to see if she could get away with more. Failing that, she would be content if she could embarrass Jackie.

Mark supervised Katie while Jackie was busy helping her mother prepare the meal. Katie was now used to John's kids, Nathan and Art, and they were used to her. They were careful with their toys and games around her. Jane's kids, Melinda and Bob, were not so well prepared. Katie asked to use Melinda's Gameboy. Mark began to suggest that they play something else but Melinda's dad, Robert, indicated that Katie certainly could play with Melinda's toy. When Katie was not able to win she threw it on the floor. When it seemed to be broken, Robert remained understanding and forgiving, although Melinda did not. Mark indicated that Katie would be responsible to pay for its replacement if it could not be fixed. Katie screamed at that idea and she screamed even louder when Mark insisted that she sit next to him while the other kids remained playing on the floor. Jane came in from the kitchen to help and when she discovered the problem she assured Mark that it was not necessary for Katie to replace the Gameboy since she did not mean to break it. Mark indicated that Katie was responsible for replacing it if necessary. Jane was interested in helping Katie to get over her distress. She told her not to worry about it since Jane knew that she could fix it. She put her arm around Katie's shoulders and suggested that Katie help her in the kitchen putting the fruit appetizer into the dishes and carrying them to the table. Katie smiled and cheerfully went with her. She had found an ally.

Katie charmed Jane. Jackie looked at them with mild amusement and annoyance. Now her sister would never believe her when she described some of Katie's behaviors. She could anticipate more comments such as, "It can't be that bad," "She's just a little girl!," or "Aren't you just a little too hard on her?"

When it was time to sit at the table, Jackie discovered that Katie had managed to have her seat placed next to Jane's. She indicated that it would be best for Katie to sit next to her. Jane insisted that it was fine with her for Katie to remain next to her. In an effort not to be "unreasonable," Jackie consented. Jane agreed to select the right portions for Katie, although it was clear that she thought that Katie was old enough to do it for herself.

Jane prepared Katie's plate and the angelic child smiled and thanked her. When Jane put the gravy bowl down next to her, Katie quietly asked if she could put the gravy on her mashed potatoes herself. Jane smiled, gave her the ladle and turned to talk with Ruth. Katie put one hand on the bowl and began to lower the ladle into the gravy. With the slightest smile she tipped over the bowl, with the gravy pouring onto the table and into Jane's lap. Jackie, seeing the whole sequence, yelled "Katie!" and Jane just yelled as she jumped up from her chair and headed for the kitchen sink. The rest of the relatives sat frozen, watching the river of gravy slowly making its way over the table cloth toward the turkey. Ruth ran to the kitchen to be of help to Jane while Jackie hurried to Katie to escort her from the table into the living room.

"I saw what you did, Katie, and that makes me very angry at you!" Jackie yelled at her. "Jane was very nice to you and you repay her by doing such a mean thing to her." Katie only yelled, "I want my dinner!" in reply to Jackie.

Robert followed Jackie and Katie into the living room and said, "I'm sure it was an accident, Jackie. Don't be hard on her."

"It wasn't an accident," Jackie said. "Katie has lost her right to eat dinner with the rest of the family."

Robert did not know what to say, so he went to the kitchen to check on his wife. A few minutes later Jane and Ruth went into the living room.

"I'm OK, Katie," Jane said. "The gravy was hot but I wasn't burned. I had to change my skirt and I'm sure that I'll be able to get the stain out."

"I'm sorry for what happened, Jane," Jackie said. "Katie, tell Jane that you're sorry for what you did to her."

"I'm sorry, Jane," Katie said in her sweetest voice.

"It's fine, Katie. I know that you didn't mean to do it," Jane replied.

"She did mean to do it, Jane, and it's not fine," Jackie said. "Katie will be responsible for making enough money to pay the cleaning bill."

"I think we should just forget it, Jackie," Jane said. "I'm sure that it was an accident. Why don't we all go back and enjoy the meal."

"I'll be there in a few minutes, Jane," Jackie said. "Katie will be sitting here while the rest of us eat. I'll get her something later."

"That's not necessary, Jackie," Jane insisted. "I said that I'm fine and I'd rather just forget it."

"It is necessary for Katie, Jane," Jackie said. "It was not an accident and she needs to be accountable for what she did."

Jane looked at Jackie with growing annoyance. Ruth tried to resolve their conflict by saying to Jackie, "Honey, why not find a little punishment for her later. This is Thanksgiving dinner and I want us all to enjoy it."

"I know you do, Mom. We all can still enjoy it. But Katie will have to eat by herself when the rest of us are done," Jackie said gently to her mother. She truly did not want to argue with her about this.

"You're becoming a bigger problem than Katie, Jackie. Why don't you just do what Mom asks," Jane was still annoyed.

"I can't. I need to do what is best for Katie," Jackie firmly replied.

"Well, maybe you're wrong. Maybe what's best is for all of us to just drop it and have a decent family meal." Jane's voice was becoming louder.

"I may be wrong, but I'm responsible for Katie and I have to do what I think is best for her," Jackie said.

"Why don't you think of the rest of the family too? Not just what you want," Jane yelled.

"I'm not responsible for the rest of the family. But I am responsible for Katie and she's not eating with us!" Jackie's voice began to rise too.

"If she's not eating, neither am I!" Jane yelled and turned and left the room.

Ruth looked sadly at Jackie. "Please, Jackie. It would mean a lot to me if we all could sit down together. We so seldom are together anymore. And I don't want you and Jane to fight."

Jackie felt the tears begin to roll down her cheeks. She took a deep breath. "I'm sorry, Mom. You don't know Katie. I've worked hard for her for the last five months. I can't give in on this or it will set her back too much."

Jackie stared at her mother, waiting for some acknowledgment of her words and acceptance for her decision. Her mother simply stood there, not saying anything. Jackie knew that she would not get the support that she was asking for.

"I'm sorry, Mom. I think that it's best for Mark and me to take the kids and leave now." Ruth still did not respond. Jackie took Katie by the hand and walked into the dining room. She looked at Mark.

"We better be going home now. I'm afraid that this just has not worked out today," Jackie said quietly.

"Let's go, kids, we'll get something to eat on the way home," Mark said as he got up from the table.

At the door Jackie turned again to her mother. "I'm really sorry, Mom, for how this turned out. I'll call you tomorrow." Ruth nodded as she stood by her chair. Jane was not in sight.

John got up from the table and came to the door. He hugged his sister. "It will work out OK, sis. You got to do what you think is best. Mom and Jane will come around."

"Thanks, John." Jackie felt the tears coming again. "I know that you're right."

On the way home, Jackie sat in the front seat, staring at the road. She heard Diane make a few angry comments at Katie. Katie screamed at her. Diane yelled at Katie and Mark told her that her comments were not helping the situation. Jackie didn't have the energy to say anything. She could only think of her mother staring at her, condemning her decision. Eventually she imagined what Katie must have looked like while Jackie was arguing with Jane and Ruth. She knew that Katie would have been feeling excited and powerful then. Jackie would not let herself look at Katie now. She knew that if she did, Katie would smile at her. She also knew that if that happened she would truly hate her and she would not bother to hide her contempt.

That night Mark took care of Katie and got her to bed. Jackie kept her distance. She had no empathy for her. She could not interact with her. She wasn't going to try.

Later Mark sat next to her on the couch. He took her hand. She smiled at him and felt very tired and sad.

Slowly she began talking. "I think she might beat me, Mark. I did it with Gabe, but I don't know if I can continue to do it for her. I have given her so much. And she spilled that damn gravy to hurt me. She knew what would happen, I truly believe it. I feel that she's evil. She's just too much for me."

She leaned against him and sobbed. After a time she said, "I don't want to love that kid. Why do I still love her? 'Like the kid and dislike the behavior' is crap. I don't like that kid. I don't want to love her anymore. Why can't I stop?"

"Honey, that's who you are. That's one of the many reasons I love you so much. Whatever you decide to do, I know it will be for the best. I support you all the way. If you think that someone else has to raise Katie, then someone else will have to raise her. If you think that you need to continue with her, then she'll stay. If you want her to stay I will do my best to be of more help to you. You're in charge."

"Maybe I don't want to be in charge. Maybe I don't want the responsibility of bringing this kid into the human race. Maybe I don't want the responsibility for her life! Her problems and needs seem bottomless. I'm afraid she's going to pull me down with her and I'll be no good to anyone."

"I know you and I know me. No kid has that power and she'll never get it," Mark said. "But if you need to have her move somewhere else I understand and support you. I know that whatever you decide will be for the best."

Jackie looked at Mark. She smiled and kissed him. "Thanks for the vote of confidence." She laughed. "I wish that I could tell what was best. I can't now. Maybe I need to get some sleep."

When she awoke the next morning, Jackie felt more discouraged than she could remember. She had hoped, with the new day, to discover her usual enthusiasm for her life and her family. Not today, not now. Maybe she should give Allison a call and tell her about her Thanksgiving disaster. Maybe she and Mark should go out for breakfast. As she lay there she heard Mark begin to grumble and stretch. After so many years she knew that he was about to awaken within the next thirty seconds. On cue, Mark reached over and gave her a hug.

"Good morning, honey," Jackie said. "Would you mind taking care of Katie for breakfast? I need to lie here for awhile and think over some things."

"Sure, Jackie," Mark said quickly. This was most unusual. "Anything you want to talk over with me?"

"Not now," Jackie responded. Mark got out of bed, dressed, and went directly to check on Katie. Nothing began in the Keller home until one was certain about Katie's whereabouts.

Jackie simply lay in bed. As her mind drifted, she began to pray. She was not surprised to find herself doing it. She generally did when she felt lost. Her faith often helped her to get through the hardest times, as well as find the direction that she needed to take. Her prayers led her through her numerous conflicting thoughts and feelings about Katie. From there she became aware of her sister's rejection of her and of her own shame over Katie's behavior at the Thanksgiving dinner. Suddenly, she became aware of how she had needed to have Katie meet her needs to be validated by her relatives over her work with Katie. Now her sister, and even her mother, thought that she was a failure in her efforts to raise foster kids. She felt shame and she blamed Katie for it! That awareness made all the difference.

About thirty minutes later, while taking a shower, Jackie knew with certainty that she was not ready to have that kid beat her. She was going to keep loving her and she was going to keep raising her. She didn't care if Katie wanted her to or not. Katie needed her and she was still able to be there for her—at least most of the time. And that was a whole lot more than most parents could do. Jackie knew that her mother would understand. She knew too that Jane would eventually come to accept what she was doing. That knowledge made it easier to decide that she was still Katie's mom. But she also knew that she would have come to the same decision regardless of her mother's and sister's responses.

Jackie was not looking forward to talking with Katie about the dinner, but it actually proved to be easier than she thought. Once she recommitted herself to Katie, the words came fairly easily. She knew what Katie needed to hear so she said it.

"Katie," Jackie said over the breakfast table when she and Katie were alone. "You managed to really mess up the dinner for all of us yesterday. I'm sure you noticed how upset I was and how angry Jane and I were at each other. I was really mad at you and I'm sure you knew that too."

Katie was listening, not sure where this conversation would be leading. Jackie continued, "After I calmed down, I realized that I should have made you sit next to me even if Jane didn't understand why. She just doesn't know you the way I do. Also, maybe I shouldn't have taken you with us to my mom's house. I could have found someone to watch you here. You weren't ready to enjoy the family holiday. It wasn't special to you at all. I know that it's hard for anything to be special to you. The next time you won't have to go if I think that you're not ready for it."

"Well, sweetie, you're still going to have to pay to have Jane's skirt cleaned. I'll be giving you some extra chores. And Mark and I are going to be making a special dinner here today for the family. Since it will probably be too much for you to handle, you'll be sitting in the living room while we eat. I'll save something for you to eat when we're done."

"I want to eat dinner with everyone too!" Katie yelled.

"Well sweetie, you're just not ready to now. Someday you'll be able to and I'll be happy for you then." Jackie got up and kissed Katie on the top of her head. Katie's pouting continued, but she did not have a tantrum. Jackie's comments must have surprised her and she didn't know how to respond. Since Katie only wanted to do things that might put her in control, she'd just have to wait and figure it out before putting energy into a tantrum.

"You sure were put through a lot, Jackie," Allison said at the next therapy session on November 30. "You probably felt like covering Katie with gravy."

"I never want to see gravy again, Allison."

"Are you struggling with anything now? You seemed to have worked through so much on your own already."

"Not really on my own, Allison," Jackie replied.

"Then how did you deal with it so well?" Steven asked.

"Well, I do hope that I have not broken any 'separation of church and state' rules, but I prayed, and I found my answers in my prayers. As long as I believe that this is what God wants for me and Katie, I think that she'll be with me. Mark helped too so I've managed to weather another storm."

"Well," Allison said. "By the time this is all over you'll be stronger than all of us together. Why don't I get Katie now. I'm curious to see where she is now after what you went through with her."

Allison brought Katie into the room with her usual, "Well, it's Katie Kiddo. Good to see you again, kiddo!" She rubbed her back a bit as Katie took off her shoes. Katie climbed into Allison's lap and rested her head onto the pillow.

"Well, kiddo, you don't look your usual cheerful self. What's up?"

"Nothing."

"Nothing is it? Say that again, say, 'Nothing, Allison.'"

"Nothing, Allison!"

"Again."

"Nothing, Allison!"

"That's the idea, kiddo. Now say, 'I'm not talking to you, Allison'."

"I'm not talking to you, Allison!"

"Way to go, kiddo. Well, if you don't want to talk, I'm just going to have to count your fingers. Let's see . . . 1, 2, 3, 4, 5 over there. Ten, 9, 8, 7, 6. There, 5 and 6, that's 11. What! You have 11 fingers! You gotta be kidding! How could that be? Let me do it again. One, 2, 3, 4, 5 on that hand. Now, 10, 9, 8, 7, 6! Six and 5, wow, you do have 11 fingers! That's incredible! You're incredible! See, that's proof that you're just an incredible kid, kiddo."

"I don't have six on that hand," Katie said. She wasn't laughing and her eye contact was poor. Allison immediately knew that engaging Katie today would not be as easy as it usually was.

"Of course you only have five fingers on your hand."

"Five and five are ten," Katie said.

"You sure know your numbers, kiddo. I'm sure not going to trick you."

Katie lay across Allison's lap. She appeared to be passively resigned to being there. This contrasted noticeably with her general air of expectant uncertainty about what would be occurring. If she wanted to convey the idea that she was bored and annoyed at wasting her time there she was doing a good job.

"My goodness, Katie," Allison began, "you sure don't seem to want to be here. It seems to me that you want to say 'I want to leave. I don't like it here. I don't want to talk about anything! I don't want to think about anything! I don't want to feel anything! I don't want to do anything! Let me go. I want to leave!' My guess is that those are some of the things that you would be saying if you wanted to tell me something."

Katie remained quiet and sullen.

"That's it, Katie. See how quiet and annoyed you can be while I talk with your mom," Allison said casually and then looked over at Jackie.

"Jackie, Katie seems to be very unhappy about being here now. Do you have any ideas what is bothering her?"

"She didn't seem upset when we drove over here, Allison. I'm not sure what's on her mind now," Jackie said.

"Well, something is getting to her," Allison said. "Did anything happen since I saw her last?"

"It was a hard Thanksgiving for the whole family, Allison. Maybe that's bothering her," Jackie said.

"Nothing's bothering me!" Katie screamed.

"Wow, you yelled that loudly, kiddo. Maybe something about Thanksgiving is on your mind," Allison said.

"No, it's not!" Katie yelled.

"What happened, Jackie, that might be upsetting Katie now?"

"Well, Allison, we went down to my mother's house for Thanksgiving dinner. When we sat down to eat, Katie spilled the gravy on my sister's lap so she had to leave the table."

"It was an accident!" Katie screamed.

"Katie had my sister and mother thinking it was an accident, but I saw her smile before she did it and I knew it was on purpose," Jackie said.

"I did not! You're lying! You're lying!" Katie yelled at Jackie.

"You sure are mad at your mom, Katie. Tell her. Say, 'I'm mad at you, Mom!'"

"I'm mad at you!"

Say, 'I'm mad at you, Mom!'"

"I'm mad at you!"

"Wow, Jackie, she really is angry with you, she won't say 'Mom.'" Allison said.

"Say, 'You're a mean mom!'"

"You're mean!"

"Say it again!"

"You're mean!"

"Why do you think she's so mad at you, Jackie?" Allison asked.

"Well, she has had to do chores to pay to get Jane's skirt cleaned. And she missed the family Thanksgiving dinner that we had at home the next day," Jackie said.

"But she's always getting annoyed at you for giving her some consequence. Generally she doesn't get nearly so mad at you."

"You're right, Allison. Maybe it's because of my reaction to what she did."

"What was your reaction, Jackie?" Allison asked.

"I was very mad at her for what she did. You see, my mother and sister got angry with me and we all left early. I was crying a lot and Diane yelled at Katie. All the way home and that night I didn't talk to Katie. That's the only time I ever stopped talking to her when she did something wrong."

"Jackie, I'll bet you're right. Katie is probably mad at you because of how mad you got at her," Allison said.

She turned to Katie. "I'll bet you were saying to yourself, 'Why is she so mad at me? Moms aren't supposed to get so mad! She's not allowed to get mad at me that much!' Right, Katie?"

Katie did not say anything. She looked toward the couch.

"Oh, Katie, now I understand. No wonder you got so mad at your mom! You could tell that she was more mad at you than she ever was before! You didn't know what that meant! Maybe she was so mad she'd never stop being mad! Maybe she would become like Sally!" Allison sat motionless for a moment and then leaned forward and said quietly, "You thought that she might be hating you. . . . You thought that she might not love you anymore. . . . You thought that she . . . might not . . . want to be your mom anymore."

Katie remained motionless. Allison then said even more quietly, "You must have started to feel . . . sad . . . .and scared. . . . No wonder you're mad at . . . your mom."

Allison began to stroke Katie's hair.

"Don't do that!" Katie screamed at Allison.

Allison pulled Katie toward her and began to slowly rock her in her arms. As she rocked her, she whispered over and over. "Katie, Katie, so sad, so scared, . . . Katie, Katie, so sad, so scared, . . . Katie, . . ."

"DON'T SAY THAT!" Katie screamed. "DON'T SAY THAT!" She screamed and screamed as she struggled and thrashed in Allison's arms.

Katie continued to scream and Allison continued to rock her, stroke her hair and shoulders, and repeat the words that reached into Katie's soul. It went on and on. Jackie waited, wanting it to stop, wanting it to never stop.

The screams continued. As the minutes passed, they changed. They originally were filled with rage. Now they were more and more permeated with despair. Her screams became cries of one abandoned to the night, forever alone.

Allison continued, "Katie . . . Katie . . . so sad . . . Katie . . . Katie . . . so scared."

Katie's cries continued too; seemingly they would continue forever.

Allison looked at Jackie, who nodded and came to the couch. Allison gently placed her into Jackie's arms. And Jackie rocked her.

"My Katie . . . my Katie. . . . you're safe . . . you're with Mom. I love you, Katie. . . . I love my Katie," Jackie whispered. Katie clung to her. Jackie felt Katie's fingers dig into her sides. She clung to her like a baby. A terrified, despairing baby.

Allison went to the corner shelf and turned on the tape player. She always kept a tape in the player that would be suitable for times like this one. This tape contained Irish lullabies, with gentle and loving tones. Allison hesitated to play it because she thought that she might be encouraging Katie's feelings of being an infant too much, causing her to resist. Katie accepted it.

Jackie stopped talking. She began to move slowly and hum in time with the lullabies. Allison simply watched. She didn't exist to Jackie and Katie. They were in their own world now. This world would heal and reach Katie much more than anything that Allison might say or do.

Eventually Allison turned off the music and indicated that the session would have to stop. There was nothing that she wanted to say. Nothing that she should say. When Jackie and Katie got up to leave, she stared at them for a moment and then she went over and hugged them both.

COMMENTARY

When Katie spilled the gravy on Jackie's sister she was engaging in a behavior that almost defines the unattached child. She was ruining a family celebration for all, splitting Jackie from her relatives, eliciting anger and rejection from her, and taking pleasure in the shambles that she created, all from one action. Children like Katie are inevitably on their worst behavior during moments like the Thanksgiving dinner. They cannot tolerate such mutual enjoyment and support, and they cannot tolerate allowing others to have that experience. To them, it is much more desirable to experience the power of destroying the experience for all and confirming their self-perception as being isolated and evil.

Jackie's response to Katie's behavior can best be understood by the dynamics of shame, similar to, but much less profound than, its meaning in Katie's life. Central to Jackie's identity is her ability to be a good therapeutic foster parent. Since Katie's behavior so infrequently confirmed her view that she was good at her work, Jackie was more vulnerable to the need for confirmation from those important to her that she was actually good at what she did. She was seeking that confirmation from her sister and mother. Katie sensed this and took advantage of the opportunity to hurt Jackie and test her commitment. The criticism from her sister and mother elicited her doubts and triggered shame, which, in turn, led to rage at Katie. Jackie was not able to integrate the rage at the time, and she distanced herself from her.

Jackie's shame is not an uncommon response among parents who attempt to raise unattached children. Their children seldom confirm that they are good parents. Their child's rejection and oppositional behaviors constantly suggest that they are failing them in some fundamental ways. They give and give to their child and the response that they most often receive is, "Is that all? I want more!" In the face of their child's rejection, they turn to friends and relatives for support and confirmation that the ordeal that they are living has meaning and their efforts are worthwhile. Often, they receive skepticism, advice, and criticism that they are being too harsh and are not meeting this poor child's needs. When professionals, therapists, teachers, and social workers concur with the opinions of their relatives and friends, these parents are extremely vulnerable to experiencing shame. From such a position, it is extremely hard for this parent to then attempt to reduce the pervasive shame experienced by their child. When Jackie experienced herself as a failure as Katie's parent, she had little energy or skill to continue to parent her.

Parental shame from raising unattached children needs to be acknowledged and addressed. If there are two parents, they need to be solidly in support of each other in the face of their child's rejection. The best source of support is often other parents of unattached children who truly understand what it is like to raise such children, and who are in the best position to know what one needs to hear and what support might be the most beneficial. Also important is the understanding and support of a therapist who knows the symptoms and needs of the unattached child as well as the various parenting strategies and support that parents need in order to have a chance to raise their child adequately.

In therapy, Allison focused with Katie more on Jackie's response to her behavior than on the behavior itself. She took her cue from Katie's initial resistance to therapy, something which was not usually present. Katie was defending herself against some intense affective experience that seemed to go beyond her actual behavior. What was the most unusual about the event was not Katie's behavior, but rather, Jackie's. Her emotional withdrawal from Katie for the rest of the day, triggered an affective response in Katie that was similar to her response to Sally's extended periods of rejection of her. She was left feeling terrified that whatever relationship might have existed with Jackie was now ended. Jackie would now most certainly insist that she move. She had finally revealed that part of herself that Jackie would find disgusting and which would cause her to throw her away.

By allowing Katie to recognize and acknowledge her fear that she was finally being rejected by Jackie, Allison was able to lead her to expressing the depth of despair into which she was now falling. Through rage, Katie initially rejected Allison's lead. Gradually she began to respond to Allison and Jackie's empathy and loving attitude and she allowed herself to express her affect fully and then accept Jackie's reassurance and continuing commitment.

WINTER ON A ROLLER COASTER

The next few months were a roller coaster ride with each hill bigger than the last. At each summit, Katie's rage outbursts were something to experience. She would hurl herself to the floor, bruising her body and knocking over anything nearby. Anger seemed to be her only way to enter into a relationship. Katie was here! So alive! With such passion! And so much hate!

At the foot of each hill, she would seem to be miles away, lost somewhere in a reality that she could not share. Katie now seemed to have turned off her emotional life. At these times, Jackie almost wished for her anger.

But Jackie first noticed another quality in Katie early in January, a few weeks after the holiday season. Katie might laugh spontaneously and begin to enjoy talking with Jackie and Mark. There was a genuineness to her interactions that had never before been evident. She seemed to be able to briefly recreate how she was during "mom time" outside of those structured times that were maintained by Jackie's attunement. At these times she did not convey her usual manipulative quality, nor did she talk in her typical chattering monologues. Katie seemed to be "an ordinary kid" at these moments. Jackie did not mention her observations to her. Often they would end suddenly with Katie saying or doing something that was certain to cause a break in any comfortable emotional quality to their time together. Jackie counted these moments in minutes, not hours. She told Allison about it and they both smiled in hope. They were careful not to expect it to continue. They needed to guard against disappointment. Also their very expectation would probably be sensed by Katie and would certainly drive her further away again. Katie had now been with Jackie for seven months. To most outsiders, Katie had not changed at all. Allison and Jackie knew that she had. They had seen moments of reciprocal enjoyment where the need to control seemed to dissipate. They saw a child who might be told something to do, and who actually, calmly, did it! They did not know if these moments would ever become a significant part of her life.

On January 27, 1995, Allison and Jackie met with Steven and his supervisor, Kathy. Kathy had told them last June that she would review their progress in six months, and she had actually given them an extra month. Steven had not been able to attend many therapy sessions over the last two months either, so the meeting would serve to give him an update.

Jackie summarized Katie's typical days with their rage and defiance, lies and destruction. She went on to describe how Katie spent a lot of time sitting quietly, working, or playing with a few toys in whatever room that Jackie happened to be. She mentioned how Katie often ate her meal alone after everyone else was done because she would often try to disrupt the meal by saying something mean to someone or by eating her food in some gross way. She indicated that Katie had only received a few small gifts for Christmas since anything more would only disrupt her functioning and ruin the day for her, and possibly other members of the family too. Katie did seem to accept Jackie's hugs and she even asked to have her give her a bottle on occasion. Jackie was excited by those moments of shared enjoyment. She explained to Kathy and Steven what her "mom times" with Katie were like and how she hoped that they would serve to open the door for Katie to experience having a mother in a new way. Katie now had another way of living in the home besides being motivated only by her pervasive needs for manipulative control. Of course, apart from the bedtime ritual, she did not choose that "other way" very often.

Allison spoke of how Katie was generally quite engaged during the treatment sessions, even though Allison was clearly in charge and relating with her in a close, emotional, manner. Allison noted that Katie still had a great deal of difficulty exploring her misbehaviors without falling into seemingly endless shame. This led to defensiveness, denial, and rage. Allison said that Katie seemed to be able to manage her shame-experiences more openly, but not consistently so. She indicated that these explorations would remain central to Katie's therapy since they were central to both the integration of herself and also her readiness to form a secure attachment to Jackie. Allison also described those therapeutic experiences of special affect and intimacy, which she took to be indicative of Katie's potential for a more significant and lasting developmental attachment.

"So far she doesn't seem to have made any significant improvements that last on their own," Kathy suggested. "She sounds just as angry and defiant as she was when she first came into foster care over two years ago. Will she ever really be able to live a normal life in a family?"

"That's our goal or we wouldn't be pushing her and ourselves so hard," Allison said. "She's still only 7 years old. She's bright and she's a fighter. We're just teaching her that she doesn't need to fight with Jackie, especially when she's having a hard time and needs her the most. If she can learn that, she'll have quite a future. Also, I really don't agree with you about her not having made any significant improvements. Certainly there are no major external changes. However, she has demonstrated more subtle changes in her ability to tolerate intense affect and closeness with me and Jackie. I think that for the first time she is beginning to notice the world of trust, affection, and reciprocal enjoyment. She hasn't stepped fully into that world, but she has noticed it and maybe gotten her toes wet."

"But will she ever do that, I mean really do it?" Kathy asked.

"I don't know. But I know that she deserves a shot at it. I also don't know who could encourage her to do it better than Jackie. She's doing a great deal for this kid and I think that someday we'll see the results."

"What do you think, Jackie?" Steven asked.

"I agree with Allison," Jackie replied. "I can't read into the future, but I know that Katie has spunk. She works hard at what she thinks is best for her. The problem is that what's best for her is almost always something different from what she works for. She just has to discover that she needs a mother, not a servant. She needs to learn how to have fun with me, rely on me, and listen to me, not control me and get me to reject her."

"She seems to have come pretty close to getting you to reject her on Thanksgiving," Steven said.

"Yes she did. But not since then, and I feel like I'm on a roll. The little turkey has met her match." Jackie smiled.

"Well," Kathy said, "this brings us to our next big question. We need to decide if we should proceed with asking the court to terminate Sally and Mike's parental rights. She has been in foster care for almost two-and-a-half years now and her parents have done very little toward reunification with her. As you know, her mother is not really interested in seeing her more than every few months, and she has done little work in her psychotherapy. Her father has done nothing and they continue to live together. Neither parent has accepted responsibility for their acts of abuse or neglect. They actually are not seeing a therapist now because they failed to keep some sessions and they need to make a payment for the missed appointments."

"It has seemed to me ever since I first saw her that this kid is not going to be reunited with her parents," Allison said. "Not only are they not doing their work, but they have left her so damaged that they could never adequately raise her again. If she went back to them she wouldn't last a week and she'd leave there so damaged that she'd never be able to make it."

"You're right about that," Kathy said. "But another important question that the court will be asking is whether or not she is adoptable. If we cannot say that we can successfully place her for adoption, I doubt if the judge will terminate her parents' rights. The court does not like to create legal orphans, no matter how improbable it is that she will ever have a meaningful relationship with her parents."

"I understand your problem," Allison said. "At this time, even if you found an adoptive home willing to try to raise her, the risk is there that the adoption would eventually disrupt. Even if the adoptive parents maintained their commitment to her, she is likely to need major services in the years ahead unless she can make significant changes. Her chances of making those changes are much greater if she can continue her work with Jackie and me."

"But the question is, will this kid be able to be adopted at some point down the road?" asked Kathy.

"I strongly believe that Katie should have the opportunity to be adopted. And I'm more than willing to recommend that to a judge," Allison said. "You know that even if the judge agrees to terminate their rights three months from now, it will still be another nine to twelve months before an adoption worker has gotten to know Katie and found the right home for her. That will give Jackie and me a lot of time to continue working with her and help her to be as healthy as possible before adoption. She is still only 7. She deserves a shot at a permanent home—although we will have to be very careful to match her up with the right family."

"Since we're still mandated to do reunification, Jackie, I have to be careful how I word this," Kathy said. "If her parents' rights were terminated in the future, do you think that you would apply to adopt Katie?"

There was silence and Jackie seemed to have trouble breathing for a moment. Finally she said, "That idea has crossed my mind any number of times, Kathy. The thought of getting her to finally trust me and then telling her that she is going to be adopted by someone else sure doesn't feel good. I had the same situation with Gabe. I cried a lot before deciding that I could not adopt him. There are various reasons, none of which made me feel any better with him. The main reason is that I truly want to continue my work as a foster parent who can help these troubled kids really learn about maternal love. I think that I'd like to do it for another twenty years or so, which means another ten or fifteen kids. I couldn't do that if I had adopted Gabe. If I had, I wouldn't be working with Katie now."

"I hadn't really thought through what you're doing with Katie," said Steven. "Now I'm wondering if this is right. Should we be setting it up so that she attaches to Jackie only to have her move to another home a year later? Is that fair to her? Are we being deceitful?"

"That's a hard question to answer," Allison said. "Over the years I have come up with two responses. First, what other options do we have? With a kid as unable to form an attachment to caregivers as Katie is, I am convinced that the odds that she could do it with

adoptive parents are not good. Most adoptive parents are not interested in adopting in order to become therapeutic parents. They
want to give their love and home to a kid who can accept what they
have to offer to a reasonable degree and benefit from living with
them. Katie would be unlikely to respond to such a home unless
the parents were able and committed to learn to parent her in a
way similar to the way Jackie is doing. It takes a certain kind of
person to parent a kid like Katie. If we are truly honest with pro-
spective adoptive parents about what really is involved in parenting
a poorly attached child, I don't think that we'll find nearly enough
families who sign up for the duration. Also, the type of interventions offered by me and Jackie are not available in many parts of
the state and country. This is a fairly new area of knowledge that
is not yet understood well enough by mental health and social
services professionals."

"Second," Allison continued, "it has been my experience that
Katie will be able to form an attachment with adoptive parents after
first learning how to do it with Jackie. When Gabe was clearly told
that he would not be staying with Jackie and that he would have
his own adoptive family, he cried and screamed for days. But this
was healthy grief over his anticipated loss of the first person whom
he ever trusted. Yet throughout the grieving he was able to turn to
Jackie for comfort! When he was ready to face the adoption itself,
he talked with her for hours about his hopes and fears about his
new family! When he finally got the photos of his new parents he
was excited and he shared his excitement with Jackie. He did not
retreat into his life prior to learning how to be attached. He did
not lose his trust for Jackie. He knew that she still loved him and
wanted what was best for him."

"How is he doing in his adoptive home?" Steven asked.

"Well, he's been living with his family for about ten months now
and it is going well," Jackie said. "He was sad for awhile, but now
he seems to feel secure in his home. He calls me and sends me
letters. It's obvious that I'm still important to him. I think I've become a special aunt to him. Most importantly, his attachment to
his adoptive mom seems to be strong. I wouldn't be surprised if by
now she is more important to him psychologically than I am."

"It's sad that Katie will have to move someday," Allison added.
"I am convinced, however, that adoption and not long-term foster

care is most likely to meet her needs. It would not serve her interests if we discouraged her learning to attach until her parents' rights were terminated and she were placed in an adoptive home. And she would have wasted two or three years of her early life when she is more receptive to learning how to attach. And she most likely would have had another three or four placements. And after all that, there's a fair chance that a suitable adoptive home could not be found. I don't have to tell you about the adolescents in foster care who do not have a permanent home and who are not likely to be attached to anyone who really loves them and is committed to their care."

"No you don't," Kathy said. "We'll be discussing this back at the office, but there's a good chance that when we go to court in the spring we will be seeking to terminate Mike and Sally's parental rights."

On February 20, 1995, Katie's one-week school vacation started. She was doing fairly well at school, compared to her home difficulties. Her teacher, Mrs. Robinson, said that she was keeping up with her class in her academics and might even be reading at a higher level. However, she really did not seem to comprehend what she read as well as did the other kids in the class. She had a hard time discussing the stories and her teacher thought that she often did not seem to understand the main theme and the wishes and motives of the characters.

With her peers at school Katie tended to be controlling and domineering. She did not seem to have formed any special friends. The other kids were not sure how she would react and they tended to give her some distance. Mrs. Robinson thought that she was socially immature compared to her peers. She also had initiated a reward system to see if she could increase Katie's on task behaviors and reduce some of her disruptive behaviors. When she talked with Jackie about implementing a similar system at home in order to have greater consistency, Jackie declined and indicated that she already had a very comprehensive and structured program in place that did not rely on concrete rewards to motivate her. Mrs. Robinson then tactfully told Jackie that Katie had told her of some of the consequences that she got at home. She went on to add that Jackie might attain greater results if she adopted a more positive approach to Katie's problems, rather than emphasizing her misbehaviors. She suggested that Jackie consult with the school behavioral specialist for ideas that would focus on the positive. Jackie explained why she doubted that such a behavioral plan would work, given Katie's significant difficulty tolerating the most basic "rewards" of fun and love. Mrs. Robinson became aware of the fact that she and Jackie really were not speaking the same language. Jackie was grateful when Katie's teacher changed the conversation to academics.

Katie continued to show the intensity of her rage at Jackie in every way imaginable. She was indiscriminate in her choice of time, place, and circumstance to unveil her hatred. She would be angry with whatever Jackie said or did, simply because she needed to be. The question that Allison posed was what did she actually need in her outrage. Rejection by Jackie? Proof of her own worthlessness? Matching rage from Jackie? Denial of her own despair? Confirmation of her expectations that the world would never meet her needs? That the world, namely Jackie, really didn't care? Allison thought that at times Katie was motivated by any or all of these factors. Jackie agreed.

Why then did she seem to appropriately engage Jackie at times? Why did she seem to be genuinely interested in something happening in the family that did not relate to her? Why did she seem to actually enjoy herself? Yes, these times lasted ten minutes, tops, but they still counted.

Without having the structure provided by school, Katie needed to have a fairly tight schedule at home if she was to function at all appropriately during the vacation week. Jackie planned some arts and crafts activities along with the usual chores. She also intended to get Katie out in the snow for a time every day although Katie would most certainly complain about being cold and quickly begin to whine about wanting to come inside.

Jackie decided after lunch to take Katie outside to build a snow horse in the back yard. After the usual grumbling, Katie did manage to find and put on both of her boots along with her snowsuit—not a small accomplishment. The snow was wet, heavy, and sticky—great to work with. In little time at all, they managed to roll together two large snowballs that would form the body of the horse. They struggled to raise a smaller ball on top of one of the large ones. This would somehow be fashioned into the neck and head. The tail would come last, if they could get it to stick to the other ball. Then they would shape the four legs and cut out an opening between the front and back legs. Surprisingly, Katie became involved with the activity and had little to complain about. After finally shaping it to their satisfaction, Katie backed up to look at it while Jackie began digging out the space under the body.

"It doesn't look like a horse!" Katie yelled.

"Sure it does!" Jackie hollered back. "You just have to use your imagination a bit."

"It looks like a big dog!" Katie yelled again and laughed.

"A big dog! What are you talking about?" Jackie smiled and got up and walked over to Katie.

"That's no dog!" Jackie said. They both continued to stare at it. "It's more like a bear!" They both laughed.

"No, it's a little elephant!" Katie said. They laughed even harder.

"I think it's a giant frog!" Katie continued to laugh.

"Katie, don't call our horse a frog! A dog or elephant is one thing, but not a frog!" Jackie teased.

"It's a goat!" Katie added as she howled.

"Katie, cut it out!" Jackie pretended annoyance at her descriptions of their work.

"It's a goat!" Katie repeated.

"You're asking for it!" Jackie took a handful of snow and threw it at Katie, hitting her on the chest with some of it going on her face. Jackie held her breath.

Katie screamed. This scream was different. It was permeated with laughter. Katie took snow into her hand and ran at Jackie. Jackie fell backward and Katie pushed the snow into her face. Jackie then screamed and grabbed Katie and they both rolled in the snow until they were wet with snow and sweat.

"Katie, why don't you sit on our 'goat' and you'll discover that it feels like a horse," Jackie finally said. They ran to their snow figure and Jackie lifted Katie up onto it. She then knelt down and continued to dig an opening under it.

Katie finally got into the spirit of their "horse." She pretended that she was riding it, holding on tight as she galloped "across the plain." Katie yelled to her horse and bounced on its back. Jackie dug further and further under the horse until she made a hole to the other side. She started to back out when Katie's final bounce broke the back of their horse and what felt like an elephant and Katie fell on top of the shocked Jackie. Katie was scared at the sudden fall and the sight of Jackie's legs sticking out of the snow under her. Jackie was frightened over Katie's fall, especially since she could not see her nor anything else until she dug her way out from under their fallen steed.

"Are you OK?" Jackie asked as she struggled from under the avalanche.

"I'm fine," Katie replied and sat motionless, not knowing what to do next.

Slowly, and then with increasing momentum, they both began to laugh again, totally taken over by their wild adventures in the snow. There was little to show for their hour of labor to build the white steed.

"Well, Katie, I guess our horse doesn't much look like anything now. But I think we must look like two soggy ducks," Jackie said while still reclining among the ruins.

"Two soggy ducks!" Katie repeated and laughed again. Then she added without thinking, "A mama duck and her baby. Stuck in the snow away from their nest."

"Well, Katie," Jackie said, taking that comment as casually as she could. "This mama duck and her baby had better get into their nest right away or they're going to get sick." Jackie got up and helped Katie to her feet.

As they walked toward the house they took one last look at their piles of snow.

"Katie," Jackie said, "now we can tell everyone that we made a beautiful horse and no one will ever know that it looked more like a goat."

Katie liked that idea. In the kitchen she told Diane about their beautiful horse that sadly collapsed. She looked at Jackie, smiled, and almost winked.

Jackie decided to give Katie a snack with hot chocolate and crackers. They both fussed about being cold and enjoying the warmth of the kitchen. Jackie wondered when Katie would do something to try to ruin the atmosphere. She had never spent so long with her when they both were having fun. The old record was about ten minutes. She was entering new territory. It could not last.

After the snack, Katie took her plate and cup to the sink. She turned to Jackie and asked, "Can I watch the movie *Aladdin* on TV now?"

Jackie knew this was the moment for the outburst. Katie had found a great reason to be angry and she just needed Jackie's cooperation.

"Not this afternoon, sweetie. I'd like you to sweep the kitchen floor and then you can play in the dining room while I do some paper work that I have to get done. I know you've had a lot of fun and it's hard to stop. Kinda sad that fun can't go on forever, isn't it? Oh well, *Aladdin* will be there some other day."

Jackie looked at Katie. She wasn't screaming or throwing herself on the floor. Neither did she reach for something to throw, nor try to run from the room. She just stood there. And she looked sad. Sad! She looked right into Jackie's eyes with nothing but sadness in her expression. Jackie did not know what to say. She patted her head and commented again about it being hard when fun stops.

"OK, Mom," Katie said quietly and walked to the closet to get the broom and dust pan. Jackie turned to the sink and almost dropped her cup. She forced herself to stay there, splashing in the water and trying to wash the dishes. She didn't want to do anything that would confuse the situation and interfere with whatever was going on inside Katie's head.

The rest of the day and evening was fairly uneventful. Katie complained a bit and tried to get Matthew upset with her. She went to bed without a fuss and seemed to enjoy Jackie reading to her and tucking her in.

As Jackie turned to leave her room, Katie asked, "Mom, can we make another horse tomorrow? I'd like everyone to see it and draw a picture of it."

"That sounds like a plan, Katie. I'd enjoy it too. We should have some time after lunch just like today."

"Good night, Mom."

"Good night, Katie Kiddo."

The next day the horse never got made. When Katie came down for breakfast she refused to eat the eggs, toast, and juice that Jackie gave her and she insisted on having pancakes. That disagreement led to her refusing to eat, refusing to wash herself and brush her teeth, refusing to "pick up" the downstairs rooms, refusing to sit and think about her choices and generally just being disagreeable, disrespectful, and a pain to be around. This led to Jackie holding her and Katie spitting at her. Katie's gloomy and cross attitude continued throughout the day.

"But why didn't you tell her how great it was that she was able to have fun with you and also that she was able to accept it when you told her 'no'?" Steven asked at the next therapy session after hearing about the snow horse.

"If I had," Jackie replied, "she never would have finished the day OK, and she probably wouldn't have another time like that for quite some time."

"But if she's not going to be praised for that, when will you praise her? How will she ever know that she's doing a good job?"

"Steven, you're assuming that if Jackie shows pleasure in what she did, Katie will be more likely to do it again," Allison said. "But that's not Katie. She's not going to be motivated to act that way because Jackie's getting something out of it. If Jackie is really pleased, Katie won't be able to see that this is benefiting her, not Jackie. She'll think that Jackie wants her to act that way for her own benefit, not for Katie's. She can't yet imagine that Jackie really is happy *for her*, and not for her own benefit. Finally, if she thinks that Jackie is pleased when she acts this way, she'll think that this is a new way to frustrate Jackie. She'll resist having fun with Jackie and instead be motivated to bug Jackie, without any focus on whether or not having fun with Jackie is of benefit to herself."

"I still don't see why it will hurt her progress if we just tell her that she's finally doing what we have wanted her to do for so long." Steven was not convinced.

"She's only going to do it when she wants to," Allison said. "She'll continue to do it, *if* she wants to. This is *her* experiment to decide if *she* wants a life based on attachment. Stating our preference for her, *at the time that she's trying it out*, will distract her from the inner feedback that I want her to notice. Namely: 'This is good.' 'I like this.' 'This isn't anything to be scared of.'"

"So when can she handle praise?" Steven asked.

"Praise is overrated as a way to raise kids generally," Allison said. "Praising kids has at least as many disadvantages to their development as advantages, if not more. Parents need to foster intrinsic motivation for the child to do what is in his long-term best interests. Intrinsic motivation is not based on external factors, whether they be rewards or personal evaluations that we call praise. Intrinsic motivation comes from parents loving their kid a lot, being good models about how to live, and communicating the need to learn to make choices and to live with the consequences of the choices that we make. Intrinsic motivation comes from feeling good inside over the consequences of one's own actions. It needs to be her judgment, not ours. Showing our kid how special she is and being interested in how she is learning to manage her life goes a lot further in fostering her development than making comments such as "good girl." I want her, and *only* her, to ever decide if she's a good person.

"Saying that she did a 'good job' is OK, but overdone, I believe," Allison continued. "Kids are often told that a hundred times a day. They know when it really is a good job and when it's routine or mediocre. When we use it too much they probably get the idea that we think they really are not very capable. And they cannot escape the feeling that we are always evaluating them. They need to feel that we enjoy and accept them most of the time and evaluate them only infrequently. Sure, give specific recognition for something that your kid is proud about. You are sharing her joy. You are affirming her inner experiences. You are loving her, not evaluating her. But don't think that your praise is what motivates and maintains a child's interests and accomplishments while traveling on his life's path."

"But Katie gets into trouble dozens of times each day," Steven said. "Aren't we evaluating her each time and doing it negatively? Shouldn't we balance it with dozens of positive evaluations, no matter how small they are?"

"When Katie is 'getting into trouble' dozens of times, we are not evaluating her those times," Allison said. "We are accepting her choice. We might be puzzled at her choice because it leads to a seemingly undesirable consequence, but we are not evaluating it. We might even say something like, 'Well, Katie, I hope that you'll be happy with your choice' or 'If you change your mind, you'll probably have another chance, tomorrow, or next week, or whenever. Maybe you do like this consequence, or maybe you'll like the other one. Oh, well, there are other days.' And we make those comments without sarcasm or an 'I know better than you' attitude. We do want her to choose what is best for her, and we will expect her to manage whatever consequence her choice brings her. If she becomes upset by the consequence, that's fine. We'll support her through her distress, but we will not eliminate the consequence."

"As usual," Steven said, "I hear you and might eventually come to agree with you. Right now, I need to give that some thought."

"Fine with me," Allison replied. "Well, it's time for me to get the kid again."

Once settled in Allison's lap on the couch, Katie demonstrated her usual curious and mildly playful attitude that suggested that she would probably be fairly receptive to Allison's interventions.

"Katie, your mom tells me that you and she made a beautiful snow horse. It must have been so sad when it broke and fell on her," Allison said innocently.

Katie looked at Jackie and smiled. "We really were *so* sad. Mom said that she had never made one so pretty," Katie said quietly before exploding in laughter.

"What's so funny?" Allison asked. "What are you two laughing about?"

"Oh nothing," Jackie said.

"Nothing!" Katie said and laughed some more.

"Something is not right here!" Allison exclaimed. "What really happened?"

"Nothing!" Katie yelled again. Then she looked at Jackie again.

"Tell me, Katie, or you're in trouble." Allison smiled.

"It's true!" She laughed.

"You asked for it!" Allison said as she tickled her and banged her head against the pillow. "Now tell me!"

"OK!" Katie yelled. "It was ugly and looked like a goat. Or a dog."

"Katie even said that it looked like a frog too!" Jackie added.

"We weren't sad when it broke. We laughed until I almost peed!" Katie shouted.

"So that's it. An ugly horse. And you almost peed in the snow. If you had peed, you probably would have told everyone that the ugly horse had done it!" Allison suggested.

They chatted some more about the great deal of snow that was falling on Maine that winter. Allison suggested that they make a snow dinosaur next. Jackie grumbled when she thanked her for the suggestion while Katie got excited about the idea.

"It will probably end up looking like a whale," Steven added.

After discussing a few more minor events of the week, Allison directed Katie's attention to her past. "Katie, we haven't talked much about Sally and Mike lately. You were hurt a lot when you lived with them in many ways. We need to talk about that part of your life more so that it doesn't hurt your life now so much."

"It doesn't hurt me," Katie said.

"I wish it didn't, sweetie," Allison said. "I think it does though. It makes it hard for you to live with your new family without having so many troubles. I think that Sally and Mike are still mixing you up inside and you don't know how to trust Jackie and Mark very well."

When Katie did not reply, Allison continued. "Today I'd like to make a play. You will be Katie and Jackie will be Jackie. But I am going to pretend to be Sally. I'll be guessing what Sally might say to you and your mom as if she were here and I'll say those things. You pretend that I'm Sally and say whatever you want to me. OK?"

Katie looked at Jackie and then nodded.

"Your mom, Jackie, will be sitting next to you on the couch. I'll leave the room and when I come back, I'll be pretending that I'm Sally. I'll sit in that chair and begin to talk with you both. Remember, the things that I say are not what I think or feel, but what I am guessing that Sally might think or feel because of how she treated you. If it gets too hard for you, let us know and we'll stop."

Allison waited for Katie to ask questions. When none came, she added, "If you can't think of something to say, Jackie will whisper something into your ear and you can say that. Jackie's job will be to help you to feel safe and to give you things to say if you get stuck. OK?"

"Yeah," Katie said, almost looking excited, but showing anxiety too. Allison got up and left the room. Jackie sat on the couch next to Katie with her arm around her. Jackie asked her if there were things that she wanted to say to Sally. Katie couldn't think of anything so Jackie gave a few suggestions. Katie added another and they sat and waited for Allison's return.

There was a knock on the door and Allison entered. Katie laughed when she saw her. She was wearing a long dark coat, and had a scarf over her hair. Katie had never seen those clothes before. Allison also held a cigarette in her hand. She had been told that Sally smoked a lot.

Katie laughed and yelled, "You don't look like Sally!"

Allison ignored what she said and then spoke to her, more rapidly than she usually spoke and with a higher pitch to her voice. "Hello, Katie, I haven't seen you in a long time. How are you doing?"

"OK," Katie replied, still laughing.

"Who is that lady, Katie? You living with her?"

"Yeah, she's my mom, Jackie," Katie replied with a smile.

"She's not your mom!" 'Sally' yelled. "I'm your mom and you only have one, so don't you call her Mom!"

"She's my mom now," Katie said, no longer smiling.

"She is *not* your mom, I said," 'Sally' yelled. "So call her Jackie!"

"I'll call her Mom if I want to," Katie said.

"Well, you're still the brat that you where when you lived with me," 'Sally' said. "I can see that they have not helped you any!"

"I'm not a brat!" Katie said, "You're a brat!"

"Don't talk to me that way, little girl!" 'Sally' yelled. Then she turned to Jackie and said in a grouchy tone, "Is she bad most of the time like she was with me?"

"Katie is not a bad girl, Sally," Jackie said firmly. "Sometimes she might make a poor choice about something, but she is *not* bad!"

"I don't believe you!" 'Sally' said. "You probably spoil her and don't make her mind! No wonder she hasn't changed."

"You don't have to believe me, Sally," Jackie said, "But I'm telling the truth. Katie is a good kid, a special kid. And I don't spoil her. I love her and teach her how to live a good life in a good home."

"Yeah, right," 'Sally' said with annoyance. "And you probably blame me for her problems too, don't you?"

"I don't blame you, Sally, but I know that you and Mike did not raise her the way she needed to be raised. Whatever your reasons, you didn't love her in ways that she needed to be loved when she was a baby and little girl."

"Right, you know everything," 'Sally' said loudly. "I was a better mother for her than you are!"

"You were not!" Katie yelled. "Jackie is a good mom! She never hits me and calls me names like you did. And you didn't care when Mike hit me hard. She'd never let anyone hurt me!"

"Shut up, kid, I wasn't talking to you!" 'Sally' said.

"I will not shut up. You said something mean to my mom!" Katie yelled.

"Why did I bother coming to see you? You're bad and I'm wasting my time!" 'Sally' said with disgust.

"You were bad, not me!" Katie yelled. "You never held me or played with me. You always told me to go to my room. You didn't want to be with me! And you slapped me just because I dropped something!"

"You don't remember how I raised you," 'Sally' said. "You're just saying what other people told you and they're lying."

"I do remember!" Katie said forcefully. "I know you did those things to me. I don't forget how mad you were at me. You never wanted me with you!"

"I'm wasting my time as long as you're living with this lady who is lying to you about me! If I got you home again you'd start acting better or I'd know the reason why," 'Sally' said.

"I'm not living with you again!" Katie yelled.

"Oh, yeah, you're not the boss!" 'Sally' yelled. "I think I might just take you with me now!"

Katie leaned closer to Jackie and Jackie embraced her more tightly. "I'm not going with you! I'm staying with my new mom!"

"That's what you think, kid!" 'Sally' yelled as she stood up and moved toward the couch. She reached for Katie's ankle. Just as she was about to touch it, Katie pulled her foot back up onto the couch.

"Don't you touch her!" Jackie yelled.

"Don't touch me!" Katie joined in.

"Come on, Katie, you're coming with me!" 'Sally' yelled.

"No she's not, Sally. It's time for you to go!" Jackie said firmly.

"Leave!" Katie yelled.

"I don't have to do what you say!" 'Sally' said.

"We're both telling you, Sally, it's time for you to go now!" Jackie said again.

"Go!" Katie said and pointed toward the door.

'Sally' turned toward the door, opened it quickly, and slammed it behind her.

There was silence in the office. Katie and Jackie remained in a tight embrace. Katie was breathing heavily. She was clearly upset.

"You sure didn't need much help from me, Katie," Jackie said quietly. "How do you feel about it?"

"I feel good. I told her that she was a bad mom, I wasn't a bad baby. How can a baby be bad?" Katie said.

"That's right, kiddo," Jackie said. "You told her the truth!"

"She said that she was a better mom than you are!" Katie said, almost in surprise at the idea. "I told her that you were a better mom!"

"I'm glad that you think and feel that way, sweetie!" Jackie said.

"I told her that I wasn't bad!" Katie said, as if surprised at herself.

"Yes, you did, Katie, yes, you did!" Jackie hugged her even tighter. They were quiet for awhile. Then Jackie added, "That was hard work! I think that we both did a good job. Do you agree?"

"Yeah," Katie said slowly and quietly. They continued their embrace for a few minutes in silence.

Allison then entered, no longer wearing the coat and scarf. She sat in her usual chair and talked as if she had not been present. "Wow, you two look like you've been through a lot. How did it go?"

"I told her that I wasn't bad!" Katie exclaimed. "She said that I was a brat and I was bad and I said that she was a bad mom and I was not a bad baby."

"You did! It sounds like you really were able to tell her what you're learning about yourself and your past, Katie. I'll bet that feels great for you!" Allison said.

"Yeah! And she said that Jackie is a bad mom and that she was a better mom! And I told her that Jackie was the better mom, not her! And she got mad at me!" Katie spoke rapidly, talking as if Allison really did not know what had been said. She then continued, "And she tried to make me go with her! But I wouldn't let her take me! I held onto Mom and we told her to leave!"

"Wow, you two really went through a lot and it sounds like you really handled it well!" Allison said. "What do you think, Jackie?"

"We sure did, Allison. But we had to work really hard. It was scary the way that she yelled at us and said mean things about us. We held each other tight and that probably helped us to tell her that she was wrong in what she said!" Jackie said with satisfaction.

"Yeah!" Katie said. "We told her that she was wrong!"

"I like the work you two did!" Allison said. "What do you think, Steven? You heard them and 'Sally.'"

"It was something, Allison," Steven said. "It was a little scary, and Sally said some mean things. She also didn't tell the truth about how she and Mike raised Katie. I was glad when Katie told her that she *was* telling the truth. I also was glad that Katie told her that Jackie was a good mom!"

"I am too," Allison added, "I sometimes have thought that Katie might have trouble telling the difference between Sally and Jackie. But it sounds like she really is learning to see the differences real well."

All four of them smiled and sat quietly for a few moments. Jackie and Katie were still hugging each other.

"I guess that there's not much more to say," Allison said. "Let's stop now."

When Jackie and Katie left, Steven stayed a moment to talk with Allison. "That was powerful, Allison. For a while I thought that it was going to be too much for Katie."

"Yes, Steven, it was hard for her. I was watching her closely and she seemed to be managing it well, though. If it had seemed to be too much to her I would have reduced the intensity or even stopped. She seemed almost driven to respond to 'Sally' and I sensed that she was doing what she needed to do."

"Is that enough or will you have to be 'Sally' again?" Steven asked.

"Well, that depends on a lot of things about Katie's functioning in the weeks ahead. Most likely though we will at least do it once again, and this time try to elicit Katie's sense of loss over Sally's abandonment of her. Sally most certainly was nurturing, caring, and responsive to Katie sometimes. I need to give Katie the opportunity to be aware of that and to feel sad, if she is able, over the fact that Sally was not able to be a better mom for her. If she can do that she might be able to accept and integrate the parts of herself that are sad, scared, and vulnerable—just as she was when she was an infant and toddler."

"If she can do that," Steven said, "I guess we'll be home free."

"If she can do that," Allison added, "I guess Katie will have a decent chance to begin to learn what a home can really feel like."

Jackie's Journal:

2/28/95. Katie seemed more withdrawn today. I suggested that she still might be thinking about "Sally" from Allison's session yesterday. She would have none of that. At school Katie apparently managed to get a toy reward for having a good day. She immediately threw it at another girl who was simply looking at her. When she was corrected for that she looked at Mrs. Robinson, stepped on the toy, and smiled. I probably shouldn't feel pleased with that, but I had a hard time not smiling when I read the note. Maybe they will gradually begin to understand Katie. Bedtime went well. She accepted my playing "eeny meeny miny mo" with her ten toes and she giggled when I was being funny. She got a few hugs too.

3/1/95. Katie seems to have found a new source of pleasure. Before dinner I gave her markers to draw with at the table while I prepared the meal. I looked away for a moment. She had stepped on the felt tip of two markers lying on the floor. What a mess! And she looked at me and smiled! I guess it was something that she just had to find out for herself. It had rattled Mrs. Robinson, would it work on me? Well, not really. I was sad that she now had no markers to draw with since she liked them so. She got a bucket with soap and water to clean up the floor. Of course she was slow, thinking that she would be saved by dinner. Wrong! The rest of us ate at the dining room table while she continued her solitary cleaning. The teenagers were extra hungry and had extras. When Katie finally finished there was nothing left for her. I gave her a peanut butter and banana sandwich, which did not impress her. Oh well! Bedtime went well. She even enjoyed our feeding each other slices of banana on tooth picks. After her dinner, I wasn't sure how that would go over, but the bananas were getting old and I took the chance. I rocked her a bit too.

3/4/95. Katie actually did her chores this morning in an hour. Usually it takes her two or three on Saturday mornings. I found out why. She and Diane went outside in the middle of the snow storm. To me, at this time of year, there is no snow that is good snow. To them, it was an opportunity to be kids. Imagine that. Katie actually choosing to be a kid. Diane seems to feel that she has permission to act younger and silly when she is playing with Katie. Katie doesn't mind. So they both were being silly and wild in the storm. Looking at them, who would know what a monumental task Katie was performing in front of my eyes. She was having fun. Really having fun! Maybe Katie is teaching us the value of 'snow therapy.' If so, I might move to northern Alaska. Sure enough, when she came in she left her wet snow suit on the kitchen floor. And she ordered me to make them some hot chocolate. I had to hold her a bit before she would sit. She had to sit for a while before she picked up her snow suit and cleaned up the puddle on the floor. She got no hot chocolate, but I offered her a choice of warm or cold water. She said that I ruined her day. To her, I seem to make a habit of that. At bedtime we played "Pop goes the weasel." Each of her stuffed animals had a turn popping up from under the covers and in doing so knocking most of the other animals off the bed. Soft circles on her face helped her to sleep.

3/5/95. Church, as usual, did not impress Katie. She finds the entire service quite boring. Since, when she is noisy during the service, she spends a fair amount of time later in the day being quiet to make up for the "thinking time" that she missed, she generally now chooses to have her "thinking time" at church to get it over with. Although today after lunch she sat with Mark and they looked at the Children's Bible together. She seems to like the Old Testament stories better than the New Testament. I have noticed that by late Sunday afternoon Katie tends to be quite irritable and restless. Maybe spending the weekend with a fairly relaxed, friendly, and active family is hard on her. She needs school to get a break from the mental stress of family life. And summer is only about 15 weeks away! Bedtime, as usual, was our main time for some enjoyment. It's as if she calls a truce during our special time each night. The rest of the day—forget it.

3/10/95. Katie is furious that her teacher made her write an apology for breaking Erica's lunch box handle. She says that she did not do it and her teacher would not believe her! Imagine that! She says that her friend Sandy really did it but lied and said that she had done it! She apparently had to be restrained by Mrs. Robinson. Oh well. The fruits of a lifetime of lying. Being blamed for something that you did not do. I told her that she could solve the problem easily by starting to tell the truth. She looked at me like I needed brain surgery. I suggested that if she ever changes her mind I might be available to help her to practice her truth-telling. In the meantime, she was on her own among the hazards of being falsely accused.

3/11/95. What a wild Saturday. Katie was horrible when she awoke. By 10 A.M. she was friendly and cooperative. At lunch she had to be sent from the table. By 2 P.M. she was doing everything I told her to do, and doing it right the first time. By 5 P.M. she was outrageous with John and not much better with me when I interceded, if only to save her life. At bedtime she was loving and laughing and just a joy to be near. Why am I going crazy?

3/12/95. Today was a dream. She was cooperative in church, helpful at lunch, a jolly companion while we explored the winter woods, and the same loving daughter that I saw last night, at bedtime. What does this mean? She must be setting me up prior to springing on me.

3/19/95. The whole week has gone well. Sure she has had her troubles, but she is managing her consequences OK and she is actually fun to be around. Maybe something is starting to sink in. Maybe Allison is right though when she says, "Trust nothing until you have seen it for 3 months." We'll see.

COMMENTARY

Katie had no idea what was happening deep within her brain. Actually none of us really do. Were connections between the 'old brain' and the 'new brain' that should have been developing during the first two years of her life now sprouting at the age of 7? Was she beginning to notice, and experience, the pleasure of reciprocal smiles and expressions? Was she starting to experience comfort, excitement, affection, and fun from being held, touched, grabbed and at times, swung in a blanket by Jackie and Mark? Was she noticing the pleasure and security that came from reconnecting to her mom after a conflict? How and when did she first notice that others have feelings? She seemed to be worried when Whimsy did not get up one morning and Jackie took him to the vet. Was she feeling empathy? For Whimsy? For Jackie?

Katie was beginning to notice the interpersonal world of the Keller home. And she was a part of it. The other family members were not simply living objects to manipulate, deceive, intimidate, or attack. Jackie did not talk with her, listen to her, feed her, comb her hair, and giggle or snuggle with her at night because she had to. Steven, Allison, Mark, and Katie herself did not make Jackie do those things. Jackie wanted to. Why? Now that was a question that still stumped Katie. It had never occurred to her that anyone would take pleasure in being with her, playing with her, and helping her. Jackie did. Why?

The questions were appearing and her mind was struggling with them. Katie tried to avoid them. Hence, her roller coaster ride of January, February, and March. If she could manage to avoid those questions, she could preserve the map of her world that she had formed with Sally and Mike. She could base her life on charm and rage, excuses and blaming others, and above all, controlling everything in order to gratify her individual needs. These questions disrupted her first assumptions, which were the fruits of her first efforts to make sense of her life. Jackie and Allison constantly raised these questions and it was increasingly hard to avoid them. Within and without, Katie was in turmoil.

The pyschodrama in which Allison played the role of Katie's birth mother, Sally, proved to assist Katie in her efforts to redefine herself and her respective relationships with both Sally and Jackie. Using pyschodrama in this way is a very intense experience that can facilitate a great deal of reorganization of a child's early working models of self and others. Allison chose not to employ psychodrama in Katie's therapy until she had worked with her for a number of months. She wanted to increase that probability that Katie would be able to assert herself, contrast Sally with Jackie, and rely on Jackie for comfort. In the early stages of therapy, Allison focused mostly on Katie's relationships with both Allison and Jackie. She gradually focused more on Katie's past relationships with Mike and Sally, thinking that she would be more able to reexperience those past relationships more fully, within the context of quite different new relationships.

Allison employed psychodrama while being very receptive to Katie's emotional response to the activity. She wanted to ensure that Katie could integrate the intense affective/sensory/cognitive

experience, rather than be overwhelmed with anxiety and disso-
ciating. Taking her cues from Katie, she determined if 'Sally' should
be verbally abusive of Katie or Jackie, if she should acknowledge
the past abuse and neglect or deny it, and if she should threaten to
take Katie from Jackie.

Allison indicated to Steven that she would have at least one
more psychodrama involving Sally, in which she would give Katie
an opportunity to experience sadness over Sally's failure to nur-
ture her and her eventual abandonment of her. In such a session,
'Sally' would acknowledge her own failings, express sorrow for not
having been a better mother for her, speak of how special Katie
was, and give her blessing for Katie's relationship with Jackie and
her future progress. She would make it clear that she did not have
the ability to raise Katie the way that she needed to be raised and
she would encourage Katie to learn to love her new mother.

Frequently professionals question the wisdom of facilitating an
attachment between a child and her foster parent when she will
be moving into an adoptive home sometime in the future. But there
really is no better option. With unattached children, it is only
through beginning to relate easily with one's caregivers that they
are able to begin to form an integrated, valued, sense of self. It is
only through participating in countless affective attunement experiences with Jackie that Katie can ever begin to understand that
relating to a parent is a source of pleasure. Finally, it is within the
safety of attunement that Katie will someday be able to integrate
and learn from shame experiences and become reattuned with
Jackie fairly quickly.

If Katie is able to form a secure attachment with Jackie, and to
a lesser extent with Allison, she will not forget how. When it is time
to leave, she will grieve, but she will be able to begin to form a
similar attachment to her adoptive parents. She can transfer the
attachment because Jackie would have become a part of herself.
Now, Katie's self would have a sense of worth and would enjoy
reciprocal relationships with others. Katie would have discovered
empathy and trust, and she would anticipate that she would be
loved and treasured.

When infants and toddlers are engaged in affective attunement experiences with their parents, they are able to experience
and integrate the positive feelings of interest/excitement and joy/

enjoyment. They are not able to generate and maintain these plea-surable inner states alone. They *need to be having* the affective attunement experiences in order *to be experiencing* the inner states of interest and joy. (This is made very clear in Allan Schore's [1994] comprehensive work, *Affect Regulation and the Origin of the Self*.) Katie was beginning to experience interest and joy, while engaged with Jackie during "mom-time" or during other brief in-teractions during the day. But she could not maintain those plea-surable states alone! She has not yet internalized Jackie, just as an infant or toddler has not yet internalized her parents. She needs the experience of affect attunement in order to have the gener-alized inner pleasurable feeling state. When Jackie is not attuned with her, the inner pleasure evaporates. This truth is crucial in our attempts to initiate attachment in these alone, and full-of-shame children. Katie will not be able to maintain a pleasurable inner state outside of Jackie's psychological and physical pres-ence. Through experiencing such presence and its associated inner state over and over again, eventually we can hope that she will be able to internalize Jackie's presence, and be able to main-tain the state when alone. She then will have an integrated and authentic developing *self*, just as do so many healthy 3-year-old children.

5

Breaking
Through

DISTRICT COURT

When Dr. Allison Kaplan arrived at the Augusta District Court in the afternoon of March 18, 1995, she greeted Steven Fields in the hallway and he escorted her to a meeting room where she met Robert Craven, the Assistant Attorney General who presented the Children's Services cases before the court in Augusta. She shook Robert's hand and sat to discuss his line of questioning and what she might anticipate from the questioning of Rachel Nutting, the attorney for Sally Thomas. Robert assured Allison that Judge Paul Caldwell was a reasonable man who truly tried to determine what was best for the child within the limits of the law.

Robert Craven was arguing before the court that it was in the best interests of Katie Harrison to have the rights of her parents, Sally Thomas and Mike Harrison, terminated, so that she could be provided with another permanent home. To do so successfully, Robert needed to convince the court that Mr. Harrison and Ms. Thomas either were not motivated or did not have the ability to provide adequate care for Katie in a time period that would meet her needs. He wanted Allison to tell the court her professional opinion as to what Katie's needs were. Allison would need to address whether foster care or adoption would best meet her needs. She also would have to address whether it would be damaging for Katie to wait another few years in foster care if that amount of time were necessary before one or both of her parents could begin caring for her. Allison was the fourth witness for the Department of Human Services. That morning Steven had given the court an overview of Katie's life since she entered protective custody and he had summarized the services provided to Sally Thomas and Mike Harrison. After Steven, Peter Jacobs, Ph.D. testified as to his findings when he provided psychological evaluations of both Mike Harrison and Sally Thomas. He had testified that neither parent had acknowledged the seriousness of the abuse of Katie. Nor had they accepted responsibility for it or demonstrated remorse. Mike expressed much hostility toward the Department of Human Services for interfering with his rights to raise his child. Sally was less angry and she expressed a desire to do whatever she needed to do to reunite with Katie. However, she minimized her role in Katie's abuse, and she did not see how she had failed to protect Katie from Mike's abuse. Dr. Jacobs had evaluated Sally in January, 1993, and again in October, 1994. He did not observe any significant differences in her degree of accepting responsibility for her actions and in her understanding of Katie's needs from the first to the second evaluation. This lack of change was evident in spite of the fact that she had attended two parenting courses and had participated in both individual and group counseling. Her participation in counseling was sporadic. She would attend more regularly only prior to a court hearing. Because of the missed appointments, her first two counselors refused to continue to provide treatment. Her third counselor had indicated that Sally seemed to love Katie, but had a hard time committing to reunification because of her relationship with Mike. Mike had completely refused any treatment. When it became evident that Sally could not expect to have her daughter returned as long as she remained with Mike, she separated from him, but continued to see him regularly. Dr. Jacobs did not believe that the court could realistically expect Sally to be able to raise Katie safely unless she began to fully accept responsibility for her failings with her, participated in therapy in a productive manner, and, after having shown significant progress, attended joint sessions with Katie in which she could win back her trust. He thought that entire sequence would take a minimum of two additional years, given her lack of progress over the past two-and-a-half years. Rachel Nutting, Sally's attorney, made it clear that Dr. Jacobs had not seen Sally in the past five months and did not know if she had made significant progress since his last evaluation. She also stressed that Sally was ready to visit with Katie, but was not being allowed to by DHS. Finally, she indicated that Sally had made it clear that she would separate from Mike if necessary in order to win custody of her daughter. Attorney Nutting suggested to Dr. Jacobs that such willingness to even leave the man she loved for her daughter did prove her commitment to Katie.

After Dr. Jacobs, Marjorie Taylor, Sally's current counselor, indicated that she had only seen her client for four months and that she was still building a therapeutic relationship with her. Sally attended most of the sessions but had two appointments that she had forgotten. Ms. Taylor indicated that Sally had not accepted responsibility for hurting Katie and had only expressed sorrow for what Mike had done to her. Ms. Taylor thought that Sally might be able to more fully acknowledge her own responsibilities for Katie's experiences of abuse and neglect once she developed a higher degree of trust for Ms. Taylor. She agreed with Dr. Jacobs that the process would take at least two years and she was unsure about the likelihood of success. She was willing to continue to work with Sally to try to achieve that goal.

When Allison took the stand she had her usual anxiety and doubts. Had she prepared as much as she needed to do? Would she be able to present her opinion of Katie's needs in a way that was thorough and believable? She worried that if she made a mistake in her efforts to make Katie's psychological needs very clear, then the court might come to a decision that she feared would truly hurt her. Making a mistake in court could be as damaging to Katie as making a mistake in therapy.

After first establishing her professional credentials and involvement with Katie, Attorney Craven stated, "Dr. Kaplan, would you tell the court your diagnosis of Katie."

"Katie demonstrates symptoms consistent with a Reactive Attachment Disorder. These symptoms include very vigilant and, at best, highly ambivalent relationships with her primary caregivers. She resists comforting, affection, and experiences of mutual enjoyment. She is extremely oppositional to her caregivers and she has consistently shown indifference to whether or not she is staying in a particular home. Her main goals in life are to be in control of anyone around her and have people give her things and do things for her. She has little awareness of parental love, and most often either resists it or is indifferent to it."

"Dr. Kaplan, what is the cause of Reactive Attachment Disorder?" Mr. Craven asked.

"At this time the consensus is that this disorder is primarily caused by neglect, both physical and emotional, as well as multiple placements. After countless experiences of neglect and/or substitute caregivers, the child turns to herself for what she believes will keep her safe. Katie's diagnosis suggests that she experienced considerable neglect of her emotional and possibly physical needs prior to her ever experiencing the abuse that led to protective custody. Because of that neglect, she lost trust in her caregivers and no longer anticipates or strives to love and be loved."

"What treatment does Katie need in order to be able to successfully recover from that disorder?" Mr. Craven asked.

"Treatment needs to be very intensive and comprehensive. By that I mean that treatment has to engage her in a deeply emotional way, prevent her from using her pervasive need to control to avoid the issues, and then teach her, at the most basic, preverbal level, that learning to trust and love her caregiver is both safe and good for her, and also deeply enjoyable. Because of those goals, Katie's foster mother, Jackie Keller, is an active participant in therapy. Mrs. Keller also has special training and skills as Katie's parent to raise her at home in ways that facilitate her ability to form an attachment with Mrs. Keller. Providing Katie with a knowledgeable and committed parent is more important than the therapeutic session itself," Allison said carefully.

"What does Katie need now, Dr. Kaplan?"

"In my judgment," Allison said in a deliberate manner, "Katie needs to be able to live in a permanent home, where her developing ability to form an attachment can be fully responded to with parents who are deeply committed to raising her into adulthood. I am referring to an adoptive home. She is almost 8 years of age. I believe that she needs to be placed in that permanent home soon so that she will have the opportunity to form a secure attachment with her parents while she is still fairly young. If we wait until she is 11 or 12 we are likely to be greatly limiting our ability to provide her with appropriate permanent caregivers, as well as her ability to take advantage of good parents."

"Given the problems that she has, Dr. Kaplan, will she be able to be provided with such 'good parents' who could meet her needs?" Attorney Craven asked.

"She has made some progress and I am confident that over the next six to twelve months we will see significantly more. If the court were to determine that she were free to be adopted, it would take that amount of time before that home could be found. She is still 7 years of age. I believe that we have begun working with her when she was young enough to benefit. I do believe that she will be able to function well in a good adoptive home."

"Dr. Kaplan, you have read the reports on Katie's parents from Dr. Jacobs and Ms. Taylor, among others. Why do you not think that it would be in Katie's interests to continue to work to reunify her with one or both of her parents?" Mr. Craven asked.

"Katie has already been in care for over two-and-a-half years. I believe that was ample time for one of her parents to have demonstrated full awareness of what was done to her, acknowledged responsibility, and made significant progress in counseling to now be able to provide her with a good level of care. Based on what I have read, that has not occurred. I do not believe that it is in Katie's best interest to wait another two or more years to see if her mother or father will eventually be committed and able to adequately parent her in a way that meets her needs. Given the damage done to Katie, it will take an exceptional parent to raise her, not a poor one or even a mediocre one. I have not read anything that gives me confidence that either her mother or her father will have the ability to provide her with the level of parenting that she will require. Katie's opposition to being parented is so intense that if she is placed in a marginal home, the placement is certain to fail and her disorder will, in all likelihood, be permanent."

"Thank you, Dr. Kaplan." Mr. Craven stated.

"Your witness, Ms. Nutting," Judge Caldwell said.

"Dr. Kaplan," Attorney Nutting began forcefully, "how can you say that Sally Thomas cannot provide Katie with the parenting that she needs when you have never met Ms. Thomas?"

"I based my opinion on my knowledge of Katie and my review of the reports of other professionals who have been involved with Ms. Thomas. If those reports are in error, then I certainly would reconsider my recommendation," Allison replied.

"But Ms. Thomas is participating in counseling and she did attend the parenting courses, Dr. Kaplan. Who's to say that if we give her another year or two that she could not adequately raise her daughter?" Ms. Nutting continued.

"I certainly am not saying that it is impossible," Allison said. "I am simply saying that after two-and-a-half years I would have much greater confidence if we could see significantly more progress. I am also saying that we are placing Katie at great risk of never being able to have permanent, loving, and capable parents if we wait another two or three years for her parents to be able to raise her and if that does not happen. Overall, she will then have waited five years without a permanent home. Such a situation is damaging for any child, and especially for a child who already has significant difficulty being able to trust the adults in her life. Before taking such a risk, I am recommending that the Court see greater evidence that Katie's parents do have the motivation and ability to be her parents."

"Dr. Kaplan," Attorney Nutting began, seemingly changing her tactic, "if your diagnosis is right, it seems to me that we should leave Katie where she is now in foster care and allow her parents to visit her. If she has attachment disorder, I don't see how moving her again to an adoptive home would be beneficial to her."

"I agree that moving Katie to an adoptive home will be hard for her after she learns to form an attachment with her foster mother," Allison said slowly. "She most certainly will grieve the loss of her foster mother if she is attached to her. But that grief will be temporary and the advantages of living in a permanent home far outweigh the temporary disadvantages of grieving the loss of her foster mother. It would have been more advantageous for her to develop her first secure attachment with her permanent parents. But that was and is impossible, given the legal situation and her level of needs. We could not afford to wait until the court decided on permanency before encouraging her ability to attach. If we waited that long, Katie might never learn, both because of her increasing age, but also because of difficulty that we would have finding an adoptive family who would and could make such a commitment to a child with such significant problems."

"Dr. Kaplan, if you are worried about finding good parents who are willing to commit to Katie, don't you think that you should look at Ms. Thomas? This is Katie's mother and she has been working to get her back, even though you don't feel that she has worked hard enough. Why not consider Ms. Thomas, Dr. Kaplan?"

"I wish I could, Ms. Nutting," Allison replied. "I would have loved to have read that Mrs. Thomas truly understands and regrets the gravity of what she and Mr. Harrison have done to Katie. If I had confidence that she could soon raise her, I would love to be able to work hard with Katie to help her to begin to trust Ms. Thomas. However, if the Court does decide to try to have Katie returned to Ms. Thomas soon, I would be terrified of the effects on Katie. I have not read anything about Ms. Thomas that would indicate that she could provide Katie with what she needs from her."

"Not now, Dr. Kaplan," Ms. Nutting said, "but in another year or two she might be able to do so."

"I have read nothing that builds my confidence in that possibility," Allison said. "And because of that, I strongly urge the court not to make Katie wait any longer."

"That's all, Dr. Kaplan." Ms. Nutting said.

There was another five hours of testimony before the Court deliberated on the petition to terminate the parental rights of Sally Thomas and Mike Harrison. On April 9, 1995, Judge Caldwell issued an order that terminated all of their parental rights to their daughter, Katie.

COMMENTARY

The devastating effect of pervasive emotional neglect is only slowly entering into court hearings and influencing the subsequent decisions that are being made regarding the lives of these children. Sexual and severe physical abuse receive a much more consistent and adequate response by the legal system. Reactive attachment disorder is one of the most severe consequences of profound neglect, and its damaging effects on the development of children is increasingly being recognized. When a child is unable to trust even the best parents, the damage that has been done to his self and his capacity to experience nurturance and a reciprocal relationship is unmeasurable. Such a child, without significant, successful interventions, will not assume a secure place in our society.

The legal and the social service systems are still too often inadequately aware of the need to provide a child with a timely decision so that he is able to move into a permanent home quickly enough to resume his developmental progress. Many children wait for years without any resolution of their temporary status in foster care. Often their parents, who were responsible for their entering foster care, are not held to be responsible enough to commit to reuniting with their child as soon as possible. Often parents have frequent delays and then make only half-hearted attempts to resolve their significant problems. What the legal system must come to terms with is the significant damage that is being done to children while they wait, year after year, often moving from one foster home to the next, to the next.

SPRING, WHERE THE SUN SHINES

In late March, 1995, Katie was functioning the way many people in Maine do when they are ready for spring and it's still weeks away. She was irritable, testy, and engaging in considerable self-pity. The week or so of fairly agreeable functioning earlier in the month had long since passed. Whereas Mainers "muddle through," knowing that they will welcome each blade of grass when it finally appears toward the end of April, Katie had no such confidence in her future. It were as if she now sensed that engaging Jackie in ways that were mutually enjoyable might, in fact, be in her best interest. However, she had her own plans as to accomplishing that goal, which were not acceptable to her foster mother. She seemed to think that they would negotiate over what was appropriate or not in the family. She would "give a little" if Jackie would "give a little." In her mind, family life was a democracy with her vote having equal weight with Jackie's. When Jackie refused to cooperate on her terms, Katie decided to "get even." She would make Jackie's life more miserable as punishment for not being "fair." She would be more defiant, sneaky, grouchy, and, in general, not much fun to be around. In her mind, Jackie deserved such treatment.

Jackie probably should have seen this response coming after noticing that Katie's periods of cooperation and seemingly genuine contentment had become evident. The stress of integrating such experiences into her self-concept and her working model of relationships would be great. Katie was not likely to be able to accept these new features of her self and her life without turmoil and regression. But Jackie did not see it coming and she did not recognize it for five to ten days. As usual, she became aware of it only after noticing her own increased tension and irritability. She also noticed that she was disappointed in some of Katie's behaviors. She had begun to expect more from her and Katie's continuing opposition had left her frustrated. She also noticed that she was blaming

Katie for her own annoyances. "If only Katie would . . . !" were frequent thoughts that left her discontent.

She was becoming like Katie! This realization hit her toward the end of March when Katie missed the school bus. She was immediately upset and felt trapped. She did not want to be "stuck" with Katie all day, and at the same time she did not feel like driving her to school. She felt like making her walk the six miles to school, and felt annoyed that was not an option. As she fussed about the situation she glanced at Katie and noticed that she was sitting at the table as pleased as she could be. She had Jackie where she wanted her. Jackie was annoyed and upset and Katie had made her that way! Jackie left the room and paced around the living room, staring out the windows and talking to herself about her plight. The mud in the driveway seemed to represent her own state of mind.

"Well, Katie, you caught me again, you little turkey!" she said to herself. "You are good at getting me to feel as miserable as you do. When you are able to 'get' me, you probably even feel a little better for a few minutes. You gave your gloom to me! Well, kiddo, the fight is not over. I figured it out, so you're getting it back!"

Jackie came back to the kitchen and cheerfully said to Katie, "Sweetie, I'm sad that you missed your bus. I know how much you want to go to school. Don't worry! I'll drive you there. But I am going to have to set aside some of my chores to take the time to get you there. So, of course you can do them when you get home! That should work out fine for me." Jackie got her coat and keys and they headed for the car. Katie grumbled and said that she was not doing any of Jackie's chores. Jackie ignored her complaints and commented on how it was too bad one could not move from winter to spring without going through so much mud. "Oh well, I guess it helps to appreciate spring even more when it finally comes. And it will come!" Jackie said in harmony with her returning optimism.

With Jackie again centered on preserving her own emotional balance and also accepting Katie's anger, resistance, and regression, life in the Keller home returned to normal. Of course when one is living with a poorly attached child, it is obvious to all how relative the word *normal* is. At least one could say that Katie was not able to distribute her distress and keep the home in an uproar. Also, Jackie began to notice that the moments of genuine enjoyment and cooperation that Katie had been showing over the past three months were again returning. By being able to protect her own inner life and the emotional atmosphere of the family, Jackie was able to make it easier for Katie to again inch closer to a newer way of living. Much of the pain of her existence was staying within Katie, where it now needed to be. Only in that way would she be motivated to find a way of living with others that would truly change her life.

Jackie's Journal:

4/7/95. Katie got a phone call from a girl in her class named Sandy. And the kid has no major problems! Her mother wants Katie to come over and play tomorrow afternoon. I suggest that she come here instead. Sandy is coming from 1:00 to 3:00. Katie's off the wall. She sits and stays near me. Can't calm down. I suggest that she sit with blindfold on, as Gabe used to do once he had made some progress. She agrees and she immediately is calmer. This would not have worked unless she felt some trust in her surroundings. I sing and she joins in. Dinner OK and she enjoys bedtime game with dolls. Thanks me for letting Sandy come over. I suggest that she's simply ready for time with friend now.

4/8/95. Some success with Katie's first friend visit. She was so anxious, she tried so hard to "be good" with her friend in order to be liked. She was able to share and let Sandy decide what they would do part of the time. Katie entered her personal space a lot and she chattered a lot. Sandy was a little frustrated. No aggression—verbal or physical. Later in day has to be sent from table—first time in couple of weeks. Hard to calm at bedtime but not oppositional.

4/9/95. After church today Katie asked many questions about Easter. She seemed to have real emotional response to fact that Jesus would die for us, so we can live. Also troubled by Judas being so "mean." Sad for Mary. With Katie, such empathy for others is rarely so strong. Mark took Katie for walk in woods. Saw fox family with babies. Initially excited, then scared when mother fox saw them. Wanted to hold Mark's hand. Comes home with her riding on his shoulders. And she told me all about it! Seemed peaceful at bedtime.

4/10/95. Hard morning getting ready for school. Anger about clothing allowed to wear. Angry about breakfast. Empathy rejected. Comes home sad! Sandy did not play with her at recess. One of few times she showed that it mattered and was not mad about it. Accepts comforting. Able to help Diane clean up porch with good mood and following directions. Before bedtime sings lullabies to dolls that I sing to her. Then asks me to sing same.

4/11/95. Happy over playing with Sandy. Possibility of friendship new experience. Healthy anxiety about it. Insecure. Asks for Children's Bible to read about Easter. Reads for more than hour. Less chatter, more conversation. Bedtime singing—asks Diane to come in and share her time with me. First time.

4/12/95. After school very angry, no clue as to why. Refuses to stay in kitchen, stays by swing set. Finally comes in at dinner time and angry that she has to first do 10 minutes of homework before eating. Eats cold meal. Misses TV show—doesn't explode, seems sad. Quiet during activities before bedtime. Accepts empathy and comforting.

4/15/95. Anticipating Easter services, excited and anxious. Has new dress. My mom and brother and his family coming for dinner. Many questions about Easter traditions. Bedtime, actually worried that she "won't be able to handle" excitement of day. Realistic fear—first time expressed.

4/16/95. Easter very special to Katie. Very alert, polite, controlled. Not want to get dress dirty. Stays very close to me at church. Follows directions well before and after dinner. My brother sees her as much improved over how she was in January. Wants quiet talk at bedtime, no games. Discusses the summer. She does not want to go to school, wants to stay home "all the time."

4/17/95. Again, hard time Monday morning. Shows distress with anger at me. Rejects empathy. I surprise her by picking her up after school and taking her to playground in Waterville, with juice and cookies. She's perplexed, since she had some chores to do after school for her behavior in A.M. When she gets home, they've been done. I can see her wondering about it for some time. I get extra strong hugs at bedtime.

4/18/95. Therapy seemed to have an impact today. Allison has been working on differences between me and Sally for months. In her grown-up voice she told Allison that Sally and I are different, as if Allison didn't know that. On the way home she tells me that she was telling Allison the truth. Of course when I sent her from the table for screaming over having to wait, she hated me. At bedtime she told me that she lied; she does not hate me, she was just mad at me. I tell her that I believe her.

4/19/95. I took Katie to store with me for a few groceries. She stole some candy, which I discovered when we got in car. Back in to return it and apologize. She does as directed and seems more sad than angry afterward. Accepts no dessert after dinner. We blow bubbles outside after dinner. Summer is coming! Bedtime goes well.

On Saturday, April 29, 1995, Jackie kept Katie busy with various small chores and activities. She had extra time that afternoon and decided to take her for a walk into the woods to search for some signs of spring. That morning they had counted fourteen robins in the yard. By now Katie was quite willing to accept what Jackie told her to do. Jackie did not think that she would continue to be so cooperative if she were to allow her more freedom. She knew that Katie had come to rely on the well-defined and structured external routine provided by Jackie. Katie could not maintain her friendly and compliant behavior without her structure. A walk in the woods would be a variation, but would still provide Katie with Jackie's decision-making.

They set out on the old trail behind the shed. It led over a rise, through a cove of white and yellow birch trees, and down by a small pond that they always avoided in the summer when the mosquitoes were out. They began their search for early spring flowers, pushing through some old leaves near the shelter of trees on the south side of a small hill. Katie actually seemed interested in what Jackie was teaching her. They moved the leaves gently, alert to what lay among them. They found a small, fragile, yellow flower that Jackie identified for her. It was a trout lily, one of Jackie's favorites. Shortly after that, they found some deer tracks and a porcupine nest. Jackie was enjoying one of her favorite places to be and Katie seemed to share her sense of wonder and peace as they slowly made their way through the birch glen.

Eventually they stopped at another likely spot to search for flowers. Katie took a more active role this time. She seemed to want to find those magical yellow flowers that Jackie liked so well. In her excitement she bent over and roughly pushed some leaves aside. When she found nothing she became somewhat agitated and began kicking more leaves. Jackie saw her and told her to be more gentle or she would hurt whatever flower she might find. Katie seemed disappointed but complied and knelt down and began her search again. After a time she saw a flash of yellow and with glee, she pulled it up and carried it to Jackie.

"Look, Mom, a trout lily!" Katie shouted.

Jackie looked up to see Katie bringing the flower to her.

"Oh, Katie, those aren't for picking! Just for looking at and enjoying!" Jackie said.

Katie heard her disappointment and reacted as if she had been hit. Jackie saw her response and tried to reduce the impact of her words. "Thanks, sweetie, for showing me what you found. I know that you thought that I'd be happy that you picked it for me to see. Thanks, honey."

Katie did not respond to what she said. She threw down the flower and turned her back to Jackie.

"Honey, I should have told you not to pick them. You thought that I'd be glad and you didn't know that I just like to look at them." Jackie tried again to recapture their mood.

Katie walked a few feet further away and then began kicking the leaves. "I don't care!" She yelled. "I don't care! I don't care!"

Jackie got up and approached her. Katie ran down the trail. She was headed toward the house so Jackie did not worry so much. "Katie, stop and wait for me. I'm not angry with you. I want you to wait for me!" For Jackie, this was one of those sudden incidents when she had to intuitively decide how to respond. Should she chase her or continue to walk and call to her to stop? Or should she not let Katie upset her and simply continue her own exploration of the woods? She decided to casually walk back home, looking at her surroundings as she went. She saw Katie dart over the rise and she assumed that she would see her at home.

As she approached the edge of the woods she paused for a moment to glance around. She was pleased that she did since she caught a glimpse of Katie hiding behind a tree about twenty feet from the trail.

"Katie, come on out so we can walk home together," Jackie said easily.

When Katie did not respond, she turned toward home, knowing that Katie would follow on her own terms. Katie was somewhat frightened of the woods, so Jackie had confidence that she would not stay there long alone.

As she approached the back of the shed she heard Katie running up behind her. She smiled and turned to see Katie hurl a stone at her. She instinctively raised her arm and the stone glanced off the side of her wrist and hit her cheek. As she yelled "Katie!" she turned down and away in a defensive position. She felt another stone hit her leg and a third flew past her shoulder. She looked at Katie again and saw that she had no more stones to throw. She took three quick steps toward her and grabbed her arms.

"Katie, I will not allow you to hurt me! I am angry at what you did! You could have hurt me badly! In our family we do not hurt each other!"

"I don't care! I hate you! I hate you!" Katie screamed.

Jackie was startled at the rage that she saw in Katie's eyes and face. She could feel the hatred. "Sweetie, I don't hate you for hitting me with the stones. But I am angry and I am not going to let you do it."

"Let me go! You do so hate me! You hate me!" Katie screamed again and tears came down her face.

"I love you, Katie. I love you!" Jackie replied and pulled her to her.

Katie screamed again and struggled to get away. She pulled backward and down and Jackie lost her balance and they fell to the ground. Katie continued to scream and yell, "Let me go! Let me go! Let me go!"

Katie tried to kick and hit Jackie but her arms were pinned to her sides and her legs were too close to Jackie to be effective. She then tried to butt her with her head and scratch her arms. Jackie held tight and the two of them were now lying in the wet earth. Jackie was glad that there were no rocks under them or near Katie's hands.

"You're safe, sweetie. I'm mad at your hitting me with the stones, but I do love you. I'll hold you as long as you need me to," Jackie said calmly.

"You hate me!" Katie began saying again. There was less intensity to her voice now and her movements had less force.

"No Katie, I don't hate you. I was sad that you pulled up the flower, but I know that you did it for me. I simply had not told you that the flowers were for looking at. I don't hate you at all, and I can understand why you were upset that I wasn't happy when you brought me the flower," Jackie spoke quietly and Katie listened.

Jackie felt her begin to relax. She raised her arm and began wiping Katie's tears from her face. "Oh sweetie, you got angry. You're learning to be close with me and you did something that you thought that I would like, but I didn't. You hit me with a stone, but I'm OK. We'll deal with the stone throwing later."

Katie now looked at Jackie and saw some blood on her cheek where the stone hit her. "You're bleeding!" Katie screamed in terror. "You're bleeding! I hurt you!"

"It's only a small cut, sweetie. I'm OK," Jackie said and smiled.

Katie stared at the cut. "No! Don't hold me. Please! I'm bad! Don't love me! Don't love me!" Katie seemed to be terrified.

"Oh, Katie, you're not bad! I do love you and I'm going to keep loving you!"

"No, don't love me!" Katie remained in distress.

"Katie, Katie, Katie. Maybe you hate yourself now, but I don't," Jackie said tearfully. "I love you and I hope that someday you will learn to love you too." Jackie began to slowly rock back and forth in the mud and grass. Katie began crying harder and she leaned further into Jackie. She buried her face in Jackie's neck and her sobs shook them both. They both continued to cry.

Katie pulled herself back to look into Jackie's eyes. She stared for a second and then said from some land of despair. "It's too hard. It's too hard to learn to love. I can't do it. It's too hard."

Jackie stared at this child who was raised on fear and loneliness. She stared at her and realized that Katie was teaching her something that she must never forget. She could never know the depths of pain that this young child lived with. Jackie's tears and the pain in her throat made it hard to talk. She pulled her close again and whispered in her ear.

"I know it's hard, Katie. I know it's hard. I want you to keep trying. I want you to learn about love. It's worth it. I want you to know that!" Jackie said.

They rested for awhile. Jackie ran her hands through Katie's hair and gently smiled into her eyes. When they began to feel cold, they helped each other up and walked home with Jackie's arm around Katie.

"What happened to you two?" Diane said in surprise as they walked through the kitchen door. "Did you fall in the pond?"

"What makes you say that?" Jackie said with some surprise. "We simply went for a quiet walk in the woods."

"Yeah." Katie smiled and looked at Jackie. "We just looked at the trees and flowers." They both laughed.

"Why don't you take a shower first, Katie," Jackie said. "I think you got a little wetter than I did."

Katie walked off toward her bedroom, more lightly than usual.

The next day, Sunday, after church, Katie and Jackie finished their walk in the woods. Jackie was able to show Katie her second favorite early spring flower—an hepatica.

At therapy the following week Allison wanted to help Katie to integrate the important experience that she had with Jackie on Saturday. She was careful not to simply talk about it rationally since Katie would most likely use the words to minimize the emotional impact the experience had on her. If Allison was to help Katie benefit further from the experience she would have to facilitate Katie's ability to have the feelings again, though without the same level of intensity as she had while alone with Jackie.

After establishing a positive and rich emotional atmosphere, and exploring various lesser events and ideas, Allison turned Katie's attention to Saturday.

"I hear that you and Jackie spent some time rolling around in the mud over the weekend," Allison said casually.

For a moment, Katie wasn't sure what she meant. When she realized what Allison was referring to, she seemed confused. It seemed that she did not know what she felt. She both wanted to laugh and joke about it and also avoid the topic and what it might elicit. She cautiously went along with Allison's light mood. "We were covered with mud and it got real cold. We had to go in and I took a shower first."

"I was surprised that you two didn't wait until the summer when it would be warmer to roll in the mud. That's what pigs do." Allison smiled.

"We didn't want to get too hot, Allison," Jackie said. "And we wanted to see if spring mud would stick to our hair."

"Did it?" Allison asked.

"Yeah!" They both responded.

"And your walk started out so quietly and calm!" Allison said. "Who would have guessed how it would end up!"

Allison waited a moment. Katie would not be volunteering anything. Allison then asked Jackie to hold her. She hoped to re-create their experience in the session.

Allison continued, sitting in a chair close to them. "It sounds like you both had a lot of feelings on that walk. It seemed to be very hard for you both, and very special too."

"It was, Allison," Jackie said.

"Katie, I can tell that you're feeling kinda upset that I'm talking about this. Tell your mom what you're feeling now."

"I don't want to talk about it," Katie said quietly.

"I'll bet you don't, Katie." Allison said quietly too. "Now look at your mom and say it again louder."

"I don't want to talk about it!" Katie said much more forcefully.

Allison asked Jackie to talk with Katie about the incident.

"I can tell that you really don't want to talk about it . . . and feel those feelings again. . . . That was so hard, . . . so hard . . . for you," Jackie said. "You were so confused when you gave the flower to me and I was disappointed that you had picked it!" Jackie began to speak more loudly. "You thought, 'She doesn't want it! She's mad at me for picking it! . . . I can't do anything right! . . . I'm no good! I can never do anything right! . . . She hates me! . . . Well, I hate her too!' All those thoughts must have gone through your mind, Katie. And you felt so upset! You were so mixed up! And so mad! . . . And so sad that I wasn't happy with your flower! You hated yourself and you hated me!"

Jackie watched Katie as she spoke. Katie was now tense and she seemed disturbed. She did not want to have those feelings again. "Don't talk about it!" Katie screamed.

"You want me to shut up!" Jackie yelled back. "You don't want to feel as upset as you felt the other day. Tell me to shut up, Katie."

"Shut up!"

"Again!"

"Shut up!"

"Again, Katie!"

"Shut up!" Katie screamed.

"Oh, Katie," Jackie said much more softly, "I wish I didn't have to talk about what happened again. But it was so confusing to you . . . and so important . . . that I think we have to talk about it again." Jackie gave Katie a quick hug, but she did not respond.

"Katie, tell your mom, how hard it was for you," Allison said. "Say, 'Mom, it was very hard for me.'"

"Mom, it was very hard for me!" Katie said, looking at Jackie.

"I know it was, Katie," Jackie replied.

"Now say, 'Mom, I was very mad at you when you didn't like the flower!'"

"I was very mad at you when you didn't like the flower."

"I thought that I'd never please you!" Allison said.

"I thought that I'd never please you!"

"I thought that you were mean!"

"I thought that you were mean!"

"I thought that you didn't love me!"

"I thought that you didn't love me!"

"That made me really mad at you!"

"That made me really mad at you!"

"Now Katie, look at your mom and really scream at her. Say, 'I'm mad at you for not liking my flower'!"

"I'm mad at you for not liking my flower!"

"Scream again, Katie. Say, 'I'm mad at you for not liking me'!"

"I'm mad at you for not liking me!"

Katie began to cry. She tried to bury her head in Jackie's side. Jackie gently took her face and turned it until she was looking at her again.

"Katie, look at your mom and say it again, 'I'm mad at you for not liking me!'"

Katie continued to cry. She moaned as she said, "I'm mad at you for not liking me!"

"Now, Katie, tell your mom, 'I'm scared that you really don't love me!'"

"I'm scared that you really don't love me!"

"I'm scared that I'll never be good!"

"I'm scared that I'll never be good!"

"I think I'll always be bad!"
"I think I'll always be bad!"
"I can't believe that you really love me!"

Katie did not respond. Allison was about to repeat the directive when she could tell that Katie was struggling to speak, but was having trouble as she shook with tears and gasped for breath. Finally, she said, in desperation and despair, "I don't think . . . you . . . love . . . me." She burst into tears. Jackie rocked her and hummed quietly as Katie cried.

After a time, Katie became quieter and she and Jackie looked into each other's eyes. Jackie wiped her tears and smoothed out her hair. Jackie leaned over and whispered, "We can do this without mud too." Katie smiled and they embraced again.

"You two really know how to hug," Allison said as she smiled. "I can see now how hard it must have been for you both the other day."

After further silence, Allison quietly added, "Katie, when you both left the woods, you threw some rocks and hit your mom twice. Tell her that you *really* thought she hated you after you did that."

Katie complied and looked at Jackie and expressed her fear that she was certainly hated when she hit her with the rocks. She spoke quietly, with eye contact, and while still remaining relaxed in Jackie's arms.

"I thought you did, sweetie. I thought that when you hit me with those rocks you probably thought that I could never love you again because you were so bad. I grabbed you then, to keep us safe, but also to try to get through to you that you were very upset and I still loved you."

Katie smiled at Jackie and squeezed her arm. She seemed so peaceful.

"Katie, tell Jackie that you're starting to figure it out, but that this love stuff is hard!" Allison said.

"I'm figuring it out, but this love stuff is hard."

"What are you figuring out, Katie?" Jackie asked quietly.

Katie paused and stared at Jackie. She then looked away and looked back. Jackie and Allison were waiting and it seemed like they would wait forever.

"I'm figuring out that you love me," Katie finally said.

"I'm glad for you!" Jackie said, smiled, and hugged her again.

"OK you two," Allison said. "Let's get back to work and save that loving stuff for the rest of the week."

"I'm going to love this kid in therapy too, Allison," Jackie said and they laughed.

"OK, if you have to," Allison said, "but I still need to find out what kind of consequence Katie got for hitting you with the rocks."

"Should I tell her or do you want to?" Jackie asked Katie.

Katie wanted to smile but seemed to be a little embarrassed. Finally she said, "I had to clean all the mud out of our clothes with a brush in the sink. And then wash them in the washing machine." Katie then smiled.

"She also had to help me to put a band aid on my cheek," Jackie added and they both smiled again.

"Well, folks, I guess we can stop for the day. Don't get lost in the woods!"

During May, 1995, Katie continued to explore her relationship with Jackie as if it were a completely new experience. And it was. She began to notice Jackie as a separate person. Jackie would find Katie staring at her frequently throughout the day. Katie would look away when Jackie smiled. When Jackie asked her to get something, Katie would comply immediately. Katie seemed to want to please her with a compulsion that almost rivaled her earlier efforts to defy her.

Katie's rage at her life did not simply disappear. She still exploded, but she did so less frequently and with less intensity. What was increasing was the rage that she directed toward herself. She began hitting herself in the face or banging her head against the wall. She did so when Jackie corrected her or when she was not allowed to do something. She seemed to want to limit her rage at Jackie and was willing to hit herself if necessary to do so.

"Well, Katie," Jackie said after school on May 16, when she noticed Katie smacking her face. This occurred right after she was told that she could not ride her bike. "You seem to be really angry with yourself. I'm sorry that you want to hit yourself when you get mad at me." Jackie walked away. If she tried to "save" Katie from her rage, she feared that these outbursts might simply increase. Katie would have found a way to frustrate Jackie that she'd be tempted to use. Jackie wanted her to see that she was the only one being hurt by her behaviors. Jackie was sad for her but Katie was not hurting Jackie.

"Katie," Jackie said the next day when she noticed Katie's self-abusive behavior following a fairly minor frustration. "Why do you think you hit yourself so much when you get upset?"

Katie stared at her for a moment before responding. "I just feel the pain . . . and then . . . it goes away."

Jackie leaned over and hugged her. "You don't have to feel that kind of pain anymore, Katie."

"It's not bad. It doesn't last long. And I feel good when it stops," Katie said without any emotion. If anything, she was confused over Jackie's concern.

"But you really don't have to feel that pain at all, Katie. If you don't hit yourself, everything will still be the same. You don't have to punish yourself for me to forgive whatever you did."

"No!" Katie responded forcefully. "I have to hurt myself. It's the only way I can feel good again. But don't worry, Mom. It's OK. It doesn't hurt much and then I feel better."

"Oh, Katie," Jackie said as she continued hugging her. "I'm sad that you think and feel that, but I can understand. It's so hard for you to feel good about yourself. My love is helping but I guess it will take longer."

"No! You don't understand!" Katie yelled. "I have to do this!"

"I do know, Katie," Jackie said. "You think that you don't deserve any better."

Katie jumped up from her chair and as she did so, it fell over backward. She looked at the fallen chair and then exploded. She ran to the back door and before Jackie could stop her, she was on the porch and with one swing of her arm, knocked over the flower pot. Jackie did not hear it hit the ground because of Katie's scream. A moment after the geraniums splattered on the ground, Katie was there, kneeling among the pieces of clay, the potting soil, the roots, stems, and petals.

"No! No! No!" Katie screamed. "You made me do it! Why don't you let me hit myself? Why don't you?" Her hands were in the dirt as she seemed to be frantically trying to put it all back together again.

"I'm not stopping you, Katie!" Jackie said. "I simply want you to know that you don't have to do it anymore."

"I do! I do! You still don't understand!" Katie looked up at Jackie through her tears. "If I don't hurt myself. . . . If I don't . . . hurt . . . myself. I'll hurt . . . you . . . or your flowers!" Katie burst into tears. She cried harder than Jackie had ever seen her cry before. She held a red geranium to her face. Jackie knelt in front of her and pulled her into her arms.

"I don't want to hurt your flowers!" Katie continued to sob.

"I know, Katie. Katie, I know," Jackie said quietly as she gently rocked back and forth.

"Why do you want me to hurt your flowers?" Katie asked from within Jackie's arms.

"I don't, Katie, I don't," Jackie replied. "And I don't want you to hurt yourself either. My flowers are special to me, but not as special as you are. That's what I want you to know someday. I also hope that you can discover that you don't have to hurt either me or you when you're mad. Your mad feelings do not have to be the boss of you, Katie. They don't have to be connected to hitting and hurting. Feeling mad is simply a feeling and can be a signal for you that something's bothering you. Try talking with me or Mark when you're feeling mad. Or finding ways to think about something else. Or write about it. Or growl in your room. You don't have to hurt me or you, sweetie, mad or not."

"I sort of understand—but I don't understand, Mom."

"Not all the way, Katie, but you're getting better at it and you're trying. Sure, you'll slip once in awhile. I can deal with that and still love you. Our love is bigger than any old mad-mistake."

Jackie noticed that Katie began to relax in her arms. She breathed deeply a few times and actually shuddered and quivered. She rocked her gently.

After 5 minutes, Katie pulled back and held the flower up to Jackie. "Can we plant these again? Will they be OK?"

Jackie gently took the somewhat mangled geranium from Katie and said, "I think so, sweetie. Run to the back of the garage. On the bench you'll see more flower pots like this one. Bring one back here."

Katie jumped up and ran into the garage. She immediately returned, with the dedication of someone carrying the Olympic Torch. She and Jackie then carefully repotted the flowers and returned them to their spot in the sun on the railing.

They stared at the geraniums, made more red by the bright sunshine.

In therapy, Allison noticed some changes too. Katie was managing their discussions of her poor choices at home without immediately entering her defensive, angry, and resistant attitude. She spoke of hitting Jackie without blaming Jackie for the incident. She actually seemed to show some remorse for what she had done and some willingness to accept the consequences. She showed some tentative signs of feeling proud when Jackie spoke about some situation that Katie had managed well.

During the session of June 5, 1995, Allison again explored some of Katie's past experiences. Katie was now much more receptive to speak about whatever memories she had.

"He hit me with his belt just because I turned off the TV that he was watching! He was always mean to me!" She spoke loudly about her father, Mike.

Allison held up a note pad with a picture of Mike that she had drawn.

"Yell at him, Katie!" Allison said, "Tell him he shouldn't have hit you!"

"You shouldn't hit me, Mike! You were bad! You shouldn't hit me!"

Allison held the picture closer. "Tell him that you weren't bad, Katie. He did a bad thing to hit you with his belt!"

"I wasn't bad! You were bad! You shouldn't have hit me! You were bad!" Katie screamed at the picture.

"Tell him you were just a little girl. You needed love, not hitting with his belt!"

"I was little! Fathers are supposed to love their kids, not hurt them!" Katie yelled.

"Katie, tell him he shouldn't have hurt you for other things, too!" Allison leaned over Katie and spoke close to her ear.

"You shouldn't hurt me! Why did you hurt me? I was just crying!" Katie screamed.

Allison leaned closer, "Say it again, Katie, 'I was just crying!'"

"I was just crying!" Katie screamed and then took her eyes away from the drawing. She suddenly pushed up with her arms, trying to break Allison's hold on her. Her eyes were unfocused. She screamed, "Let me go, I can't breathe! I can't breathe! Please, let me go! You're not letting me breathe!"

Allison continued to hold her as she struggled. "Oh, Katie, this is hard for you. You're really scared now. But you can breathe, you can breathe."

"No, you won't let me breathe, please let me go!" Katie screamed.

"Katie, you're safe, this is so hard, . . . Oh, Katie, I'll never hurt you, . . . you're safe, you can breathe," Allison said quietly as she stroked Katie's hair and shoulders. She did not touch her face now, fearing that Katie would interpret it as covering her mouth.

"No! No! Stop! I can't breathe!" Katie screamed.

"You're safe, Katie. This is so hard. You're so scared. You're feeling Mike hurt you now . . . like you felt it years ago. I'm not Mike. I'm Allison. You're safe. I'll never hurt you."

"AIIIEEEEEE! AIIEEEEEE!" Katie screamed and shook and screamed again. Allison continued to hold her, keeping her safe while she struggled and kicked out and shook her head. "AIEEEEEE! AIEEEEE!" Over and over.

For what seemed like hours Katie screamed. Her screams gradually became loud cries of despair. Allison still held her, but did not pull her closer for fear that Katie's conviction that she could not breathe would return.

"Katie, you need your mom to hold you now," Allison said quietly when Katie lay with little movement in her lap. Allison stood up while still holding Katie. Jackie sat in the couch and reached for Katie when Allison lowered her into her arms. Katie squeezed Jackie tightly and cried even more intensely. Jackie embraced her and rocked slowly. "Katie, Katie, you're safe. You're with Mom. You're safe. Mike will never hurt you again."

Katie burrowed further and continued to cry. Jackie looked to Allison for confirmation that she was doing what Katie needed. Allison nodded.

"Katie let herself remember more about her abuse from Mike than she probably ever did before," Allison said quietly to Jackie. "Katie seemed to remember Mike hurting her for crying . . . Katie felt herself being hurt. . . . I think that Mike must have choked her when she cried. Or he might have smothered her with a pillow.

He terrorized her for crying. . . . He terrified a little girl for crying
. . . for crying."

Allison waited quietly at her desk for fifteen minutes while
Katie and Jackie gradually pulled apart a bit, smiled, and Jackie
ran her hand gently over her face and through her hair. They began to talk quietly and even began to laugh. They looked at Allison.

"When you draw a picture, you really make it seem real, don't
you!" Jackie said and they all laughed.

Allison sat next to them on the couch. She put her arms around
them both. After a moment she said to Katie, "Sweetie, I wish that
you didn't have to go through so much hurt in order to be well. In
order to learn about love from Jackie. I really do. I'm sad that this
is so hard for you. You really thought that I was not letting you
breathe! How scary that must have been! You thought that I was
hurting you!"

Katie simply stared at Allison, who continued, "I really think
that learning to love good parents is worth all of this pain. But I'm
not you, sweetie, I can't imagine how hard it must be for you."

Allison noticed the tears rolling down her own cheeks as she
rested her hand on Katie's. Katie lifted her hand and squeezed
Allison's. Then she closed her eyes and snuggled closer to Jackie.
Katie, Jackie, and Allison rested.

COMMENTARY

When Katie began to show signs of making progress, Jackie was
understandably pleased. However, Jackie went beyond simply
feeling satisfied over her gains and she began to expect that the
progress would continue uninterrupted. When Katie began to regress Jackie then began to feel annoyed with her and to resent her
problems, which, a few months earlier, would have left her quite
satisfied.

Jackie had drifted into imposing a standard of improved behavior on Katie and then resenting her when she did not meet those
standards. She began to act as though Katie's behavior suggested
either that she was a poor mother or that Katie was not trying hard
enough. Without being aware of it, Jackie was no longer accepting

Katie as she was. Katie immediately sensed this, experienced it as rejection, and also knew that it gave her an opportunity to gain control over Jackie's emotional life. Only through becoming aware of her beginning to lose the acceptance quality of her therapeutic attitude would Jackie be able to regain control over her own emotional well-being as well as the overall atmosphere of the family.

The five qualities of The Attitude are very interwoven. When Jackie began to have difficulty *accepting* Katie's behavior, she also had less *empathy* for the difficulties that she had to face if she were to learn to attach. She most certainly had less *curiosity* about the choices that Katie would make and the reasons for making them. She was less *playful* in her own response, since she was invested in having Katie act a certain way. Finally, her *love* for Katie, although it may have remained strong in being committed to her, lost some of its affective tone of enjoying her. Once she reestablished her overall attitude, Jackie was able to again find it much easier to be attuned with her affective life and to assist her through her shame experiences.

When Katie was beginning to want to please Jackie she was taking an important step in forming an attachment with her. For the first time since she was a toddler she was being motivated by wanting to be liked by her parent, rather than finding a way to manipulate her. These efforts reflected the new meaning of having a relationship with a parent as well as her new realization that she had enough worth to be able to bring pleasure to an important person in her life. For these reasons, it was very important for Katie that she be successful in her early efforts to please. When she picked the flower for her and discovered that Jackie was not attuned with her affect and was not pleased, Katie experienced the act as a rejection of her. She had failed in this new endeavor! The shame that she felt was intense and she immediately fell into rage at Jackie.

When children like Katie begin to want to genuinely please their parent they are certain to fail periodically. While Jackie might have been more sensitive to how important it was for Katie to give her the flower, she cannot be expected to be constantly vigilant about not responding with attunement to her efforts. While being aware of the importance of these efforts in Katie's overall progress, she still needs to be able to give her a realistic response to the impact of her behaviors on her. If Katie was not successful in her efforts to please, Jackie again needs to turn to The Attitude to help her through the shame that is elicited in her failure. If Jackie can do that consistently, eventually Katie will be able to integrate the disappointment that she feels when her efforts to please are unsuccessful and gradually learn what will actually bring pleasure to Jackie.

Often when the unattached child is beginning to want to please her parent and to seek experiences of mutual enjoyment with her, she discovers that she does not know what to do with her periods of anger toward her. Katie was beginning to try to avoid having angry outbursts toward Jackie, yet she was still often subject to misperceiving Jackie's motives and behaviors toward her. At times she felt that Jackie did not want to be with her enough or that Jackie was being unfair. What was she to do with her anger toward Jackie when she did not want to become angry at her? Katie's solution, as is often the case, was to turn the anger toward herself. Some unattached children have a history of self-abusive behaviors. Others show little of such behaviors until they are beginning to form an attachment. Katie would rather hurt herself than risk hurting Jackie or their developing relationship. Also, she was actually feeling anger toward herself, thinking that her anger toward Jackie simply reflected the "bad self" that she still needed to control. She was making more progress realizing that Jackie was not "mean" than she was realizing that she was not "bad."

When Jackie tried to discourage her from hurting herself, Katie felt trapped. By following her solution to managing her anger, she was displeasing Jackie. Yet one of her motives for doing it was to please Jackie, since by hurting herself she was not hurting her! Also, Katie knew that the pain that she felt when she hurt herself was minor compared to the pain that she would feel if she lost what was beginning to be the most important relationship in her life. Why couldn't Jackie understand that?

Both Katie's efforts to please Jackie as well as her efforts to manage her anger by directing it at herself represented significant progress in her psychological development. Her intrinsic motivation now included her emerging relationship with her mother. Rather than simply being driven by efforts to manipulate and control, she was integrating this relationship into her sense of what was in her best interests. Her solutions might not yet be the healthiest, but they were qualitatively different from, and better than, the self-destructive motives that emerge from being unattached.

When Allison was holding her and exploring her relationship with Mike, Katie experienced an intense reenactment of the experience of Mike having smothered her when she cried. Although such experiences do not occur frequently, they do happen when working with abused children in this emotionally intense and directive manner. They actually serve to assist the child in resolving the trauma. A child remembers more than he or she is able to integrate. The high degree of emotional and physical nurturing and support that this treatment offers provides the child with the degree of psychological safety that he needs to allow himself to recall the trauma. Such reenactments tend to occur only after the beginning stages of treatment and following some progress in facilitating the attachment.

If the child does reexperience the trauma in the acute manner suggested by Katie, the therapist needs to maintain her accepting and empathic attitude, communicating how hard the experience is for the child. The therapist also calmly communicates that the child is not being abused now and the child is safely with the therapist and parent. The therapist also clearly defines the incident that the child is reexperiencing as having been abusive, and elaborates, if possible, on the physical, sexual, and/or psychological ways that the child experienced the abuse. The therapist also speaks about how the child may have interpreted the meaning of the abuse at the time (i.e., I was bad), and provides a new interpretation for the child to integrate (i.e., he acted badly).

SUMMER, THE SECOND TIME AROUND

On June 9, 1995, for the first time, Katie completed one year of living in the same foster home. Jackie wanted to acknowledge the anniversary, but as usual, thought it best not to make it into too big a deal.

That morning she made Katie's favorite breakfast—sausage and pancakes—and presented it to her when she sat at the table.

"Here you are, kiddo. This is the anniversary of your moving here one year ago today," Jackie said. "You get to pick dessert for dinner and I get to give you an extra hug." She reached over and hugged her. Katie noticed the breakfast more than the hug.

"What does it mean?" Katie asked. "What does having an anniversary mean?" She had eaten most of her meal before she demonstrated that she had been thinking about what Jackie told her.

"It means that you have lived with us for one whole year. Twelve whole months—365 days," Jackie replied.

Katie thought about it some more. "Do you mean that every day will be the second time that I lived with you on that day?"

"That's the idea, sweetie," Jackie replied. "So on July 4th, fireworks day, it will be the second time you'll be with us on fireworks day. It's the same for your birthday in August and my birthday in September. Each time will be the second time."

"Can I have a big party on my birthday?" Katie asked. "Can Sandy and Emily and Elise and Erica come?"

"Your birthday is still quite a ways off, sweetie. If you can handle a big birthday then, you will have a big birthday," Jackie replied. "I'll let you know five or ten days before your birthday if I think that you can handle it."

"I'm different now, Mom. Can't you tell?"

Jackie put down her fork and looked at Katie. What was she getting at? Did she mean that she was bigger, or smarter, or simply older? "How do you think you're different, sweetie?"

Katie sat for a moment. "I'm not bad anymore."

"You've never been bad, sweetie," Jackie said. "And you are learning how to make good choices a lot better."

"I used to always feel bad," Katie said slowly. "I just didn't know I felt bad. Now, I don't *feel* bad anymore."

"Oh, Katie," Jackie said as she reached over to put her hand on her arm. "I'm so glad for you. It must have been so hard always feeling that you were bad."

Katie smiled at Jackie without looking away.

"Why do you think you've changed?" Jackie asked.

"You and Allison taught me that I am a good girl," Katie calmly said.

"How do you think we did that?" Jackie's amazement continued.

"I don't know," Katie quietly said. "But I think 'cause you love
me."

"I think you're right, honey. And I do. . . . I do love you."

"I know, Mom."

Jackie got up and embraced Katie. "I don't think I'll cry now,
sweetie, because you might start crying too, and you have to get
off for school in five minutes. I am going to miss you while you're
at school today."

"It's OK, Mom," Katie said. "I'll be back this afternoon. And I
only have two more school days before summer."

Jackie smiled. They finished their breakfast. Katie hugged her
mom and got on the school bus.

Jackie needed to talk with someone. Although Allison had always cautioned her not to get too excited about anything until it
had been around for awhile, Jackie decided that this would be an
exception. Allison would see that Katie had just confirmed that
something special had been happening for awhile now. Jackie
called Allison and shared the good news. Allison agreed that something special had been happening.

Jackie's Journal:

> 6/15/95. First day of summer vacation. Katie seems happy and
> relaxed. Really think that she wants to be home now much more
> than ever. She was happily working in the garden with me, tying
> up the peas, both of us feeling kinda hot. She says, "The sun never
> shined in Augusta." I didn't know what she meant. She said, "When
> I lived in Augusta with Sally and Mike, the sun never shined
> there." I told her that I understood how it must have felt that way
> to her. She replied, "No, Mom. It *really* never shined there." I said
> that I was glad that the sun shined in Vassalboro and she agreed.
> Nothing else to say.

> 6/17/95. I told Katie that tomorrow was Father's Day. She spent
> most of the afternoon working in her room. She drew six pictures
> of things that Mark had done with her like swinging her in a "ham-
> mock" blanket, taking her to see the foxes in the woods, and fix-

ing her bed lamp that she had broken in anger the month before. At the top of each she wrote, *My dad does.* On the seventh page she wrote, *That's why I love my dad.* I helped her to make them into a book after promising that I would not tell.

6/18/95. Father's Day was a success for Katie. Mark was surprised and touched. He looked to me for the OK to get excited about it. I said fine. He grabbed her and spun her around before sitting her on top of the fridge. He told her that he would be doing a lot of different things with her so that she would have even more pictures to draw for him on his birthday. He does seem to be more important to her.

6/22/95. First tantrum since school got out. Upset that she could not go swimming with Diane. Blamed me although I had nothing to do with it. Stomped around the kitchen and porch. I suggested that she stomp around the garage five times and she did. To give her a rest I "let" her weed the garden with me. She said that I was tricking her but she only smiled and then helped. On the way back to the house I squirted her with the hose to keep the dirt from getting into the kitchen. When I had to return to the garden to get the pail that I had forgotten, she was waiting for me with the hose and she cleaned off my dirt.

6/25/95. Her school friend, Emily, visited this afternoon. They were in and out forty times. Katie actually reminded me of Diane when she was her age. Once she screamed at Emily for getting her doll dirty, but she recovered fast and apologized before bringing her favorite dolls back inside. I might try having her visit Emily at her house next. She calmed down easily after Emily left. She seemed relieved that she was gone and she didn't have to control her behaviors so much. Quiet and close bedtime.

6/28/95. Trip to K-Mart. Katie sees a mother scream at her little boy and roughly pull a toy out of his hand and drag him, screaming, down the aisle. She became upset at how the boy was being treated. She said that the mother must have problems because she was mean to him and did not know how to tell her son to put the toy back. She asked if the boy would need a home like hers to be safe and to learn how parents can love their kids. She seemed disappointed when I told her that kids really had to be hurt bad, like she was, before Child Protective Services would remove a child from his home. She was confused about how someone could decide what was bad enough.

During Katie's therapy session on July 2, 1995, Allison decided to show Katie some pictures of Sally and Mike that Steven had managed to get from them. He had visited them to request information and pictures for Katie's Life Book that would be used in preparing her for adoption. This book would contain her history from birth to adoption and be something that she would have throughout her life to refer to when she looked back on her difficult first years. Allison had separate pictures of Sally, Mike, and Katie. A number of pictures of Katie showed her as an infant, with a few others having been taken when she was older. There was one picture of Katie being held by Sally and another of Katie and both of her parents posing for a photo.

"Well, Katie Kiddo," Allison said, "your mom tells me that during the last couple of weeks you've seemed to be fairly happy and making some pretty good choices. It that how you see it?"

"Yeah," Katie replied. Then she added, "I'm having fun this summer."

"That's pretty neat. And you did well even though you didn't see me last week because of my vacation. I wonder what that means?"

"It means that I don't have to see you anymore!" Katie smiled.

"Not so fast, kiddo," Allison replied. "You think that you can get rid of me that easy? No way. I want to be able to pick on you till you're 50 years old!"

"No, you won't. I'm learning how to be a regular kid in Jackie's home and you said that was what you were seeing me for." Katie smiled.

"Well, listen to you!" Allison said. "And Jackie also said that you are. Now what does that mean?"

"I don't think I'm bad anymore," Katie said simply.

"Gee, I'm happy for you that you figured out that you are a good kid," Allison said. "You've really been working at this, I can tell."

"Yes, and Jackie says that I can handle a stream of fun now," Katie said proudly.

Allison looked at Jackie curiously.

"Remember, Allison, a long time ago we were telling Katie that she could only handle a trickle of fun at a time, so we were careful not to give her too much. Well, lately I've decided that she can handle a stream of fun, so she's getting more than she used to. And just in time for the summer too!"

"Soon I'll be able to handle gobs of fun!" Katie said.

"Gobs! Listen to you! OK, fun girl," Allison said. "So you don't think that you're bad anymore, and you're making good choices, having fun, and loving your mom easier. You have had a busy year."

Katie looked at Jackie and smiled. Jackie winked.

"Your mom tells me that you made a really neat present for your dad for Father's Day," Allison said. "We never talk about your dad much. Sounds like things are going well with him too."

"I made pictures of things that he did with me," Katie said rapidly. "And he said he was going to do a lot more with me so I would make him more pictures for his birthday."

"What a great plan that is, sweetie," Allison said. "He sounds like a pretty special dad to me."

"He is." Katie smiled at Jackie again. Jackie winked.

"What a difference between Jackie and Mark, your mom and dad now, and Sally and Mike, your first mom and dad," Allison said.

"Sally and Mike said I was bad, and Jackie and Mark say I'm good," Katie said. "And Jackie and Mark love me. Sally and Mike were mean!"

"Those are big, big differences, Katie," Allison said. "I felt sad for you when it was hard for you to see how different Jackie and Mark are from your birth parents. You used to get so mad at Jackie when she would not let you do something or when she had you sit for awhile and stay near her."

"I thought that she was being mean too!" Katie said. "I didn't know she was giving me . . . consekences."

"Yeah, you thought that she was being bad to you and that you must be bad too!" Allison said. "I wonder how you figured out that you both were not bad."

"Jackie kept loving me when I was mean to her," Katie said. She seemed to be able to go right to the central truth. "And I don't have a wall around my heart anymore."

"You know, Katie, I think that you're right," Allison said.

"I am," Katie said.

Allison and Jackie looked at each other and smiled. Katie smiled too, then she winked at Jackie. They all laughed.

"Well, Katie," Allison said, "we've still got some work to do."

Katie looked disappointed and then calmly looked at Allison.

"Steven gave me some pictures of you when you lived with Sally and Mike and other pictures of your birth parents," Allison said. "I'd like to look at them with you now, and see what you think. Jackie, would you hold Katie on the couch while she looks at these photos?"

"Sure, Allison," Jackie said.

Allison gave Katie a picture of her when she was about 3 months old, lying on her back on a blanket on the floor.

"That's me?"

"Sure is, sweetie."

"Oh, Katie, what a cute baby you were!" Jackie exclaimed. "What large, lovely eyes. And your hair was so light."

Katie stared at her picture. Jackie and Allison waited for her. Finally, Katie looked at Jackie.

"I wish I could have cared for you when you were 3 months old," Jackie said.

"What would you have done?" Katie asked.

Jackie pulled Katie toward her in her arms. She began to sway slowly and then she said quietly, "I would have looked into your eyes and saw how wonderful you were. I would have rocked you like this, and looked at your tiny fingers like this. Then I would have squeezed you gently like this and quietly sung you a lullaby. And I would feed you and hold you carefully. And I would do it for hours every day and you would know that you were good and special and that I loved you."

Jackie continued to stare at her until Katie reached up and hugged her tightly.

"I wish you had been my mom when I was born," Katie said. "I wish I had been inside of you like Diane and Matthew were."

"That would have been wonderful to me, too, Katie," Jackie said.

They smiled and winked and laughed again. Then Jackie sat her back up next to her and Allison showed her some more pictures of her.

When Allison gave Katie the picture of her at about 18 months with both Mike and Sally, Katie became quiet and tense. She stared at the photo, looking at each person intently.

"Pretend Sally and Mike are here, Katie, just like they are in the photo," Allison said. "Say whatever you would like to say to them."

Immediately Katie began to talk to the photo. "Why were you mean to me? Why didn't you take good care of me? You were bad the way you treated me. Parents aren't supposed to treat their kids that way! You made me think that I was bad! You hurt me a lot. Why didn't you take good care of me?"

Katie stopped and stared at the picture some more.

"Tell them that they'll never hurt you again, Katie," Allison said.

"You'll never hurt me again. Jackie is my mom and she keeps me safe. She loves me and shows me I'm good," Katie said. "I'm good and you won't be mean to me anymore."

Allison took the photo and then gave Katie one of Sally alone. "What would you like to say just to Sally, Katie?"

"Why didn't you take care of me? Why did you let Mike hurt me?" Katie looked at the photo quietly. "Sometimes I still miss you and wish that you had taken good care of me. Sometimes I wish that you loved me the way Jackie loves me."

"It is sad, Katie," Jackie said, "that Sally didn't do a better job of caring for you and loving you. I know that sometimes you miss her and love her too besides being mad at her. Sometimes, I'll bet Sally did hold and rock you and show you that you were special to her. It's just that she couldn't do it as often as you needed. As often as any baby would need. I can see why you sometimes wish that she had cared for you better so that she could still be your mom and be a very good mom to you."

After a few moments, Allison showed Katie a picture of Mike. "What would you like to say to Mike, Katie?"

"I don't miss you! You were very bad and mean to me. You never held me and you never loved me. Sally did but you didn't! I don't miss you at all!" Katie was strong and certain in her words. She felt only rage toward Mike at that time, and possibly for a very long time to come.

After placing the photos on her desk she told Katie that Steven would be making a photo album for her with those photos and many more from her life in foster care, including her first three homes.

"I don't want pictures of my other homes," Katie said.

"Why is that, Katie?" Allison asked.

"Because I wasn't happy in those homes. I don't remember them or think about them," Katie replied.

"What do you remember about those first foster homes?" Allison asked.

Katie thought for a moment. "I remember that they didn't know how to care for me. They got mad at me a lot. They didn't take care of me the way Jackie does."

"How is Jackie different from the way Ruth and Susan were?" Allison asked.

"Jackie didn't hate me back when I hated her," Katie said. "I don't know if the other moms hated me, but I felt that they didn't like me so I didn't like them even more!"

"It sounds like you still felt that you were bad when you lived with the other moms and they didn't know how to teach you that you're good," Allison said.

"Yeah," Katie said. She was beginning to lose interest. Allison decided that this girl, not yet 8 years old, had worked enough. She told Katie that she had earned a short session so that she could now get back home and turn on that stream of fun again. Katie agreed and Jackie winked at her.

When Jackie and Katie left, Steven remained for a few minutes to speak with Allison.

"What has been happening?" He asked. "This is not the same kid that I knew six months ago or even three months ago."

"I think you're right," Allison replied. "Katie is a different kid."

"Why? What did the trick?"

"Not one incident. Jackie and I have been working with her for thirteen months. What happened during the first week and the first session was as important as what happened last week. She finally was able to notice what Jackie was offering her and to begin to integrate that into a coherent self that does not have pockets of self-hatred, rage, isolation, despair, and fear. With Jackie, she has begun to feel safe and so she has been able to depend on her, trust her, be comforted by her, and have fun with her."

"How come so suddenly?"

"It's been happening for quite awhile," Allison said. "We noticed moments of self-reflection, acceptance of authority, and an ability to have fun and experience genuine affection back in January. An internal process of self-integration and self-acceptance has been occurring that mirrors an external process of coming to know, trust, and form an attachment with Jackie. What we are now seeing can let us assume that she is internalizing Jackie, something that she had never done this way before with anyone, including Sally."

"Is this likely to be permanent?"

"I believe so," Allison replied. "Certainly under conditions of stress in the future she may well regress. When that happens Jackie will simply be "present" for her again, focus again on maintaining The Attitude, and then reduce the choices that Katie has that she can't manage. As soon as she's ready, Jackie will present her with her "gobs" of fun and love again.

"But the basic psychological realities for Katie have changed in ways that I am convinced will be lasting," Allison said. "She now knows what love is all about. I can't imagine that she'll turn her back on it again like she did when she was an infant. She also knows, I mean *really* knows, that she's a good kid, a great kid. She may have doubts about that from time to time, but she has started to realize that truth, *in her gut*, and she's not likely to forget it.

"Some kids struggle with this for a longer time than Katie has. For that, we're fortunate. Some kids never get it to the degree that Katie seems to be getting it. Her whole world is opening up, with new awareness that she never had before. Empathy, remorse, deep laughter, friendships, excitement that is truly enjoyed, being curious, discovering her talents. These were all just words before for Katie that had no relevance to her real life. Now they do. Wait till you see her a year from now."

"But before we talk about a year from now, we need to discuss adoption," Allison said. "I imagine DHS will be starting to work with her on adoption soon. I'm certain that she'll regress so we'll get a chance to see how much she has integrated the gains that she has made."

"I'm glad you brought that up," Steven said. "I managed to get Kathy to give me permission to remain Katie's case worker through the adoption process. I'll have a different supervisor for her now who can show me how to prepare her for adoption. Actually I'm planning to call Jackie and you soon and set up a meeting where we can come to a decision about how best to talk with Katie about being adopted and moving."

On July 6, 1995, Steven called Jackie to say that he and Janis, his supervisor for the adoption work, would like to meet with her and Allison to talk about making plans for Katie's adoption. He said that they needed to discuss how the adoption process would go, who would tell Katie about it first, and how long the process was likely to take. He finally said that she should give thought to the type of parents who would be most suitable for Katie. He said that Allison was free on Monday, July 10, and Jackie agreed to meet then.

That evening, Jackie and Mark talked about the phone call and what that would mean for Katie and them. Jackie was feeling protective of the child who had now lived with her for over a year. She knew that she had made some real gains, but shouldn't she have more time to really stabilize the progress that she had made? Was she ready for the regression that being told that she would be moving would cause? Was her attachment to Jackie strong enough to withstand the fact that she would be told that someone else would be her mother? Would she let Jackie comfort her?

"Mark, I just don't know. I knew with Gabe. There was something about him that was more open and trusting. Maybe it's simply that we had more time with him and we were certain that he was going to make it before we started working on moving on."

"I see what you mean," Mark replied. "Katie still has a lot of work to do; more than he did. I don't want her to lose all the gains that she made either."

"I'm worried that she doesn't love me enough yet to be able to grieve my loss. If she doesn't do that, I'm afraid that she'll never be able to attach to someone else. Still I know that she's almost 8 and we can't expect her to wait another year before she can begin to attach to her adoptive parents," Jackie said.

"Why do we have to put her through it?" Mark asked. "Let's adopt her."

Jackie pulled back and stared at her husband.

"What? What did you say, Mark?"

"Let's adopt her," he replied.

"You want to adopt her?" Jackie asked. "You really do?"

"Allison and Steven and the others seem to be saying that adoption is best for her," Mark said. "You love her, I love her. As much as she can, she's learning to love us, and she sure needs us. So. . . . Nothing else really makes much sense."

"You never said anything about that before," Jackie said.

"It's only recently been talked about. And I didn't want to make you feel guilty, if you didn't want to adopt her. You do just about all the work with her. It's easy for me to say 'Let's adopt' when most of the follow-up is your responsibility. So I haven't said anything, waiting till you brought it up."

"Why did you say something now then, Mark?" Jackie asked, truly puzzled.

"I see the look on your face when the word *adoption* is spoken. I know you. You've been trembling in front of my eyes. I know you want her as much as you want the rest of us."

"You're not saying that we adopt her just for me, are you, Mark?" Jackie asked.

"I'm saying that we adopt her because she's already in our blood. Let's make it legal," Mark said. "Now do you want to cry first, or hug me, or do them both at the same time?"

They did both at the same time.

On July 10, 1995, Steven and Janis Marshall, the adoption supervisor, met with Jackie and Allison to talk about adoption. Janis had instructed Steven in the general procedures that they would be following in preparing Katie. They met at Jackie's home to discuss how to proceed.

"I figure that I should come to your house and tell her formally that I will be working with her on her Life Story. I'll explain what that is and why it is important before we start looking for the right home. I'll make sure that she knows that her thoughts and feelings about the right family are very important, so she'll be a big part of the process," Steven said without much enthusiasm.

"Before we go further, Steven," Jackie said quietly, "I'd like to say something."

They gave her their full attention because they could tell that Jackie was hesitant and at a loss for words, something that was rare for her.

"Mark and I have been talking about this a lot," she finally said. "We do not want her to move."

There was silence. Janis eventually managed to say, "But, she's only 7, Jackie. I don't think that we'd be able to consider long-term foster care."

"I know," Jackie replied. Again, silence. Then she smiled.

"Jackie!" Allison yelled, with an intensity that Steven had never heard before other than when she was giving Katie a hard time with her repetitions. "You want to adopt Katie!"

"Yes, Allison. We do."

"Oh, Jackie!" Allison got up and came to Jackie and embraced her. Steven and Janis sat and stared. They felt a little uncertain. This was not what they had anticipated.

"I'm happy with your decision, Jackie," Steven finally said. "But a few months ago you said that you were not going to adopt her. What changed your mind?"

"I don't know, Steven," Jackie replied slowly. "I have some sense that Katie is different from Gabe. I knew that it would be hard for Gabe to leave us, but I also was sure that he would be able to attach to his adoptive family and have a good life. Somewhere within me, I have doubts with Katie. I don't know if she could transfer what she is learning with me to another mother. I don't know if she would be able to understand why I did not choose to keep her after all we've been through together. I don't want to lose her now, Steven."

"I hear what you're saying Jackie," Allison said quietly. "I know how much this kid has come to mean to you. I also know that she is making real gains now and that if she is told within the next few weeks that she'll be adopted sometime during the next year by another family, that she will be able to make the transition. You don't have to feel trapped and think that you have to adopt her, Jackie."

"I don't feel trapped, Allison. Mark and I want to adopt her," Jackie said with increasing firmness in her voice. "If I were as sure as you that she will be healthy enough to move on to another home, I don't know what we would want to do. But I don't have your confidence. That's my reality. But we're not martyrs. We know that we don't *have* to adopt her. We want her. We choose her. We love her. She is part of our family now and we want her to remain in our family. If she continues with her progress we will celebrate her future. If her progress stops, we still want her. She's a part of me now in a way that I cannot express."

"We certainly will give priority to your application to adopt her," Janis said. "We can't give you the OK today though since there's a home study that we have to complete. This will include interviews with the whole family, including Katie."

"I know that, Janis," Jackie said. "Mark and I have discussed it. We have mentioned it to the three older kids and they are support- ive. We certainly have said nothing to Katie. But I wanted you to know now since I imagine that this will affect what you say to Katie and when you do it."

"Jackie," Allison said, seeming to have some difficulty speak- ing. "I know that you love her. But again, I want you to be sure about this. Preparing her for adoption by others is a valid choice. Do you really *want* to adopt her or do you feel you *have* to?"

"Allison," Jackie said, "in many ways I love you more than a sister. Without your knowledge and support I would never have been able to raise Katie. Or Gabe. I trust your judgment more than I can say." She paused; it was hard for her to speak.

"Now I am asking that you trust me," Jackie said with tears in her eyes. "My love for Katie has brought a knowledge of her that just does not fit into any category. She is part of me and I am part of her. *Wanting* to adopt her or *having* to adopt her is a false distinction. I trust your judgment that she can make it in another home. Trust mine that this is necessary for Katie, and for me. I do have a choice, but I don't have a choice. She can make it somewhere else, but for some reason she must make it with me. I know that this is necessary and right. I am filled with joy and fear, with gratitude and humility. This must be the way it is."

Allison stared at this woman as she had often done over the past few years. Now she was understanding Jackie in a new way. She was understanding differently the work that she and Jackie had been doing. Jackie's love for Katie took her to a knowledge of attachment and of Katie that left Allison observing from a distance. Of course Allison would trust her judgment. How could she not do so?

"I have no doubts, Jackie. You know her and your family bet- ter than I ever will," Allison finally said, and they smiled when they noticed that they both had tears, just as happened so often in the past.

"Mark and I have one question for you," Jackie said to Allison. "It's about Gabe. When he discovers that we are adopting Katie, and did not adopt him, will that cause any problems for him in his adoptive home?"

"I don't think so because he is doing so well," Allison said. "He seems to have a very secure attachment with his new parents, and I think that he will simply feel now that his moving from your home was best for him and he probably won't wonder why. If he were not doing well in his adoptive home, I might worry about the effects on him of Katie staying with you."

Steven thought about what he needed to say next. The meeting certainly had gone off in an unexpected direction. Finally, he smiled too and got out of his chair. "Can I have a hug too?" he asked with some hesitation. He wasn't sure if this would remove him from being Katie's adoption worker. He'd worry about that later.

COMMENTARY

Often when unattached children have begun to make significant progress in forming an attachment with their new parents, they express the realization that they are "different now." The level of insight that they have into the changes that have occurred within themselves and also their relationships with their parents can be amazing, as well as being eloquently expressed.

Katie is discovering what other children, raised with a secure attachment by their birth parents, take for granted. At the same time she is discovering how to use words to communicate her inner life of thoughts and feelings. When she becomes aware of love, mutual enjoyment, being comforted, sharing joy, playful teasing, and quiet times of learning about the world together, she often spontaneously comments on this new reality. The words are obviously genuine. They indicate that the hardest work is now behind her.

Jackie's decision to adopt Katie does not change the fact that many children can form an attachment with their foster parent and then successfully move to an adoptive home. These children definitely grieve the loss of their foster placement, but they show the ability to work through the stages of grief and become receptive to being adopted by another family. This alternative is much better than trying to discourage the child from learning to attach in his foster home and wait a few years until he is in an adoptive home. Those are wasted years and the difficulties with learning to attach would be much greater when he is that much older. Also, many adoptive parents would not commit to bringing an unknown child into their home if they were aware of the significant problems associated with lack of attachment. These children do not learn to attach easily.

Steven, Jackie, and Allison might well have made it clear to Katie from the moment of her placement in Jackie's home that she was not there on a permanent basis. Jackie might at times have casually wondered about her moving someday, possibly while saving some things that she liked to show her birth or adoptive parents in the future. It is best to tell a foster child that it is a temporary home, and that eventually he or she will either be going back to the birth parents or to an adoptive home. Even when the foster parents think that they might choose to adopt their child when he or she is free for adoption, they should still maintain that it is a temporary home. It is much easier for a child to be first told that it is temporary and then later discover that it is permanent, than it is for a child to think that it might be a permanent home and then be told that it is temporary.

FEAR AND JOY

On July 14, 1995, Katie was weeding the garden with Jackie when Steven drove into the yard. This was the day that he would begin talking with Katie about adoption. Jackie was not sure how Katie would respond. Her sense of security and her expressions of attachment to Jackie and Mark seemed to be stronger every day. Would this discussion about her future set her back or would she take it in stride?

"There's Steven, sweetie," Jackie said. "Run over and say 'hi' and take him into the kitchen. I'll be in a minute. You can get out the lemonade and crackers. If he wants coffee, I'll take care of it when I get there."

Katie needed no encouragement to end weeding early. She greeted Steven as if he were her best friend from school. By the

time Jackie entered the kitchen, Katie and Steven were both enjoying their drinks.

Somehow Katie had discovered that Steven had a little girl
named Rebecca, who was now 2½ years old. Steven showed her
Rebecca's picture and Katie happily handed it to Jackie.

"Isn't she cute!" Katie said.

"She sure is!" Jackie said. "She reminds me of the pictures of
you that we saw at Allison's office."

"I wasn't that cute," Katie said.

"Say that again, sweetie," Jackie smiled, "and I'll have to give
you a 'mom circle' right in front of Steven."

"No!" Katie giggled. Eventually they finished their crackers and
lemonade.

"Katie," Steven said, "I came here today to talk with you."

This was unusual. Steven's serious tone immediately brought
Katie to her hypervigilant state and she instinctively stood up and
moved toward Jackie.

"I can hold you if you'd like, sweetie," Jackie said. She pulled
the now tense child into her lap.

"Katie," Steven continued, "I told you a few months ago that
the judge said that you would not be going back to live with Sally
and Mike. He said that they had not learned how to be better parents and that you should not have to wait anymore to find out if
you would be living with them."

Katie stared at Steven, motionless, so he continued. "Now that
we know that you'll not be living with Sally and Mike again, it's
time to decide what home you'll be growing up in. You need to be
able to just have a family like other kids and no longer be a foster
kid who has to worry about moving all the time."

"I want to stay here. I want to stay with Jackie," Katie said in
one breath.

"I know you do, Katie. This is a wonderful home. But right
now I cannot promise that you can stay here. First, Jackie and
Mark have to apply to adopt you. Then I will be coming back and
ask them and you and your sister and brothers a lot of questions
so that I get to know a real lot about your family. I have to be
sure that this is the best place for you before I could promise you
that you can be adopted by Jackie and Mark," Steven said with
difficulty.

"I want to stay here, I don't want to go anywhere else!" Katie yelled. She looked frightened. She turned to Jackie. "Tell Steven, Mom. Tell him I can stay here." When Jackie hesitated she looked terrified.

"Sweetie, I know you do and I'm very happy that you want to stay with us. We want you to stay. Mark and I want to always be your parents," Jackie said quietly as she held her closer. "We love you so much and we have asked Steven if you can stay with us."

"Why can't you decide, Mom?" Katie asked in confusion.

"Because when you moved here, Katie, Steven asked us if we would be your family to help you. We were asked to be a Helping-Kid Home for you. Now you need to have a Growing-Up Home and that's different. Daddy and I will apply to adopt you and then Steven will have to get to know our family better, like he said, before deciding if we would make the best growing-up home for you."

"You are, Mom! You're the best home for me!" Katie needed to put an end to this fear. She needed a promise that she could stay forever.

"Katie," Steven said, "Jackie and Mark are a great home. I am really happy that they want to adopt you. They want to always be your parents. I think that they would be great parents for you. But I can't promise now that they will be adopting you. Jackie and Mark and I will work hard to make sure that this is the best family for you to grow up in."

"Tell me now!" Katie screamed.

"I can't, Katie," Steven said. "I will tell you as soon as possible."

"No!" Katie erupted. She pulled herself away from Jackie and ran from the room. Jackie heard her bedroom door slam shut.

Jackie looked at Steven. "She's scared to death. She so much needs to know for sure that she's staying with us. I know you can't make false promises, but please, do whatever interviews you need with us and the kids as soon as possible so you can decide soon. Please, Steven. Waiting for her will be torture. Every day will be an agony."

"I'll talk with Janis this afternoon," Steven replied. "I'll try to call you with a general idea of how long this will take."

"Thanks," Jackie said. "I know you'll work as fast as you can."

Steven soon left and Jackie went to find Katie. She knocked on her door. There was no response but she heard Katie crying. She opened the door. Katie was rolled up in a ball on her bed. She held her large stuffed rabbit in her arms. Tears streamed from her eyes onto the rabbit and the spread. She was gasping for air and staring into the corner.

Jackie quietly closed the door and walked to the bed. She lay down behind Katie, wrapped her arms around her and pulled her against her chest. She whispered her name into her ear and then she was quiet. Her breathing soon matched Katie's. She felt her shivering in her arms. The tears continued, seemingly forever. Jackie's enveloping touch would have to reach her.

"Mom." Katie began to talk at the time that Jackie had thought she would never again hear her voice, only her ocean of tears. "Why is it . . . never . . . easy? Why is it always so, so hard? Why, Mom? Why will . . . I . . . never be happy?"

"Oh, my Katie. I know how scary this must be for you. I know how much you want a promise that you can stay. I hope you can. I think that Steven will know that it's best for you to stay. Mark and I will answer all of his questions and he'll really get to know us. I think that he'll agree with us that this is where you need to stay."

Jackie was quiet again and she continued to rock slowly in the bed and to hold Katie tight. Then she whispered, "You and I will be scared together, sweetie. As long as we have to wait for Steven to decide, I'll be scared with you."

Katie turned around to face Jackie. She hugged her and the rabbit got squished between them. Then she kissed Jackie's cheek. "OK, Mom. If one of us is scared, we'll hold each other's hand."

On July 17 Steven called to say that Janis and Kathy had recognized the need for a quick decision and had allowed him to work almost exclusively on their home study so that they could make their decision rapidly. Usually the adoption worker spent time with the child getting to know her, but since Steven already knew her quite well that time would be saved. After the home study was complete, they would review Jackie and Mark's application and make the decision. The Life Story could be done later. Since they already had a home study done when they got their foster care license, the actual study would not take as long as usual. What was usually a process that took months might be able to be completed in weeks. Jackie was relieved and told Steven of her gratitude. They made arrangements for Steven to begin his interviews with Jackie and Mark that Friday. They already had completed most of the application forms and had arranged for medical exams on July 24. If Jackie had her way, they would be setting a record for the shortest amount of time it took to obtain approval for adopting a child. Of course, Katie had lived with her for thirteen months, and she thought that should count for something.

On July 23, after church, Katie was told to hang up her clothes and make her bed before she could go swimming at Weber Pond with Diane. Ten minutes later Diane and Katie climbed in the car wearing their suits and carrying their towels. Jackie was amazed how easily they got along now. During the winter Diane often wondered about the wisdom of having this angry and sneaky girl living with them.

Jackie found Katie's shoes in the living room and she decided to put them away for her. She opened her bedroom door and saw Katie's church clothes on the floor and the bed unmade. She had gone off without doing her work! Katie hadn't done that in a couple of months. Jackie had plenty of time to consider her consequence.

When they returned from their swim two hours later, Jackie met them at the kitchen door. "Sit down, Katie. How was your swim?" Jackie began.

"Great, Mom. Diane says that soon I won't have to wear my life jacket."

"That's wonderful, sweetie," Jackie replied. "But I've been wondering why you went off without making your bed or hanging up your clothes?"

"I forgot, Mom," Katie said quickly.

"But I had just told you, Katie," Jackie said. "So my guess is that you really wanted to leave quickly and did not want to have to wait while you got your work done."

"I forgot!" Katie yelled.

"I know that this will be hard on you, sweetie, but so you work harder not to forget your chores," Jackie said, "the next time Diane goes swimming you won't be able to go."

"That's not fair!" Katie yelled. "I forgot. I'll make my bed now and pick up my clothes."

"Yes, Katie," Jackie said quietly. "I would like you to do that now. But you still can't go swimming the next time."

"You're mean!" Katie yelled.

She threw her wet towel on the floor and ran to her room. She threw open the door and began kicking her clothes. Jackie followed her closely and saw her rage.

"Katie, don't do that to your clothes," Jackie said.

Katie spun around and kicked Jackie. Then she screamed and ran toward the window. Jackie caught her before she hit the window with her fist. Jackie picked her up and carried her to her bed. She sat with her, holding her to her chest while she fought and screamed.

Katie struggled hard for over fifteen minutes before finally beginning to lose her strength. It was another fifteen minutes before she was quiet. Jackie spoke quietly to her as she struggled, accepting her anger, telling her that she was safe, allowing her to set her own pace. Katie initially screamed at her to stop talking. Gradually she became quiet and Jackie could not tell what she thought and felt.

Finally Katie said quietly, "You don't want me anymore. I hurt you again. I'll never stop hurting you so you don't want me!"

"Oh, Katie, I do still want you. I'll never stop wanting you. You just got mad at me and kicked me. I don't like being kicked. You know that you don't hurt me nearly as much as you used to. Do you think one little kick is going to get me to stop loving you? Oh, sweetie, my love doesn't work that way."

"Why Mom?" Katie asked. "Why do you still love me?"

"Because, Katie," Jackie replied. "Because you're my kid. That's all there is to it. Nothing you do, or say, or feel, or think, can stop me from loving you. I'm your mom, sweetie. And that's the way it is."

Katie sighed. She relaxed further in Jackie's arms. Jackie continued to sway slowly and hum to her. Five minutes later, Katie was sleeping! Tears came to Jackie's eyes. She was again amazed how often Katie could get her to cry. Now she cried simply because the kid fell asleep in her arms!

Jackie quietly lay Katie on her bed, covered her, and slowly crept out of the room. An hour later, when she checked on her, Katie was coloring at her desk. Her bed was made and her clothes were picked up.

"What are you up to, kiddo?" Jackie asked.

"I'm drawing a picture of Diane and me swimming. She's holding my foot in her hand and she's going to throw me."

"Neat."

"What's for supper, Mom?"

"Chili and muffins with our garden salad, which you're going to help me pick."

"Neat."

Jackie left. If they were going to eat on time, the muffins needed to be started.

Jackie's Journal:

7/24/95. Today I talked with Katie about her birthday next week. I said that she could invite four friends for the afternoon. Diane and I would take them swimming, we'd come back for a dinner that she picked. Then we'd have cake and ice cream and open her presents. I told her that the family would have a party for her the next day. She was both ecstatic and terrified. She wanted reassurance that I really thought that she could handle that amount of excitement.

7/25/95. Katie called her friends. Sandy will be away on vacation. But Erica, Emily, and Elise will all be able to come! She couldn't believe it. She had to tell me what she likes about each one. According to her, they are the three greatest kids in all of Maine. No, the whole country. I suggested that we would then have the four greatest kids in the country that day. She asks me to go over the whole schedule with her. It seems that she might need to have every minute of the day programmed. Later, I had to go shopping and Katie stayed with Diane. They were up to something when I was gone. Lots of looks and giggles together over dinner.

7/27/95. Mark took Katie and Diane camping for 2 days. She was so torn! She would run around trying to help them pack and asking dozens of questions. Then she'd run back to me, finding a new reason each time for me to go with them. They would be camping up at Moosehead Lake and Katie reassured me that they would not set up the camp too close to the water. She and Diane are still doing a lot of whispering. When they finally left, Katie gave me an extra long hug, and then grabbed Diane's hand without looking back. She had made up her mind and she was going through with it, by golly!

7/29/95. At 2 P.M. I heard the car coming up the drive with Katie honking the horn. She hopped out of the car and almost knocked me over. Did she talk! I learned about every adventure they had. They saw a moose and a bear. They rented a small boat and had lunch on an island in the lake. Their hot dogs were delicious, but their soda was warm. The first night Katie heard noises and she woke up Diane. That wasn't much help so they both woke up Mark. Their brave leader managed to poke a flash light out of the tent and he discovered a skunk family going through the garbage that our three outdoorsmen had failed to put away properly. They did not sleep well that night.

7/30/95. After church and lunch Katie and Diane asked the rest of the family to come outside. Katie sat me and Mark down on the porch and she ran to the driveway. Her jump rope from last year's birthday appeared. As she and Diane called out a rhythm, Katie jumped. She missed the beat a couple of times at the beginning. She was so earnest. Then she had a long spell with no misses and she was bursting with excitement. She ran to the porch and hugged me and Mark. She insisted that I jump too. She chuckled when I missed a number of times. Then she offered advice and was supportive, like Diane must have been with her. She clapped when I got it. She was proud of me.

8/1/95. Therapy tends to be fairly typical now. We discuss the week. Actually the discussions tend to become involved conversations of routine events. There's usually a lot of laughing and teasing. Allison always makes a fuss about what a neat and crazy family we have. When we discuss something that she has done wrong, Katie handles it with little or no stress. If she got any consequences she is quick to tell Allison what they were and how she managed them. Today Katie asked Allison directly if she would tell Steven that she was in the right home and should not have to move to another one. Allison indicated that she had already told Steven that, and in fact, had written a letter with that recommendation. Katie asked to see the letter. Allison showed it to her. Katie read the letter to me, with some help from Allison over the tricky words. The letter seemed to give Katie confidence. She left the session holding my hand like she now had everything under control.

8/4/95. The day finally arrived. Katie is 8. As is the custom in our home, I left her a small present on her pillow while she slept. She awoke to find a new outfit for her favorite doll. She was so surprised and pleased. Last year she got no such surprise! She quickly dressed up her doll to look nice for her friends when they came. Erica, Emily, and Elise, the 3Es Diane calls them, what a group! The four of them laughed and swam and talked and ran all afternoon. Thank goodness for Diane's youth to keep up with them. A few times during the day Katie would come running to me, give me a quick hug, and go running back to her friends. When I put her to bed she gave me the biggest hug, I could hardly breathe. She whispered "Thanks, Mom," as she fell asleep holding her doll. It's been quite a year, actually 14 months.

On August 18, 1995 Steven was able to tell Katie the good news. He was going to visit and tell Jackie at the same time, but she would have none of that, so he told her when he called to arrange for a time to meet with Katie. She did not tell Katie that he was coming until after lunch, about an hour before his arrival. Katie spent the hour cleaning the house. Jackie decided that Katie was becoming more like her every day!

When Steven arrived, Katie waited on him with milk and crackers. It was her idea and she even joked about it, saying that she did not spill one drop. Mark asked to be served too. With a look of mild annoyance at a father who did not know when to tease and when not to, Katie managed to get him some milk and crackers too.

After an eternity to her, Steven said, "Katie, as you know, I've been talking to your whole family and even some of your mom and dad's friends, about you and your home. Back at the office we all talked about your family and we've decided that . . . this is the best home for you. We want you to be adopted by Jackie and Mark."

Katie shrieked. She jumped up from her seat and hugged Jackie. She pulled back, looked at her, shrieked, and hugged her again. The minutes went by with Mark and Steven sitting in the silence. Finally, Katie pulled back and stared at Jackie.

"You're my mom forever and ever."

Then she hugged Mark and said, "I love you, Dad."

Katie turned and hugged Steven. Then she was off. They heard her run upstairs looking for Diane, Matthew, and John. She found two out of three, and Jackie, Mark, and Steven heard them cheer. She ran downstairs calling for Whimsy. The old dog found some lost energy and they rolled around on the living room floor. Katie was back in the kitchen, with Whimsy following close behind. Out the door they ran with the adults following. Katie jumped and skipped, grabbed her bike, and tore down the driveway. Whimsy barked and even seemed to skip himself as he ran beside her. By the road she slammed on her brakes, turned, and sped back toward the house.

Her bike was left by the car as she ran through the garden, swung around her swing set, and darted out into the field. She and Whimsy were rapidly losing their momentum as they headed back toward the house. But she was not done yet. She turned and made a line toward the swing under the maple tree. She pumped the swing half a dozen times and cheered until finally leaping off without waiting for it to stop. She stood panting and searching for something that she may have forgotten. She suddenly spun around. She took three giant steps and then hugged the tree. Whimsy ran around it a few times and then sat beside her.

Jackie, Mark, and Steven stood on the porch motionless and in silence.

Finally, in awe, Jackie said, "She's claiming her home."

"She is!" Mark said. "She's now at home."

"And she's claiming herself, too."

"Yes."

"Our crazy, lovely, and wonderful daughter," Jackie said as she put her arm around Mark. "Katie Keller. Our daughter. She cries and laughs . . . and weeds the garden . . . and swims and jumps rope. You know, the basics.

"Oh, and she hugs trees too."

She paused and smiled.

"In Vassalboro, Maine. Where the sun shines."

6

Principles
of Parenting
and Therapy

PARENTING

For Jackie to parent Katie well she needed to maintain general principles that would guide their interactions and help to maintain her own family well being. (See Appendix 3 for a summary of the interventions needed to effectively raise an unattached child.) It was necessary for Jackie to rely on more than one technique. A child like Katie would find a way to make any technique ineffective within an hour. If Jackie could follow these principles, she would be more likely to think of a unique intervention that fit a given situation. She might never use that intervention again, since Katie was likely to have developed a strategy to resist it.

The therapeutic *attitude* described throughout this work was central to Jackie's ability to adequately maintain the emotional tone of the interactions with Katie as well as the overall atmosphere of the family. An accepting, empathic, loving, curious, and playful attitude was most able to meet the psychological needs of both Katie and the entire family. It enabled her to protect her own healthy manner of relating and living so that she could eventually share it with Katie.

Jackie was aware that she had to provide her with countless *affect attunement* experiences and that Katie needed to gradually begin to accept and enjoy them. These experiences were characterized by eye contact, smiles, touching, rocking, and movement. They often occurred with humor, gentle teasing, and surprises. They consisted of songs, repetitive activities and movements, and various "preschool" messy activities. They occurred regardless of whether or not Katie was making good choices. They had to occur because they were the wings upon which Katie flew in order to develop a core of affective pleasure and its equivalent core of trust in Jackie.

Such attunement experiences occurred spontaneously and unexpectedly throughout the day. If Katie seemed to have difficulty accepting direct expressions of affection, she might be more receptive to moments of humor and relaxed "small talk." She would then feel close to Jackie without realizing it and without having to acknowledge that she wanted to be close. Jackie also might surprise Katie with a brief, fun-filled activity so that Katie would gradually begin to trust that when the unexpected happened in Jackie's home, it would be enjoyable and not traumatic. Katie would gradually begin to trust in a future that Jackie, not Katie, controlled. Jackie would present those surprises to her because she was her mother and they were good for her. They would not occur because Katie had a tantrum, threatened, manipulated, or charmed Jackie into doing them. Since they were unexpected, it would be harder for Katie to sabotage them.

When attunement experiences do occur at a predictable time, they are likely to be resisted initially, but gradually they take on special meaning. Jackie decided to have a special time, which she called "mom time" every evening before bed. Katie would discover that "mom time" occurred every day regardless of her behavior. It would enable her to begin to relax and feel secure at the end of the day, no matter how angry she had been with Jackie throughout the day.

Since Katie had difficulty being aware of and expressing her inner life of thought and emotion, Jackie constantly would have brief conversations with her that involved the expression of thoughts, feelings, wishes, fantasies, plans, and memories. Jackie would initially do most of the talking, both about her own inner life and also about what she thought Katie might be experiencing. Jackie needed to be very patient, knowing that it would be months or longer before Katie was likely to make the conversations truly reciprocal.

Conversations that Jackie held with Katie also would involve explorations of the past and future. Katie's past was filled with shame-based experiences, and Jackie, by calmly mentioning those experiences, was communicating that she knew and accepted all aspects of who Katie was. Jackie would also share her own past with Katie, in an effort to help Katie to feel more a part of the continuity of the Keller family. By discussing the future with Katie, Jackie would be communicating confidence in their future life together, inviting her into family rituals, and helping her to manage her anxiety about the unknown by familiarizing her with guideposts that she would meet along the way. At times, Jackie would wonder about the years ahead with Katie, expressing hopefulness about the person she would someday become.

Along with attunement experiences, it is equally important for Jackie to provide Katie with daily *shame-reducing* experiences. Katie was certain to engage in many provocative, defiant, and aggressive behaviors that would function to disrupt the family and attempt to maintain control of its emotional tone. Such behaviors also were evidence to her of how bad and worthless she was. She invariably experienced discipline as a statement of her inherent evil, rather than being an effort to teach her how to live within the social realities of family life. Jackie needed to socialize Katie if she were to ever live in harmony with others.

Jackie's therapeutic attitude served as the best context in which Katie's experiences of shame could occur. When Jackie needed to discipline and structure Katie's behavior, she was eliciting her shame. By remaining emotionally available and reassuring to her immediately following the discipline, she would be limiting the experience to the actual behaviors and reducing its impact on her vulnerable sense of self. In this manner Katie is gradually able to tolerate and then accept her experiences of shame and finally to integrate them into her self identity. At the same time, through reassuring her following the experience, she is enabling Katie to gradually learn how to accept being comforted following distress. This reassurance has been called "Interactive Repair" by child development theorist E.Z. Tronick (quoted in Schore, pp. 245–247).

Frequently, discipline involves a parent being mildly annoyed with her child for her behaviors and then giving her a consequence. If the child objects, the parent might become even more annoyed and give a greater consequence. This practice of discipline would be completely ineffective with Katie. The annoyance would immediately increase her sense of shame and be experienced as rejection. For this reason, Jackie needs to consistently maintain the therapeutic attitude when she disciplines Katie. She is then able to accept and have empathy for Katie's defiance and resistance. She also can communicate a curiosity about Katie's subsequent responses and she can choose to be playful, rather than defensive, during the interaction. A good description of how to provide consequences to a child's behaviors while maintaining an empathic, matter-of-fact attitude, can be found in *Parenting with Love and Logic*

(1990) by Foster Cline and Jim Fay. Deborah Hage (1995) presents a good summary of the principles that she employs, as a parent and therapist, in her work with unattached children.

Jackie knew that she would have to *hold* Katie often if an attachment was going to develop between them. Initially most of the holding would most likely be for containment of Katie's rage outbursts. Jackie would hold her when Katie was unable to control her own impulses, and thus was a risk to the safety of herself or others or she was being destructive to their home. By holding her, Jackie would be giving her the control that she could not give to herself. However, she also would be communicating her acceptance and empathy for Katie's distress and she would be facilitating Katie's ability to establish an emotional bond with her at a time when she most needed it and was most likely to permit it. Katie's attachment tendencies would be likely to intensify during those periods of distress, and they would become strengthened if Jackie is able to be emotionally receptive and available. In those circumstances Jackie knew that one day Katie's emotion would be likely to move from screaming rage to gentle tears and also to giggling smiles.

Jackie also would gradually hold Katie in a nurturing and affectionate way, bringing her close to her just as a mother holds her infant. Such holding is the best replication for the affective attunement experiences that Katie missed during her first year of life. Jackie began by approaching her with quick touches and brief hugs, using this physical contact as the bridge to longer periods of snuggling, rocking, and caressing.

While it was helpful for Jackie to be predictable in her attitude toward Katie, it was less beneficial for her to be predictable in her choices of consequences for her behaviors. Children like Katie often misbehave in order to feel that they have control over what consequences their parent will give them. They often seek consequences that will give them a reason to be angry and to feel that their parents are mean. Katie might choose to misbehave in a compulsive effort to make Jackie get angry with her and reject her. For these reasons, Jackie needed to keep her off balance by choosing a variety of consequences for a given behavior.

Paradoxical responses are often helpful in preventing a child from gaining control over the consequences. For example, if Katie were to scream loudly in the kitchen while she was working, Jackie might have told her to scream more loudly and then time how long it lasts. Or she might have suggested that she practice screaming twice a day, at a given time and place. Jackie might also have taped the scream to play at therapy. Or she might have screamed along with her and asked the other children to judge who was the best screamer. Such paradoxical responses work in a great many situations with various behaviors, as long as Jackie is able to accept the behavior that she is telling Katie to do. See *Troubled Transplants* (1993) by R. Delaney and R. Kunstal for many examples of paradoxical interventions.

A final general parenting principle that Jackie used with Katie involved providing her with *regression* experiences. These experiences served to acknowledge and accept that Katie's affective development more closely approximated that of a toddler than a 7-year-old. They involved both *nurturing* experiences that facilitate affective attunement, and *structuring* experiences that reduce shame and serve to facilitate socialization. *Nurturing* experiences included giving Katie a bottle, singing and playing toddler songs and games, washing, dressing and combing her hair, and quiet cuddling with books and music. They involved eye contact, smiles, movement, and touch. For ideas of such activities see *Games Babies Play* (1993) by Vicki Lansky, and also *Messy Activities and More* (1993) by Virginia Morin.

Structuring experiences involved providing her with a well-organized routine that alternated active and quiet activities. Within that routine, Jackie could be near her and supervise her closely just as she would if Katie were 18 months old. Finally, just as she would if Katie were a toddler, Jackie made most of her choices for her, even including what she would wear and eat. Such structuring experiences were as important in enabling Katie to take advantage of regression as were the nurturing ones. Through providing Katie with the opportunity to rely on her physical presence and decision making, Jackie was providing her with a very safe environment. Katie gradually felt very secure within that circle of physical and psychological proximity that

Jackie maintained for her. Within that safety, Katie was more able to reduce her own need to be in control and to rely on Jackie as being present, in control, and the source of interests, comfort, and enjoyment. She was accepting Jackie for who she was. Namely, her mother.

PSYCHOTHERAPY

The psychological treatment of Katie involved a series of complex integrative affective and cognitive experiences. (See Appendix 4 for an outline of the central treatment principles.) The central features of her treatment involved affective experiences of both attunement as well as shame reduction. By providing a setting in which both she and Jackie were closely attuned to Katie's affective states, Allison was providing a context of trust that approximated the setting in which the healthy mother-bond occurs. Within this atmosphere of trust, Allison and Jackie employed empathy and acceptance to explore with Katie various experiences of shame from her past and present life. Shame-reduction occurred both by bringing the incident to Katie's awareness, and also through Jackie and Allison immediately reattuning with Katie's new affective state. This enabled her to integrate her fragmented self, increase her sense of self-worth, and enhance her ability to form an attachment with Jackie.

When Allison sensed and was responsive to Katie's affective states she became attuned with her. When the experience occurred in a manner that involves eye contact, facial expressiveness, rich and varied voice modifications, and a wide range of gestures and movements, the level of attunement was the most therapeutic. Allison's voice moved easily from loud to soft, rapid to slow, with periodic long latencies in which she and Katie were wondering about a problem and its solution. Allison giggled and laughed, moved her face close and pulled away, and she showed sadness, anger, or fear quite readily in her facial expressions. While exploring the immediate interaction as well as a recent or distant event, she was likely to be holding Katie or at least touching her. Such physical contact greatly facilitated the communication of shared affect. Physical contact was as effective as voice tone and facial gestures in conveying various emotional themes of joy, excitement, shame, anger, sadness, and anxiety.

Along with voice modifications, facial gestures, movements, and touch, Allison was able to maintain affective attunement with Katie through saying and doing the unexpected. This created an air of expectancy and Katie was likely to be quite responsive to the affect being communicated. Allison might comment on Katie's posture, gestures, exclamation, or groan, often with empathy, humor, or curiosity. Such reflections helped to keep Katie somewhat off balance and engaged. What is important in such interchanges is not the content, but the therapeutic *attitude* that Allison was conveying. Without using words, Allison was, in essence, saying:

> Katie, you are an interesting and delightful girl. I want to get to know you, play with you, and discover who you are. I want to know all about you, child. With me and your mom, there need be no secrets that diminish you in shame. *You* are welcome here, and that includes your rage, your fear, and your desire for warmth and joy. We will hold you and guide you on this journey. We will stay with you no matter where this journey takes us.

Just as paradoxical responses prove to be effective discipline strategies at home, so too are paradoxical interpretations, that reframe a behavior or incident, quite effective in therapy. Thus, Allison suggested that Katie's anger at her mother was a sign that she was beginning to love her. Or the anger could be framed as a sign that she was still somewhat frightened of her love for her. Katie's threat to hurt their dog might easily have framed as representing her desire to ask her mother for extra supervision so that she would not hurt the family pet. Allison could also easily insert "double binds" into her conversation with her. Katie might be told to show how much she enjoyed therapy by smiling, screaming, being silent, or by doing something else. Whatever she did, she was enjoying therapy! Allison frequently interpreted her resistance in therapy in a very positive manner, suggesting that Katie was wise to go slowly now, or suggesting that she had an important message that she was communicating to Allison, who then "uncovered" the message. The *attitude* qualities of curiosity, playfulness, empathy, and acceptance each facilitated this manner of relating with Katie.

Therapeutic suggestions can easily be incorporated into these affectively rich and reciprocal conversations. Allison might have asked her if she would like to learn to reduce her anger first or become more relaxed first. If she accepted the limits of the choices available to her, she was going to make progress. Allison might have wondered if her progress would be fast or slow, if she would first show progress in an area that they had already explored, or if she would choose to surprise them by making progress in something that they had never talked about. These interventions, as well as the underlying therapeutic attitude, have many similarities with the work of Milton Erickson (see Erickson and Rossi 1979).

Finally, Allison also used music at times to support the affective tone of a conversation with Katie. Playing music can set a calm and relaxed tone or it can offer a supportive atmosphere for Katie while she was dealing with shame-inducing experiences. Nurturing reattunement experiences between Jackie and Katie were also supported by music.

Along with providing affective attunement experiences, for therapy to be effective it needs to also provide shame-reduction experiences. Attachment sequences, which involve attunement, emotional separations created by shame, and reattunement, occur frequently throughout the therapy session. Katie's denial of an event was an effort to reduce the emotional pain of shame. Her pervasive sense of shame permeated her definition of self as being bad and left her in isolation and despair. Her only recourse was to deny the experience. This led to lies, excuses, distortions, and very often, to rage. By exploring the shame-based experience, in the context of the therapeutic *attitude* being conveyed by Allison and Jackie, Katie managed to reduce the shame and integrate the experience into her sense of self. She then became more receptive to becoming reattuned with Jackie as well as to maintaining a higher level of attachment throughout the day, since her sense of self as being more worthwhile could now integrate movements toward such a relationship. She needed not be so afraid of loving and being loved. For Katie, eventually reciprocal enjoyment needed not be frightening.

Throughout Katie's therapy, Allison had her *repeat* certain phrases and direct them toward Jackie or Allison. By associating these phrases with specific affective tones, Allison was able to lead her toward bringing certain themes to awareness and experiencing them at a therapeutic affective level. This is a very powerful strategy that often enabled Katie to begin to face the harsh realities of her life so that she could gradually begin to integrate them into a more cohesive self. The words alone did not reach Katie's inner experience; they needed to be presented along with meaningful affective expressions. Shock, surprise, sadness, rage, excitement, joy, interest, and fear were frequently conveyed while asking Katie to accept and express certain phrases as representing her own inner life.

When asking her to engage in these verbal and affective repetitions, Allison remained attuned with Katie's affective states so that she would discard a phrase progression that did not match an aspect of her inner life. At times Katie might refuse to repeat a phrase even when Allison's statement did accurately reflect her thoughts and emotions. Allison simply accepted her refusal and spoke for her, and then waited to see if Katie was demonstrating an affective response to Allison's words and affect.

The conversational strategies described above, which are useful in maintaining affective attunement, are equally useful in helping Katie to remain engaged while the shameful experience is explored. These therapeutic principles and strategies are also developed in my previous book, *Facilitating Developmental Attachment* (1997).

Finally, it is important to note that the therapy provided to Katie was very difficult work for Katie, Jackie, and Allison. This difficulty needs to often be acknowledged by the therapist in order to facilitate their continuing motivation to change. It also should be made explicit in an early session and acknowledged in writing. See Appendix 5 for a generic form detailing the commitments that the child, parents, and therapist need to make if the treatment is to be successful.

Therapeutic affective attunement experiences that are crucial to Katie's therapy are also considered to be central to Ann Jernberg's *Theraplay* (1979) and Viola Brody's *Developmental Play Therapy* (1993). Both emphasize many qualities of the mother–child relationship during the first two years of life. These approaches emphasize physical contact, eye contact, facial gestures, movement, and reciprocal enjoyment. The relationship between the therapist and child is the primary therapeutic focus. The therapist also provides training and consultation to the child's parents regarding ways to maximize the quality of their relationship at home. The "floor-time" approach of Greenspan and Wieder's (1998) *Psychotherapy with Children* contains strong components of affective attunement.

What distinguishes the therapeutic approach illustrated in Katie's story is the belief that unattached children need to directly deal with their constant experience of pervasive shame. Affective attunement experiences need to precede and follow an exploration of experiences that are associated with profound shame in order to reduce this shame and integrate the need for appropriate socialization into the child's life. Simply providing affective attunement does not reach into, explore, and integrate the "bad self" which so permeates the life of the unattached child.

Martha Welch (1989) in *Holding Time*, presents a treatment model that is centered on the child's attachment with her mother. In her model the affective attunement and shame-reducing experiences all occur between the child and her mother, with the therapist taking an ancillary role. Only the mother holds her child, since the goal of attachment is between parent and child, not child and therapist. While holding her child, the mother forcefully expresses the full range of her own affect to her child, within the context of her total love for her. While maintaining her intense affective and physical connection with her, she insists that her child also expresses her range of affect to her mother. Such intense reciprocal expression of affect leads to a "breakthrough" of intimacy that strengthens the attachment and enables the child to utilize this attachment in resolving her developmental difficulties. Welch's model of treatment is presented as applicable for a wide range of problems in childhood, and not restricted to children who are unattached.

Foster Cline (1992, 1995) emphasizes physical contact, eye contact, facial gestures, movement, and reciprocal enjoyment as the supportive context that is necessary for his Attachment Therapy. Cline also believes that it is necessary to focus a great deal on the child's significant emotional and behavioral problems. He states that "All true bonding has elements of trauma, pain, difficulty or uncertainty followed by gratification and/or relief" (1995, p. 3). Thus, Cline focuses on the act of reestablishing a bond with the child following the emotional "separation" due to trauma, pain, and so on. He does not speak of shame as being the primary source of the unattached child's rage. Rather, he believes that the rage is a response to habitual unmet needs.

Cline emphasizes that it is first necessary for the child to feel "helpless and hopeless" before he will be driven to receive the nurturance that is available to him. He also believes that for these children, who are so rigid in their pathology, it is necessary to first "disturb the disturbed," and thus destabilize their maladaptive defenses, if they are to begin to be attached to their parents.

Cline's therapeutic stance first increases shame and its associated rage. The therapist forcefully challenges the child's behaviors and gives him directives. The therapist's anger intensifies shame and when it increases, the sense of being worthless necessarily intensifies. When the child experiences himself as truly being bad, the therapist and parent show their compassion for and commitment to the child by treating him with a degree of understanding and support far greater than anything he thinks that he deserves. The child is then very likely to increase his dependence on his parent and the therapist. Since he experiences himself as worthless, no one else is likely to give him the support and understanding that he is now receiving. He believes that he is bad, but his parent loves him anyway! Over time, as he comes to form an attachment with his parent, he can then use that attachment to gradually reduce his sense of being worthless. While he may have initially thought that his parent loved him in spite of his being bad, he gradually believes that his parent's love for him demonstrates that he actually is good.

Beverly James (1994) and others have expressed concern that the bonding developed through Cline's Attachment Therapy is a form of dependency that is trauma based. She has compared it to "brain washing" while others compare it more to the intensive indoctrination experiences of "boot camp." Dr. Cline believes that all bonding is created in response to the distress of unmet needs which have elements of trauma. He believes that in Attachment Therapy, the child's distress is only created to meet the needs of the child, not the adult, and the child is able to work through the distress and engage in accepting nurturance. For this reason, he believes that the child is experiencing an attachment-bond and not a trauma-bond. Cline and therapists who employ his techniques have also indicated that while such procedures are indeed very intrusive they are necessary when being employed with children with severe attachment disorders. They suggest that less intrusive interventions should be employed first. However, they maintain that if these children do not receive interventions that are effective in significantly reducing their psychopathology, then they are at high risk for having profound psychological and interpersonal problems throughout their lives.

My stance in therapy and at home is to comprehensively work to reduce shame from the onset rather than to increase shame in treatment, in contrast to Cline's work. In therapy I will calmly focus on a shame-inducing experience in the child's life and the act of exploring it does often precipitate a shame-rage response. I then accept the response, explore it too, and enable the child to reduce and integrate it into his developing sense of self. I do not create shame in therapy by becoming angry with the child. I supportively bring out for resolution the hidden shame that was already present within him. This stance involves the belief that when shame decreases, the associated rage will also decrease. As shame decreases, the child becomes more receptive to entering into attachment with his parents through both attunement experiences as well as through being supported and comforted following experiences of shame. When this treatment is successful, the child's sense of self-worth develops together with his attachment to his parents. Rather than coming to believe that his parents love him in spite of his being worthless, he begins to discover *at the same time* that both he and his parents are worthwhile and that the attachment follows naturally from this realization. Over the past five years, the treatment interventions at The Attachment Center at Evergreen (Colorado) have become increasingly similar to the approach that I am recommending.

These children already experience habitual profound shame because of the countless traumas and deficiencies in their early attachment history during the first eighteen months of their lives. A treatment stance that acknowledges and reduces their preexisting shame, rather than first increasing it, seems both theoretically and humanely to be the more reasonable intervention approach, *if it is successful*. When such an approach fails to produce therapeutic benefits within a given child, then parents and therapists might well consider whether or not the more intrusive Attachment Therapy developed by Cline is indicated.

All of these treatment approaches for unattached children lack a research base. Such research, that focuses on treatment that provides preverbal experiences to address the profound deficiencies in the child's first twenty-four months of life, is crucial if we are to know what interventions are necessary to have significant therapeutic benefit. Are therapeutic experiences that are provided by *Theraplay* and *Developmental Play Therapy* sufficient, or should they be combined with interventions that also directly focus on the shame-inducing experiences of a child's life? When focusing on shame, should it be done with empathy and support only, or is it necessary to intensify shame through directing anger at the child? How is it best to involve the child's parents in the treatment process? As co-therapists? What parenting qualities and interventions are necessary and how best to teach those traits and interventions? Such questions, and others which focus on selectively matching interventions with children or symptoms, as well as discovering the most beneficial intervention sequences and combinations, need to be answered through an integrated body of clinical research and experience.

The work of Beverly James (1989, 1994) represents an important effort to increase the effectiveness of play therapy with children with attachment deficits. Some of her interventions may be easily incorporated into the therapeutic format suggested in this book. The same can be said for the gestalt strategies and stance of Violet Oaklander (1978). Finally, narrative therapy developed for children by J. Freeman, D. Epston, and D. Lobovits (1997) demonstrates a manner of relating with a child about his problems that has similarity with the playful and relaxed style adopted by Allison in her work with Katie. Their approach also externalizes the problem in a manner that might well enable the child to address it with less shame.

Cognitive-behavioral interventions are primarily verbal efforts to conceptualize the problem and provide the parent and child with specific cognitive and behavioral strategies to reduce the behaviors of concern and increase alternative, adaptive behaviors. The therapist is directive and recommends a similar directive, problem-solving strategy to the parent. In general, therapists who rely on a cognitive-behavioral framework emphasize neither the importance of attunement, nor shame-reducing experiences in the child's psychological development and therapeutic interventions, although incorporating those experiences and developing strategies to facilitate them, is not incompatible with their framework. Too often this framework does not adequately recognize that, with children with attachment deficits, the usual social reinforcers are not effective, and also that the concrete reinforcers often provided to these children are not effective for any period of time, and do not generalize to ongoing interpersonal behaviors. These children experience their greatest reinforcements in manipulating the reinforcement program and then causing emotional distress in their parents because of their inability to control them. However, as is the case with certain play therapy interventions, cognitive-behavioral strategies can be incorporated in the framework suggested by Katie's story.

Appendices

Developmental Attachment Patterns[1]

1. BIOLOGICAL REGULATION (0 to 5 months)
   (FOOD AND SAFETY)
   Biological rhythm (feeding, sleeping, waking, elimination) of infant becomes coordinated with an available, responsive, and intervening parent, leading to "reciprocal coordination of actions."
   A: disinterested and apathetic
   B: over-alert, excited, upset, and unfocused

2. AFFECT MODULATION AND ATTUNEMENT (0 to 12 months)
   (ATTUNEMENT)
   Emotional, joyful, and reciprocal interaction with infant, highly focused on eyes, smile, expressions, and gestures of parent. Affect is immediate, shared, increasingly modulated.
   A: avoids eye contact and touch, withdrawn and rigid
   B: indiscriminately clinging, demanding

3. BEHAVIORAL ORGANIZATION (9 to 18 months)
   (ATTACHMENT SEQUENCES)
   Integration of autonomy and attachment. Socialization with shame. Wide range of socially meaningful feelings and behaviors are expressed and organized. Much interest and joy. Much initiative while accepting limits. Impulse control emerges.
   A: passive and withdrawn, repetitive, asocial behavior
   B: rapid shifts in mood and behavior, demanding and stubborn, repetitive

---

1. Patterns based on the work of Stanley Greenspan (1988), Margaret Mahler (1975), Allan Schore (1994), and Daniel Stern (1985).

4. COGNITIVE CAPACITY (18 to 36 months)
   (INNER STATE COMMUNICATION)
   Internalized attachment. Words are used to indicate wishes, in-
   tentions, and feelings (inner-state language) in an organized
   manner. Self-reflection, monitoring.
   A: descriptive, not inner-state, words
   B: disorganized, fragmented chatter

5. COGNITIVE DIFFERENTIATION (30 to 48 months)
   (RECIPROCITY)
   Internalized, differentiated, attachment. Words are used to sepa-
   rate self from non-self, and to relate to others across a wide range
   of emotions and ideas.
   A: withdrawn; words used for things
   B: little focus and direction, indiscriminate

General Symptom Patterns of Poorly Attached Children

Lack of Affective Attunement
Lack of joy, humor
Lack of reciprocal enjoyment
(fun, love)
Lack of eye contact
Lack of selective attachment
indiscriminately charming
Lack of empathy
Lack of guilt/remorse
Lack of appropriate
communication
Lack of inner-state language
Lack of cause/effect thinking
Lack of awareness of bodily
functions
Lack of appropriate physical
boundaries
Lack of a continuous sense
of self

Excessive Shame
Excessive need to control
Oppositional-defiant behaviors
Intense negative affect
rage, terror, despair
Hurting others and self
emotional, physical
Poor response to discipline
frustration, responsibility
Lies, excuses, blaming
Good/bad splitting
Sense of entitlement; demanding
Victimhood identity
Destructive, stealing, hoarding
Manipulative affect and behavior
Dissociation and/or
hypervigilance

These symptom patterns reflect failings in the developmental differentiation and integration of one's basic body-self, affect, behavior, and cognition that is occurring during the first three years of life. Each symptom most likely reflects a combination of both a lack of affective attunement and excessive shame.

Parenting Guidelines
for Attachment

ATTITUDE: 1. Accepting   2. Curious   3. Empathic
4. Loving   5. Playful

To Facilitate the CAPACITY FOR FUN AND LOVE:

1. Affective attunement
2. Maintain attitude
3. Eye contact, smiles, touch, hugs, rocking, movement, food
4. Regression: nurturing experiences
5. Emotional availability in times of stress
6. Surprises
7. Holding your child
8. Reciprocal enjoyable activities
9. Reciprocal expression of thoughts and feelings
10. Humor and gentle teasing
11. Basic safety and security
12. Opportunities to imitate parents
13. Spontaneous discussions of past and future
14. Routines and rituals to develop a mutual history

To Facilitate EFFECTIVE DISCIPLINE
(Shame-Reduction and Skill Development):

1. Set and maintain your favored emotional tone, not your child's
2. Maintain attitude
3. Accept thoughts, feelings, and behaviors of child
4. Provide natural and logical consequences
5. Be predictable in your attitude (#2), less predictable in your consequences
6. Reattune following shame-inducing experiences

7. Regression: structuring experiences
8. Interrupt cycles of resistance: "mom time"
9. Use paradoxical responses
10. Use permission, thinking, practicing, having restrictions, being supervised
11. Employ periodic anger (60 sec. scolding), not habitual anger or annoyance
12. Clarify for all concerned that it is the child's problem, not your problem
13. Use the child's anger to build a stronger connection
14. Establish discipline as simply being one part of a healthy attachment cycle
15. Be in charge, but also be attuned to the affect of your child
16. Greatly limit your child's ability to hurt you, either physically or emotionally

Psychotherapy with Poorly Attached Children

PSYCHOTHERAPY:

1. Will be a joint endeavor which involves the parents, child, and therapist, focusing on all aspects of relationships and self, at home and in the office, past, present, and future.
2. Will create many experiences of affective attunement with the child.
3. Will be directive in order to prevent the maladaptive effects of the child's pervasive need to be in control of all interactions.
4. Will accept the child's strong resistance to the directiveness.
5. Will reduce the negative impact of shame-inducing experiences on the child's sense of self and relationships through providing attachment sequences (attunement, shame and distress, reattunement).
6. Will convey an attitude that is accepting, empathic, curious, loving, and playful.
7. Will endeavor to differentiate the new family experiences from the old and, in so doing, assist the child in integrating the new.
8. Will support and facilitate an emotionally rich and nurturing family atmosphere to which the child is likely to form a secure attachment.

PARENTAL PARTICIPATION PROVIDES OPPORTUNITY FOR:

1. Affective attunement and emotional support for their child
2. Mutual enjoyment with their child
3. Differentiating their relationship from previous parental relationships

4. An increase in similarity between interactions in therapy and in home
5. Sharing their thoughts and feelings with their child
6. Challenging lies, distortions, excuses
7. Providing expert knowledge about their child
8. Reinforcing parental authority
9. Providing safety for child and therapist
10. Receiving support, ideas, and validation of their parenting.

Contract for Parent, Child, and Therapist

COMMITMENTS

Parent's Commitment:

I will relate to _____ today in a way that facilitates his/her attachment to me. I assess how well I do, not how well he/she does. If I focus on my functioning, his/her progress will take care of itself. I can control how I love _____, not how she/he loves me.

I will remain aware of _____ need for fun and love experiences with me that were so lacking in his/her early life, and I will provide him/her with many such experiences now. For his/her sake and for my own, I will be in charge. I will expect _____ to face his/her problems and mistakes which cause him/her shame, and I will do so while knowing that it is hard for him/her and also while maintaining an attitude that makes it possible for him/her to benefit from the activity. I will protect and maintain a healthy emotional atmosphere in our home, so that she/he can become like the rest of us in the family, rather than our assuming his/her anger, fears, and sadness.

signed,_____   _____

Child's Commitment:

I acknowledge that I am very unhappy and that I need my parents and therapist to teach me how to live in a way to increase my happiness. While it is very hard work, and I often do not understand what attachment means, I will work to learn because I really do not have another option if I want to be happy.

I agree that I don't do well at having fun with my parents and enjoying their love. I think that I'm bad and don't deserve better. I will remember that I might be wrong so I'll try to learn to enjoy fun and love with them. It is very hard to look at what makes me feel that I'm bad, but I need to do it and I will try to accept their help so that it's easier. I agree that I do not make good choices and that my parents need to teach me how to make them better. I will probably think that they are being mean to me and I might hate them. I will remember that I might be wrong and I'll deal with it. I know that they need to be in charge if I'm going to learn all this stuff. I hate that, but maybe someday it won't seem so bad so I'll deal with it now.

signed, _____

Therapist's Commitment:

I will relate to _____ and _____ in a manner that assists the development of their bond. I will not forget how hard it is for parents to successfully develop and maintain a bond with their unattached child. Nor will I forget how hard it is for an unattached child to learn to form an attachment with her/his parents. I will work with them with respect and humility in the face of the ordeals that they must face.

I will communicate that the parents are in charge and I will constantly support their authority. I will work to create in the session an atmosphere of reciprocal enjoyment. I will engage the child in a manner to facilitate his/her ability to integrate experiences of affective attunement and shame, and I will maintain this attitude while we explore experiences that impede the natural development of attachment. At the conclusion of our work, I will provide a party for the _____ family.

signed, _____

References

Brody, V. (1993). *The Dialogue of Touch*. Northvale, NJ: Jason Aronson.

Cicchetti, D. (1989). How research on child maltreatment has informed the study of child development: perspectives from developmental psychopathology. In *Child Maltreatment*, ed. D. Cicchetti and V. Carlson, pp. 377–431. New York: Cambridge University Press.

Cline, F. W. (1992). *Hope for High Risk and Rage Filled Children*. Evergreen, CO: EC Publications.

——(1995). Understanding the essentials: bonding/attachment theory. In *Give Them Roots and Let Them Fly*, ed. C. A. McKelvey, pp. 1–9. Evergreen, CO: The Attachment Center at Evergreen.

Cline, F. W., and Fay, J. (1990). *Parenting with Love and Logic*. Colorado Springs, CO: Pinon Press.

Delaney, R. J., and Kunstal, F. R. (1993). *Troubled Transplants*. Ft. Collins, CO: Horsetooth Press.

Egeland, B., and Erickson, M. F. (1987). Psychologically unavailable caregiving. In *Psychological Maltreatment of Children and Youth*, ed. M. R. Brassard, R. Germain, and S. N.Hart, pp. 110–120. New York: Pergamon.

Erickson, M. H., and Rossi, E. L. (1979). *Hypnotherapy: An Exploratory Casebook*. New York: Irvington Publishers.

Freeman, J., Epston, D., and Lobovits, D. (1997). *Playful Approaches to Serious Problems*. New York: Norton.

Greenspan, S. I., and Lieberman, A. F. (1988). A clinical approach to attachment. In *Clinical Implications of Attachment*, ed. J. Belsky and J. T. Nezworski, pp. 387–424. Hillsdale, NJ: Lawrence Erlbaum.

Greenspan, S. I., and Wieder, S. (1998). *The Child with Special Needs*. Reading, MA: Addison-Wesley.

Hage, D. (1995). Therapeutic parenting, part 1 & 2. In *Give Them Roots and Let Them Fly*, ed. C. A. McKelvey, pp. 177–214. Evergreen, CO: The Attachment Center at Evergreen.

Hughes, D. (1997). *Facilitating Developmental Attachment*. Northvale, NJ: Jason Aronson.

James, B. (1989). *Treating Traumatized Children*. Lexington, MA: Lexington Books.

——— (1994). *Handbook for Treatment of Attachment-Trauma Problems in Children*. Lexington, MA: Lexington Books.

Jernberg, A. (1979). *Theraplay*. San Francisco: Jossey-Bass.

Kaufman, G. (1996). *The Psychology of Shame*, 2nd ed. New York: Springer.

Lansky, V. (1993). *Games Babies Play*. Deephaven, MN: The Book Peddlers.

Mahler, M., Pine, F., and Bergman, A. (1975). *The Psychological Birth of the Human Infant*. New York: Basic Books.

Morin, V. (1993). *Messy Activities and More*. Chicago: Chicago Review Press.

Nelson, G. E., and Lewak, R. W. (1985). *Who's the Boss?* Boston: Shambhala.

Oaklander, V. (1978). *Windows to Our Children*. Moab, UT: Real People Press.

Schore, A. N. (1994). *Affect Regulation and the Origin of the Self*. Hillsdale, NJ: Lawrence Erlbaum.

Stern, D. N. (1985). *The Interpersonal World of the Infant*. New York: Basic Books.

Welch, M. G. (1989). *Holding Time*. New York: Fireside.

Index